ROUTLEDGE LIBRARY EDITIONS: AGING

Volume 27

AGEING IN MODERN SOCIETY

AGEING IN MODERN SOCIETY

Contemporary Approaches

Edited by
DOROTHY JERROME

LONDON AND NEW YORK

First published in 1983 by Croom Helm Ltd

This edition first published in 2024
by Routledge
4 Park Square, Milton Park, Abingdon, Oxon OX14 4RN

and by Routledge
605 Third Avenue, New York, NY 10158

Routledge is an imprint of the Taylor & Francis Group, an informa business

© 1983 Dorothy Jerrome

British Library Cataloguing in Publication Data
A catalogue record for this book is available from the British Library

ISBN: 978-1-032-67433-9 (Set)
ISBN: 978-1-032-69386-6 (Volume 27) (hbk)
ISBN: 978-1-032-69409-2 (Volume 27) (pbk)
ISBN: 978-1-032-69408-5 (Volume 27) (ebk)

DOI: 10.4324/9781032694085

Publisher's Note
The publisher has gone to great lengths to ensure the quality of this reprint but points out that some imperfections in the original copies may be apparent.

Disclaimer
The publisher has made every effort to trace copyright holders and would welcome correspondence from those they have been unable to trace.

AGEING
IN MODERN SOCIETY

CONTEMPORARY APPROACHES

Edited by

DOROTHY JERROME

CROOM HELM
London & Canberra
ST. MARTIN'S PRESS
New York

©1983 Dorothy Jerrome
Croom Helm Ltd, Provident House, Burrell Row,
Beckenham, Kent BR3 1AT
Croom Helm Australia, PO Box 391, Manuka,
ACT 2603, Australia

British Library Cataloguing in Publication Data

Jerrome, Dorothy
    Ageing in modern society.
    1. Ageing——Social aspects
    I. Title
    305.2'6   HQ1061
    ISBN 0-7099-1422-9

All rights reserved. For information, write:
St. Martin's Press, Inc., 175 Fifth Avenue, New York, NY 10010
First Published in the United States of America in 1983

Library of Congress Cataloging in Publication Data
Main entry under title:

Ageing in modern Society.

    1. Aged——Research——Great Britain——Addresses, essays,
lectures. 2. Aged——Services for——Great Britain——
Addresses, essays, lectures. 3. Great Britain——Social
policy——Addresses, essays, lectures. 4. Social work
with the aged——Great Britain——Addresses, essays,
lectures. I. Jerrome, Dorothy.
HQ1064.G7A65 1983   305.2'6'0941   83-13684
ISBN 0-312-01388-4

Printed and bound in Great Britain

CONTENTS

Introduction by Dorothy Jerrome   7

1. NEW APPLICATIONS OF OLD DISCIPLINES

   Introduction   11
   Chapter One: Associational
     Participation in Old Age,
     by Christopher Harris..................   14
   Chapter Two: Elderly Women and
     Disadvantage: Perceptions of Daily
     Life and Support Relationships,
     by Helen Evers......................   25
   Chapter Three: Crime and the Elderly:
     Experience and Perceptions, by
     R.I. Mawby............................   45
   Chapter Four: Elderly Vagrants,
     by Martin Blacher....................   61
   Chapter Five: Ageing in the Inner City:
     A Comparison of Old Blacks and Whites,
     by Kenneth Blakemore..................   81
   Chapter Six: Stereotypes of Old Age: The
     Case of Yugoslavia, by
     Dianne Willcocks......................   104
   Chapter Seven: Accounts of Onitsha Market
     Literature: Perceptions of Age and
     Wisdom, by Pamela Shakespeare.........   124
   Chapter Eight: "Just a Song at Twilight":
     Residents' Coping Strategies Expressed
     in Musical Form, by Jennifer Hockey....   129
   Chapter Nine: Loneliness: A Problem of
     Measurement, by Clare Wenger...........   145
   Chapter Ten: The Potential for Learning
     in Later Life, by Paula Allman.........   168

2. STUDIES OF CHANGING POLICY AND PRACTICE

Introduction   188
Chapter Eleven: The History of Provision
    for the Elderly to 1929, by Pat Thane..   191
Chapter Twelve: From Public Assistance
    Institutions to 'Sunshine Hotels':
    Changing State Perceptions About
    Residential Care for the ·Elderly,
    by Robin Means and Randall Smith.......   199
Chapter Thirteen: Short Term Residential
    Care for Elderly People: An Answer to
    Growing Older   by Peter McCoy.........   227
Chapter Fourteen: A Profile of Residential
    Life, by
    Dianne Willcocks, Sheila Peace and
    Leonie Kellaher.......................   240
Chapter Fifteen: Friendship and Isolation:
    Two Sides of Sheltered Housing,
    by Laura Middleton.....................: 255
Chapter Sixteen: The Nursing Home:
    Professional Attitudes to the
    Introduction of New Forms of Care
    Provision for the Elderly, by
    Gillian Dalley.........................   269
Chapter Seventeen: The Hospice Concept and
    the National Health Service, by
    Hedley Taylor..........................   282
Chapter Eighteen: Groups of Old People in
    the Community: A Preliminary Report, by
    Jeanette Brewster, Bob Chard and
    Gregorio Kohon.........................   292

Details of Contributors.................   301

Index   302

INTRODUCTION

Dorothy Jerrome

The twentieth century has seen twin developments in
Britain: changes in the pattern of employment,
producing the institution of retirement; and demographic changes resulting in an ageing population.
These phenomena have stimulated interest and concern
in political, professional and academic circles.
The growing interest in ageing has encouraged the
development of social gerontology as a new area of
intellectual activity in Britain.

The chapters in this collection draw attention
to the changed circumstances in which ageing takes
place, at the subjective level, at the level of care
and provision, and at the level of theory. Some
challenge prevailing notions about the characteristics, needs and capacity of older people. Others
are about the changing perceptions of policy makers
and practitioners. The collection as a whole offers
a view of social gerontology, and illustrates the
integration of theory and practice. Taken together,
the contributions reflect the view that the contemporary experience of old age needs to be seen against
a background of social change and cultural diversity.

An important area of change to which the book
draws attention is the study of ageing. The
emphasis in research over the past four decades has
been on the scientific, quantitative approach.
Increasingly, though, use is being made of intensive
anthropological and biographical methods in pursuit
of more adequate conceptualisation and an understanding of the subjective experience of ageing.

Changes in official and professional perceptions of need area product of several developments.
The first is the increasing number of elderly people
in relation to the rest of the population, and their
relegation to the status of "retired", forcing the
ageing process on the attention of academics and

7

policy makers. The concerns of policy makers and
professionals have provided a basis for enquiry into
ageing, traditionally stressing policy and welfare
considerations.

The second influence on the character of recent
social gerontology has been the cultural movements
of the 1960s and 1970s. These decades were marked
on both sides of the Atlantic by a growing emphasis
on individual rights, emotional needs, and particularly the right of underprivileged groups to self-
determination and fulfillment. In the United
States this shift in consciousness gave birth to
various liberation movements - Black Power, Women's
Liberation, Gay Liberation, and the Gray Panthers.
In social gerontology it produced a way of seeing
elderly people as victims of an oppressive, work-
and youth - oriented society. Dependency in old age
was seen to be a product of the social, economic and
political forces of modern capitalist society. At
the same time, the emphasis on the social construction of reality, and of "old age" in particular, led
to a concern for the perspectives of older people
themselves and the meanings they attached to events
and relationships. Concepts such as loneliness,
friendship , privacy, dependency, and old age itself,
were subjected to closer scrutiny and refinement.
This led to a recognition that the normal pattern of
ageing might not, perhaps, be that of the few frail,
lonely or dependent old people who were known about
because they were receiving help.

Thus traditional interests - policy and welfare
oriented, with an emphasis on social and individual
pathology, needs and coping strategies - have made
room for research on normal ageing, personal
resources and the continuity of   experience. The
balance is still, however, in favour of research on
needs, service provision, policy implications and
practice. It is still largely oriented towards
social rather than sociological problems. The literature as a whole provides more material on policy
and practice than on issues of predominantly
theoretical interest. This situation is reflected
in publications and professional meetings which
embrace a wide range of interests and are generally
undiversified in content. The juxtaposition of
theoretical and methodological discussions of ageing,
accounts of policy implications and prescriptions
for professional practice, is partly based on the
fact that ageing itself is a multifaceted experience.
Another reason for the integration of theory and
practice is a lack of resources which would enable

8

gerontologists to develop their interests and form
distinct subgroups of specialists. The current integration of theory and practice is reflected in
this book. It contains few chapters of purely
theoretical interest. Half are specifically on
policy and practice, informed in some cases by discernible theoretical frameworks. The theoretical
chapters themselves tend to focus on elderly populations who are likely to be future, if not current,
recipients of services, and the implications for
policy and practice are spelled out.

This arrangement reflects the distribution of
research interests in gerontology which in Britain
are governed by utilitarian values and a pragmatism
born of dependence upon government and voluntary
agencies for funding. It is unfortunate that the
current situation does not permit the growth of
understanding which is not tied to immediate action.

The chapters in this book are based on papers
originally presented at a conference of the British
Society of Gerontology on the theme of <u>Old Age in a
Changing Society</u>, in September 1982. They have
been arranged here in two parts. The first, more
theoretical part, includes new applications of
social science disciplines - anthropology, psychology, sociology - to the study of ageing. These
chapters deal with the degree of isolation and
social involvement of old people in different categories (gender, social class, ethnic); with changes
over the life cycle and the relationship between
past and present; with images and models of ageing;
and with the diversity of experience in the elderly
population. Some provide insight into new needs
and hitherto unrecognised needs, and indicate some
positive aspects of ageing. Others offer illuminating ways of looking at both longstanding situations
and novel ones, and attempt to understand the ageing
process from the point of view of the social actors
themselves.

The second part of the book consists of studies
of changing perspectives on ageing, and sets out
to examine official, popular and professional perceptions of need and capacity in later life through
an analysis of changing policy and practice in
residential, health and community care. It includes
also an account of innovatory work by practitioners
responding to new definitions of capacity and need
which acknowledge the positive aspects of ageing
and the validity and continuity of experience.
Through group work, cognitive change and development is effected. Through self-analysis in

Introduction

collaboration with other older people and with
professionals, group members show a capacity to
develop emotionally and to achieve satisfactory
relationships with their environment.
    The chapters in Part Two lead to the conclusion
that practice sometimes develops in a policy vacuum,
in that policy does not meet real needs. There is
an eviden gulf between intention and implementa-
tion because designers and policy makers do not
understand the subjective experience of the people
affected. One solution which emerges is a reversal
of the professional-client relationship. The
professional assumes a non-directive role and the
client is restored to independence through self-help.
Other chapters offer less radical (perhaps less
romantic) prototypes for effective policy and
sensitive professional practice.
    Running through the book as a whole is the
implication that, as the theories and methods of
social gerontology grow more sophisticated and our
understanding of the nature of ageing increases, the
interests of older people will be better served.
Academics who read this book will acquire a more
illuminating picture of old age and will appreciate
the need for analysis which takes into account the
elderly person's life experiences and definition of
the present situation. Policy makers who read it
will realise that they should not make assumptions
about the needs of the people whose interests they
are seeking to promote, and practitioners will
realise that they must respect the autonomy and
individuality of elderly clients. Both will recognise the importance of treating older people as
people, not things, and of giving their needs
priority over the needs of organisations.

PART ONE. NEW APPLICATIONS OF OLD DISCIPLINES

INTRODUCTION

The contributions in this part are largely theoretical, and most are written from sociological or
social anthropological points of view. They attend
to the relationship between subjective experience
and objective circumstances, and call for a recognition of the diversity of experience in old age.
    The chapter by Harris offers a theoretical
framework for the analysis of ageing. It stresses
the importance of gender and social class and shows
that these variables can account for the limited
popularity of old people's clubs. The second
chapter, by Evers, goes further in recognising the
importance of gender, though she challenges the
usefulness of conventional class categories when
applied to women. Evers argues for a phenomenological, rather than a structural, approach. She
shows how the former reveals meaning of activity and
dependency for frail elderly women and argues that
such knowledge is vital for the provision of adequate care.
    The following three chapters deal with the
circumstances and experience of various minority
groups. Mawby examines the myths and realities of
crime in relation to elderly people, both as victims
and perpetrators. He uncovers a discrepancy between
fears of crime and the risk of it, and relates it to
marginality and an absence of security on a
general level, particularly among old women.
Blacher develops the deviance theme by considering
a special group of elderly lawbreakers: vagrant men,
many of them alcoholics with criminal records.
Like the anxious old people described in the previous chapter, these men are apparently isolated.
But viewed from the perspective of the vagrants

themselves daily existence is structured by a
satisfying pattern of activities and social contacts.

Their distinctive lifestyle and unconventional
values make these men a cultural minority. In the
following chapter Kenneth Blakemore introduces a
cultural minority of a different kind. The elderly
West Indians and their white neighbours are not
"deviants" but "respectable" elderly people. Yet
they suffer from a sense of alienation, a discontinuity between past and present, the loss of
anticipated patterns of ageing. Their lack of
control over their environment produces different
responses, from resignation and self-blame in the
blacks to resentment and anger in the whites.
Again, gender emerges as a significant variable,
though it is complicated by race. While old black
women are supported by their churches, old white
women are isolated and alienated. Like the other
authors Blakemore concludes that, despite similar
objective circumstances, subjective experience
varies and needs to be taken into account in the
formulation of social policy.
Chapter six and seven lead in a new direction
though they, too, are concerned with cultural
variation. Willcocks, like Harris, offers a theoretical framework for the study of ageing. Drawing on
theories of deviant behaviour she suggests that
negative stereotypes modify the experience of ageing
and she uses material from Yugoslavia to illustrate
the point. Shakespeare, similarly, chooses another
culture in which to examine perceptions of old age.
Relationships between old and young in a rapidly
changing society - Eastern Nigeria - are perceived
through a content analysis of market literature.
The anthropological approach is evident also
in the following chapter. For Hockey, as for
Shakespeare, words have special significance. This
time the symbolic meanings of a set of verses are
drawn out, in the setting of an English old people's
home. We see how elderly people speculate upon and
come to terms with death and decline, using the song
as a coping strategy. The song, a symbolic statement of the concerns of the residents, lends purpose,
meaning and dignity to their experience.
The next contributor, also an anthropologist,
discusses the theoretical and methodological problems
of studying loneliness. Wenger argues that a more
critical approach to the concept produces surprising
revelations which can be explained only by attention
to the subjective element. Loneliness or its

absence are governed by expectations based on
previous experience, and present states are best
understood through a biographical approach.

The final chapter again raises theoretical and
methodological issues.   Allman, the only psychologist writing in this part, suggests that widespread
beliefsabout intellectual decline in later life are
based on popular images and compounded by faulty
research.   She is critical of both psychological
theories and techniques of measurement which are
geared to childhood and youth, and inappropriate for
later life.   Allman thus reaffirms the belief -
spoken or unspoken - of the other contributors: that
our knowledge of the variety and potential of old
age will be enhanced by more sophisticated concepts
and methods of study.

Chapter One

ASSOCIATIONAL PARTICIPATION IN OLD AGE

Christopher Harris

INTRODUCTION

The work on which I shall report issues from a re-
analysis of the material yielded by the study of
family and kinship in Swansea, South Wales, undertaken by Rosser & Harris, 1959-1963, published as
The Family & Social Change (Rosser and Harris 1965).
The re-analysis is contained in my doctoral thesis
(Harris 1975) entitled The Process of Social Ageing.
The work is concerned with changes in the pattern of
social activity over the whole life cycle of the
adult, in so far as these can be inferred from data
originating at a single point in time. It does however include special material on the elderly in the
population and on old people's clubs.

Its basic theoretical stance is to understand
old age as a social state - as one of deprivation in
both the subjective and objective sense relative
both to the earlier life experiences of the elderly
and to the situation of their younger contemporaries.
This social deprivation is not an inevitable consequence of physiological deterioration. Nor is it
simply economic or resulting from economic factors.
Social deprivation of the elderly must be seen as
socially produced: as related to social processes
occurring regularly within the society which have
that effect. To describe old age as a period of
social deprivation is to claim that our society is
such that social processes compound organically based loss of capabilities among the old rather than
socially compensating them for that loss. The problems of old age, as we commonsensically understand
them, are not therefore to be seen as derivable in
toto from inevitable and universal natural processes, but as being, in substantial part, socially produced and hence (in principle) capable of allevia-

tion. 'Old age' is a social as well as a natural product.

Much of the empirical analysis involved four categories of people obtained by permutating the two gender categories with two 'class' categories. 'Class' is not used here in the Marxist sense but as it was used in the Swansea study. The classification used involved two attributes: membership of occupational group and self ascription. We divided the Registrar General's classification into three: Professional and managerial; routine white collar and supervisory manual; skilled manual and below. Our occupational classification also involved allocating both respondents and their parents to one or other of those three groups. By this means we were able to distinguish, on the one hand, a set of respondents who were in Professional or Managerial occupations, whose parents had been in such occupations and who thought of themselves as 'middle class' and, on the other, a set of respondents who thought of themselves as 'working class' and who, like their parents, fell into the 'skilled manual and below' occupational group. We were able to show a very steep class gradient between the categories, thus defined, on associated variables, and used these associated variables to determine the allocation of the residual mixed categories to one of the two main groups. 'Middle class' therefore means upper socio-economic strata, exhibiting a bourgeois culture/ style of life, claiming membership of the upper set of strata, and 'working class' means the opposite.

The rest of this paper is concerned with the problem of understanding variation in the level and type of what will be termed social participation over the life course, the function and determinants of associational participation, and the conceptualisation of the notion of age and ageing.

AGE AND AGEING

Age, purely chronological age, is not an explanatory variable. It is not possible to make any inference about differences in behaviour from differences in age; it is not possible to infer that, because someone is now ten years older than s/he was ten years ago, s/he will therefore behave in certain different ways. Indeed to make such a simple supposition is to fall into the trap of 'ageism'. Of course what has happened in those ten years will make a difference to the behaviour of the person concerned; but what difference will depend upon what has happened.

Hence regularly found differences between age categories will depend on social regularities in what
happens to people: patterns in people's careers
through life.

The understanding of social ageing therefore
requires some way of analysing and characterising
the transitions typical of the life course. However
as soon as one attempts to do this one is forced to
take into account the different life trajectories of
people in different classes and of different gend-
ers. In thinking about the life course it is also
necessary to take into account both activities and
relationships.

Activities

For men, the central life activity has been and still is, paid work, and the chief activity transitions are therefore from education to paid work and
paid work to retirement. For women the central life
activity has been and still is (for the majority)
concerned with reproduction and domesticity. Here
the chief activity transitions are from paid work to
marriage, marriage to child bearing and rearing and
the loss of the opportunity to continue that activity. For men, ageing in the activity sense involves
the progression through a series of paid employments
constituting a career. For women, ageing has involved a succession of domestic occupations, whose
nature and duration has been determined by the shape
of the reproductive cycle and the composition of the
domestic group. The character of the 'employment
career' and the 'domestic career' will both be powerfully influenced by social class membership: that
is by different class cultures, by the location of
different class members in the labour market, and by
their different situation in the market for consump-
tion goods.

Relationships

It is also possible to discern distinctive patterns
as between sexes and classes in terms of relationships. In order to trace those differences I wish
to distinguish between relationships that are chosen
as opposed to given, and relationships which are
personalised or particularistic and those that are
more impersonal or universalistic. We are all born
into a given set of personalised relationships consisting of family, kin, friends and possibly neighbours. To these relationships are added other equally given (not chosen) but universalistic sets of
relationships involved in participating in education

and paid work. A further set of given, particular-istic relations is added by marriage through which one acquires affines (in-laws). This applies to both sexes. After marriage, however, the social sphere of women contracts in so far as relationships through employment are frequently lost, and social interaction becomes confined to a limited number of given, personalised relationships, concentrated in the domestic sphere, a social situation men do not face until retirement.

ASSOCIATIONAL ACTIVITY & SOCIAL PARTICIPATION

Associational activity has the effect of extending the number of relationships available to an individual within which personal selection may be made. Associational relationships are not chosen, as friendship relations are, but neither are they given. The set is chosen by virtue of a person's choice of an association within which to participate. The members of this set are given. If extension of an individual's set of social relationships is seen as a good, we would expect extension to occur at those points in the life cycle which make it possible; and where existing relationships were lost; and where, for whatever reason, existing social relationships were experienced as depriving rather than rewarding. Obviously, associational participation is not the only means of achieving extension, but we should expect to find associational participation occurring whenever extension occurs and other forms of extension are not available.

Variations in associational participation are to be understood therefore in terms of the progression of individuals through the stages of life-course trajectories typical of the class-sex categories to which they belong. Loss of occupation, domestic or paid, provides the opportunities for associational activity; loss of relationships provides the motivation to extend the range of relationships available. (It is perhaps necessary to make clear that this way of approaching the problem does not involve making generalisations about the behaviour of individuals. It is not to claim that if anyone is a human being they will regard extension as a 'good', and always seek to extend relationships when their set of relationships contract. Individuals obviously vary as to how much social participation they want, and how they balance social participation as against other goods. While this theoretical approach does not yield hypotheses which can be mechanically applied to each and every individual, it does yield hypotheses about the variations in the rates of social and associational participation as between categories of people who have or have not lost activities and have and have not lost relationships).

The theoretical approach put forward permits predictions to be made about variation in social and associational participation over age by class and sex, once descriptive models of the life course of the four class-sex groups has been established which specify the age related (though not age determined) pattern of activity and relationship loss and gain.

PEER GROUPING

It is more true to say however that this theoretical approach would permit such inferences, were it not for a confounding factor. This confounding factor is one of central interest to those who are concerned, not only in social ageing over the life course, but especially with old age itself. The confounding factor is peer grouping. Associational participation can function as a means of extension or as a means of peer grouping or have both characteristics. This opposition between extension and peer grouping maybe illustrated by a consideration of old people's clubs (OPCs). Where, as in the Swansea study, OPCs are set up by the old people themselves, we need to ask the question: what is the need that they supply ? Are they essentially concerned with providing companionship for lonely old people (the extension function), or are they concerned with providing the opportunity for interaction with similarly situated persons - in this case with age peers ? Are OPCs clubs for the 'lonely'; or clubs for old people ? Are they, that is to say, mechanisms of extension or mechanisms of peer groupings ?

In order to clarify this problem we need another modest theory: a theory of peer grouping. Peer grouping is believed to occur when the life experiences of successive age cohorts are radically different, leading to the creation of distinctive age related cultural styles, leading, that is to say, to the creation of 'generation' in the sociological sense. It is also found at points in the life course characterised by transition between statuses and by normative confusion. The most obvious example is peer grouping in adolescence. Half way between child and adult, the adolescents are uncertain which role to adopt on any given occasion and the adults are equally uncertain as to which should be adopted.

There is a parallel between adolescence and old age. The old are half way between the adult and the dead. They are still within social life but apart from it - 'at arms length from the social structure' in Townsend's phrase (Shanas, Townsend et al, 1968). Moreover just as adolescents are moving from a narrow set of given and predominantly particularistic relationships to a wider set including universalistic relationships, which permit autonomy and choice, so the old are moving in the reverse direction. On these grounds we might expect to find peer grouping in old age as in adolescence.

There is a third reason to expect peer grouping in old age however, and this is connected with the deprivation of the old relative to their contemporaries. Peer grouping is a mechanism whereby deprivation is accommodated by restricting interaction to similarly situated persons, thus avoiding interaction with members of categories relative to which those comprising the peer group are deprived, which interaction inevitably sharpens the sense of that deprivation. If the later part of the life course is, in our society, characterised by a number of forms of social deprivation, one would expect to find peer grouping occurring late in the life course to accommodate it. It is likely to occur at those points where people lose occupations (domestic or paid) and relationships and hence will vary in its timing with gender and class membership. Peer grouping is most likely to occur when the degree and abruptness of the deprivation is great, and in those situations where deprivation includes loss of prestige and authority.

It is important to note that peer grouping is not the same as joining a peer group. A person who concentrated his or her interaction among siblings and diminished that with children would be peer grouping within the familial sphere. A golf club member who played and drank with members of similar age as opposed to those of younger ages would be peer grouping within the associational sphere. The need to peer group will not necessarily affect the level of associational participation therefore, nor should we expect increases in associational participation at the points in the life course at which social deprivation occurs - unless peer grouping is impossible with existing sets of relationships. Where it is impossible, however, we may expect the field of relationships to be extended by increased associational participation to permit peer grouping. Moreover, we may also expect the development of

associations whose purpose is peer grouping; that is
the development of peer groups.

I believe that it can be shown from my survey
data that the later part of the life course is associated with increase in associational activity corresponding to the points at which activities and relationships are lost. The spontaneous development
of peer groups (old people's clubs) is to be explained, however, not as a mechanism of extension, but
as a response to the loss of opportunities to form
peer groups within existing sets of relationships.
The increase in associational activity and the formation of peer groups late in the life course has a
paradoxical consequence. If the latter part of the
life course is characterised by a socially produced
movement away from relationships chosen among sets
of universalistic relationships to given, particularistic relationships, then the upturn in associational activity and the formation of peer groups must
be understood as an attempt by older people to resist what is happening to them. Age grouping functions as a mechanism of resistance to the role transition which is socially being forced upon them. To
say this is not to deny that society disengages from
the elderly, but it is to deny that the elderly necessarily willingly disengage from society. Hence
from the disengagement theory perspective, old
people's clubs are deviant responses. They are ways
of resisting what 'society says' should be happening
to them. To say this is not to suppose that elderly
people are engaged in a forlorn struggle to behave
like middle aged people or that they exhibit a path-
ological inability to accept the inevitable consequences of their location late in the life course and
the loss of capacity that this entails. It is rather to claim that they refuse to accept that their
life course location entails the deprivation of
social activity and participation and the restricti-
on of interaction to the narrow sphere of family and
neighbourhood.

ASSOCIATIONAL PARTICIPATION AND PEER GROUPING:
DIFFERENCES BY GENDER AND CLASS

Having, if somewhat cryptically, presented the major
thesis, it is necessary briefly to dicuss differences between the four class-gender categories, each
category being distinguished in terms both of paid
work career, and reproductive cycle. The brevity of
the discussion will mean that the difference noted
will be somewhat crudely expressed.

Men

In dealing with men, no reference will be made to
the cycle of their domestic roles, because though
important these can be inferred from what will subsequently be said about women. In the sphere of
paid work we may note that men are deprived both of
their central life activity - and the whole set of
relationships built around it - suddenly and abrup-
tly, and this is in marked contrast to the process
of loss experienced by women. Men also lose their
central social status (e.g. steel worker) whereas a
woman does not lose her status (wife/mother). They
also experience loss of income (as of course do
women). The class differences to which I draw attention are first that, in so far as middle class men
have careers in the popular sense of the word, retirement constitutes the sudden reversal of a lifelong upward progress between sequential statuses.
In this sense the middle class man is more deprived
than his working class counterpart, who typically
will have been in the same occupational grade throughout the major part of the life cycle. In my sample, both classes of men experienced an income fall
of an equivalent proportion, but the income of working class men fell to a much lower absolute level,
hence they were less able to maintain relationships
with those still in employment which required the
expenditure of money. Working class men, throughout
the life course, were less heavily involved in associational activity and had less opportunity for
peer grouping within associational groupings after
retirement. As predicted, therefore, an increase in
peer group membership was found in old age among
working class men, but not among middle class men.
It would appear that among the middle classes previous associational membership can be retained because of their higher income, and age grouping can
occur within associational life. For working class
men however, peer group membership is necessitated
because they have fewer associational memberships on
retirement and cannot afford to maintain them after
retirement. Those who are most deprived are deprived also of the means to compensate for the deprivation.

Women

Unlike men, women's loss of occupation is not abrupt
and does not involve the loss of the relationships
associated with it. However, the fact that women
retain a domestic occupation after the loss of their
child rearing activities, means that the loss of the

husband's occupation is not accompanied by any change in the woman's activity. Rather her loss of occupation occurs when she finally becomes widowed.
Conversely in middle age, when she loses child care
activity, there is no corresponding change in her
husband's activity pattern. Hence the role cycle
of the spouses are out of phase, which makes activity loss difficult to accommodate within marriage by
a redefinition of marital roles. Moreover changing
demographic features have been restructuring the
domestic cycle, so that even were a woman to retain
her child care activities by participating in the
care of grandchildren, there is now a period, late
in the life course, where she loses that occupation,
while increased life expectation at later ages combined with the differential longevity of men and
women, mean that there now exists a significant period at the end of the life course in which women
lose all occupation. Women are, in this sense, coming to experience 'retirement'.

There are major differences however in the experience of women in the two classes. Because of
smaller family size, and swifter dispersion of adult
children resulting from their wider marriage range
and greater geographical mobility required in the
higher occupational strata, the middle class woman
loses her child care activities at a far earlier
point in the life course than the working class woman does. Hence in the sample the first female activity loss had occurred in middle age for the middle
class but not until late middle or early old age for
the working classes. Moreover a greater proportion
of the working class women had gone out to work upon
the maturation of their own children compared with
the middle class women. Activity loss was thus earlier and sharper in middle class, and less frequently compensated for by paid work, while associational
activity was found to increase in middle age among
middle class women. As a result, the middle class
woman in old age was in a position similar to her
husband: able to take part in peer group activity
within pre-existing associational groups.

In contrast, the working class woman experiences in old age a series of abrupt losses; of child
care activity; of paid occupation; and with the
death of her spouse, of her domestic occupation as
well. Of all four class gender categories, working
class women participate least in associational
activity over the cycle and hence are least able to
accommodate deprivation by peer grouping within associations. Their world is the world of kinship: and

yet it can be shown that over the life course the number of available kin declines and the geographical dispersion of kin increases, sibs later in the life cycle being particularly widely dispersed. The elderly working class woman needs assistance; (1) because working class health is worse than middle class health, (2) because old men tend to get ill and die while old women get ill and tend to live on and on. When she needs assistance it will probably be provided by one child, usually a daughter, near to with whom she has previously been living and assisting with child rearing. In consequence, for the working class woman, not only is deprivation multiple, abrupt and severe, it is also characterised by a role reversal involving loss of occupation, authority and status.

Theoretically one can predict, and I in fact found, that of all the four class gender categories, working class women showed the sharpest upturn in associational activity very late in the life course, i.e. in 'old age'. Their rates of activity were not high of course: lack of previous membership, lack of money, and poor health prevented that. But they were the only category to show a marked increase in these rates of activity in old age.

Old People's Clubs (1)
The 'catch 22' of peer grouping is this. If you peer group with other deprived persons, you avoid the experience of deprivation while in the group, but reinforce it in other social contexts since your membership is a public proclamation of your deprived state. This is a powerful disincentive to club membership: club members are seen by non-members as social failures ('lonely'); scroungers ('they only go for the free trips'). Hence middle class people (however much they age group within associational life) tend to avoid age specific associations - unless of course they run them. At the other extreme is the man's 'trade union' group which is conceptualised as carrying on the principles of Trade Unionism (i.e. the struggle of the oppressed for justice) into old age.

The image of the clubs as associations for the socially inadequate is a powerful disincentive to female membership, except where the label 'O.P.C.' can successfully be avoided, or the clubs, being self-organised and run, can be represented as feats of social capability and ingenuity.

An analysis of what goes on in the (mainly working class) clubs powerfully reinforces the analysis put forward here, since it centres on the public expression and communal appropriation of life experiences peculiar to a generation, and to people who share a common life situation which is explicitly conceptualised as one of deprivation and struggle against adversity.

It is appropriate to conclude by reporting an incident which conveys the gist of what has been said and conveys the paradoxical - 'part of, but apart from' - position of the elderly in our society:

'Tell them, said the secretary of one club as I stepped across the threshold, 'tell them, we aren't finished yet'.

NOTES

1. The data on clubs are derived from a survey of clubs and observation in forty of them.

REFERENCES

Harris, C.C. (1975) The Process of Social Ageing Unpublished Ph.D. Thesis, University of Wales (Swansea)

Rosser C. & Harris, C.C. (1965, 1983) The Family and Social Change, Routledge, London

Townsend. P. (1968) in Shanas, E., Townsend, P. et al Old People in Three Industrial Societies Routledge, London

Chapter Two

ELDERLY WOMEN AND DISADVANTAGE: PERCEPTIONS OF DAILY
LIFE AND SUPPORT RELATIONSHIPS

Helen Evers

There is evidence that elderly women as a category
have distinctive characteristics as compared with
men. They greatly outnumber men, and in various
ways they are on the whole relatively disadvantaged
members of society. Since the topic of women in old
age is potentially vast, I shall restrict myself to
looking, first of all, at some of the evidence of
disadvantage. Following on from this, assumptions
about gender order, implicit in aspects of current
health and social policy for the elderly, will be
discussed. Community care will be taken as an ill-
ustrative example, in order to identify some of the
issues as they affect women: both as providers and
receivers of support services. In the final part
of the chapter I shall discuss two themes emerging
from research into the daily lives of old women living alone. These themes may have practical implications for modes of service provision by professional
and other paid workers.
        There are many reasons why we should be think-
ing specifically about elderly women.
1.   It is not uncommon that practitioners, researchers, gerontologists, policy makers and lay people
fail to distinguish operationally between old men
and old women. The tacit assumption seems to be
that men and women are for most purposes members of
the same category.
2.   The popular mythology of ageing and old age in-
corporates many stereotypes of older women, usually
highly derogatory: 'old crones', 'old bags',
(Preston 1975) 'mutton dressed as lamb' (Fairhurst
1982). Many elderly women themselves share these
stereotypic images of old age, through a lifetime of
conditioning. Of course, old men are also the subjects of derogatory stereotypes, but as Sontag
(1972) argues, old women suffer the double jeopardy

25

of ageism and sexism: for women, ageing may threaten attractiveness, sexuality and the very core of identity and esteem much earlier and much more profoundly than for men. The myths and stereotypes require serious analysis.
3.   Beeson (1975) suggests that gerontologists themselves have failed to challenge many of the stereotypes of older women. Reviewing research of the 1960s and early 1970s, she shows that many writers assumed some of the transitions of ageing - e.g. retirement and loss of a spouse - to be far less traumatic for women than for men, as well as being less of a threat to women's self esteem and general social status. Yet there was and is plenty of evidence from non-academic writing which suggests this is not the case. A likely reason for the conflicting views from research on the one hand and popular literature on the other is, Beeson suggests, a theoretical and methodological one. Researchers have assumed too readily that dominant social values - e.g. the importance of paid work roles - are synonymous with subjective individual experience. Those dominant values tend to relate to the more powerful groups of a society - who are usually men - and to its 'public institutions'. Thus the derivative sociological concepts and theories, for example much of role theory, may be quite inappropriate if applied to less powerful groups living their lives and deriving their identity predominantly in private, i.e. in the domestic sphere rather than the public sphere. Beeson calls for greater attention to phenomenological research to develop a new set of concepts which would be more relevant to understanding women's subjective experience.
4.   The position of elderly women in society is one of relative disadvantage as compared with men. This situation derives from gender divisions which can be seen across the whole lifespan. The women's movement has of course made us aware of arguments about sex-role segregation and of some of the discrimination and injustice women suffer in education, employment, childbearing and family care in general. But in this country, the women's movement has paid little attention to the older women. As Phillipson (1981) observes, we need to look at the nature of sexual divisions in late life, and the ways in which they are maintained. He also suggests that as the women's movement develops, and its early members move closer to old age, interest in older women is beginning to gather momentum in the U.K. (Phillipson 1982).

5.   We have in this country (and many others) rising numbers of very elderly people, the vast majority of whom are women, a substantial proportion of
them living alone. This raises some practical questions, given also other demographic trends and changes in family life. For example, what are the implications of static or slightly decreasing numbers of
younger-old, particularly the women, who carry most
of the responsibility for caring for elderly parents,
and later, widowed mothers ? How are traditional
caring networks within families going to be affected
by rising divorce rates, the lower probablity of re-
marriage for women, and smaller sized families ?
Are the trends towards increasing workforce participation by women going to continue, and what are the
implications both for availability of female carers
for the elderly, and for the material resources and
expectations of the current generation of working
women when they themselves reach old age ?   In a
society featuring static or diminishing resources
devoted to needs of the elderly and their families,
such questions become particularly important.
     These are some of the reasons why we should
look at old women qua women. Relevant research in
N. America is now well established, from its beginnings in the mid-70s. Work in the U.K. is as yet
more limited, though there are important researches
in progress, e.g. Fairhurst and Lightup (1981), on
the menopause, and Jerrome (1981) on the nature and
importance of friendship in later life.
     In focussing particularly on women, one import-
ant pitfall to be avoided is to assume that elderly
women form a homogeneous category - of course they
don't: there are age and class divisions, divisions
in terms of health, illness and dependency, and in
relation to social and family networks. But it will
prove less pedantic, sometimes, to err on the side
of some generalisations which will oversimplify.

OLD WOMEN: DEMOGRAPHY AND DISADVANTAGE

Differential male/female life expectancy has led to
a gross imbalance between proportions of elderly men
and women; an imbalance which increases with increasing age. Between 75 and 84 years, women outnumber
men by 2:1 (Rowlings 1981). Widowhood is therefore
the norm for old women. In 1974, 65% of women over
75 were widows. It is also common for women to live
alone: the General Household Survey for 1980 showed
45% elderly women, but 17% elderly men, lived alone.

Elderly Women and Disadvantage

There is evidence that elderly women tend to have a
higher incidence of housing problems than elderly
men (Tinker & Brion 1981). A higher proportion of
women as compared with men receive very low incomes.
Abrams (1980) shows that 44% of women over 75 living
alone were receiving supplementary benefit, as compared with 28% of men living alone. Ermisch (1982)
and Ward (1981) highlight the relative disadvantage
of women with respect to pension rights. Walker
(1981) points out that the tendency for women to be
at a disadvantage in the labour market - e.g. receiving lower earnings - is perpetuated into old age:
women are less likely than men to retire early, but
much more likely to give up work in order to look
after someone (other than their husbands). Townsend
(1979) in his study of poverty in the U.K. shows
that elderly women, particularly widows, are among
the poorest members of society. Rowlings (1981) has
remarked that this may be no more than a perpetua-
tion into old age of the tendency for women to be
relatively disadvantaged right across the lifespan.
     Besides material disadvantage, survey research
evidence shows elderly women differ from men with
respect to patterns of family life, and use of leisure time. Differences also emerge between women
living alone and those living with others (Abrams
1980): family relationships are fewer and more tenu-
ous for the former, feelings of loneliness and depression more widespread. There is also evidence of
gender-specific trends in health and illness in old
age. The data will not be systematically reviewed
here, but a study by Hunt (1978) and data from the
General Household Survey show that women tend for
example to be more likely to report mobility problems and chronic illness.
     Ethnographic studies illustrate characteristics
of the lifestyles of elderly American women.
Matthews' (1979) interactionist study looks at how
elderly American women try to maintain their identi-
ties. She shares the contention of Walker (1980)
and others that the so-called 'problems' of old age
are largely social constructions, legitimated and
institutionalised through legislation, health and
social policy and so on. Through case studies, she
shows how elderly women seek to maintain self-identity and avoid labelling themselves as 'old'. Ageing
in a setting one knows and where one is known, rather than moving to a new place, helps, Matthews suggests, to avoid identity becoming synonymous only
with 'oldness'. Regarding family relationships, an
exchange theory analysis shows how the power

position of the widowed mother weakens as she ages, and maintenance of quasi reciprocity often depends on the elderly mother fitting in with the expectations of the younger generation. Matthews' study is important because it both provides insights at individual level and sets the analysis in the context of social institutions which tend to foster stigmatising social mores and images of old age. Matthews does not make the comparison between women and men, but the substance of her data leads one to suggest that systematic differences would emerge.

Jerrome's (1981) British study of friendship of elderly middle class women also generates many themes which would appear likely to be gender specific. Jerrome shows how friendships can become an important adjunct or alternative to other roles and activities enjoyed during earlier stages of life. Friendships thereby serve an important purpose in maintenance of identity. Loneliness and being alone are stigmatising conditions, and generally friends are sought with whom pleasurable pastimes can be shared. New friends are often sought in the context of formal or voluntary organisations. Friends - old and new - are important not only in relation to maintaining continuity and identity, but also as practical helpers, confidantes and companions.

WOMEN AND SOCIAL CLASS

So far, the discussion has oversimplified by ignoring ethnicity - which will not be dealt with in this paper - and social class divisions. The latter is a particular problem to women in old age. A number of feminist writers - e.g. Delphy (1981) - have argued forcefully that notions of social class as relating to occupational status are very dubious when applied to women, who do not occupy an equivalent status to men either in the labour market or the domestic sphere. The convention is to classify married women by husbands' occupation, and the process becomes that much more dubious for elderly women. Many of them are widows, and many others will have husbands who have retired from their main occupation, some perhaps having taken up lower status part time work. Cartwright and O'Brien (1977) suggest that cultural position and life style of elderly people may well be related to previous occupation but their prestige and economic position are bound up with their status as pensioners. Townsend (1979) remarks on the problems of class analysis of the elderly, particularly women. He shows that means and resources of late

life for both women and men are in a relationship
with their status as retired people with limited
access to the labour market; and with class of origin and class of own or of spouse's occupation for
married women i.e. professional people are likely to
continue to be in a relatively advantageous position
in old age.

Having said that, the evidence nevertheless
shows a majority of older women, particularly widows
- unless they have access to family wealth or other
resources - to be less well off materially and in
terms of income than old men.

In view of the extent and diversity of evidence
pointing to the importance of gender in old age, the
next section will explore the relevance of this in
the context of health and social policy and service
provision. Examples will be taken from the field of
community care, since aspects of this form part of
the agenda for my current research, to be discussed
in the final section.

OLD WOMEN AND THE RHETORIC OF COMMUNITY CARE

A cornerstone of U.K. policy on the elderly is and
has for a long time been the premise that home care
is the best form of provision for those who need
help. The DHSS white paper of 1981, Growing Older,
and many other recent DHSS documents, make it clear
that services are supposed only to support the primary care provision which comes from families and to
a lesser extent neighbours and others. The evident
assumption is that the traditional carers within
families - that is, women - will routinely take on
the job of caring for the elderly. The arguments
put forward in favour of community care have taken
on slightly different forms over the years, but the
messages stay essentially the same: look after old
people at home because it's what they prefer and
because it's cheaper. (The latter assumption has
often been questioned: e.g. Opit 1977).

This policy, and its manifestations in terms of
our current patterns of service organisation and
provision, has important and (until recently) unnot-
iced implications for women. The effects of the re-
cession and demographic changes underscore the urgency of taking these implications seriously.
1. Specifically vis a vis old women, there is evidence that different, but seldom explicit, criteria
are used in allocation of services to old men and
old women. A study by Bond (1980) suggested that
home help organizers have different decision rules

for men and women when allocating home helps. Very
often a woman is assumed to be able to cope to a
greater extent with household chores than a man who
has apparently comparable limitations on his ability
to look after himself. It may be that for an elderly woman, accepting the services of a home help is
more stigmatising than for an elderly man. But evidence about service allocation and need in relation
to sex is patchy: often, research offers data on
male/female utilisation of services, but seldom are
the rules that were used by practitioners made explicit, and seldom do we know anything about potential clients who were rejected - not to mention
those whose potential need never becomes visible.
2. In their old age, many married women become
carers of their ailing and dependent spouses. This
happens more frequently to old women than to old
men: women tend to marry men older than themselves,
and they also tend to live longer. We know very
little about women in this situation, how they cope
and how they feel about the often heavy burden they
must face when perhaps they themselves are becoming
frail.
3. A third issue about the community care policy
is reliance on unpaid or low paid women workers.
Recent papers by Ungerson (1981) and Finch and
Groves (1980), the Bond (1980) study of the home
help service, and Rossiter and Wicks (1982) point
out that the policy of community care in practice
often means care on the cheap by families, and almost always means care by women. Care given by old
women has already been mentioned. Some recent studies - by Nissel and Bonnerjea (1982), and by the
EOC (1980, 1982) - shed further light on the impact
upon families of caring for dependent elderly relatives. Nissel and Bonnerjea's research was a detailed analysis of care work done by 22 families and
the material, social and psychological costs incurred. Women were the main carers. Help from outside
sources was not distributed equally between those
with similar problems; those who coped were left to
get on with it, those who shouted persistently got
some help. Main stresses were physical work and
psychological stress: the feeling of total, sole and
continous responsibility as well as isolation, frustration and resignation. Nissel and Bonnerjea note
that married women are subject to the ridiculous
discrimination of being ineligible for the Invalid
Care Allowance, a legacy from the past assumption
that women are the property of husbands. Any man
and single woman can claim it, if they give up work

in order to look after a relative who is entitled to
Attendance Allowance. Nissel and Bonnerjea conclude
that the supposed benefits of home care to the
elderly may amount to little more than saving public
money, and ensuring that dependent elderly people,
their problems and those of their carers, remain in-
visible.
4.   Questions are now being raised about the consequences, not only of demographic trends, but also of
changing patterns of family life for the future
availability and requirements of carers for the
elderly: and indeed the requirements for care of
elderly people themselves. An important piece of
research is being carried out by Elaine Brody in the
U.S. The subjects of the research are three generations of women: grandmothers, middle aged daughters
and adult grand daughters. Part of the research
looks at the attitudes of each generation regarding
family care of the elderly, and gender appropriate
roles. Another part of the research programme is
looking at actual caregiving of middle-aged daughters in relation to their elderly mothers. Brody's
(1981) main concern is the stress for the woman in
the middle, who is often in her middle age, caught
between obligations to parents and to offspring, and
perhaps also the desire (and necessity, maybe) to
remain in, enter or re-enter the labour market.
Brody is also concerned about trends for the future,
and policy implications. Among the findings, it
emerges that there was general agreement among the
three generations about gender-appropriate roles.
But the trend was for each successively younger generation to endorse more strongly propositions about
women sharing domestic tasks and care work, and
women having access to educational and employment
opportunities. All three generations strongly af-
firmed the traditional values of family responsibility for care of the elderly.
    Some interesting specific findings are noted:
more than threequarters of the granddaughters
favoured helping their grandmothers, but only 22% of
the grandmothers agreed with this. The grandmothers
were more likely to favour paying for care of the
elderly rather than obliging a working daughter to
provide care, and to believe that formal services
can often replace family care so far as instrumental
tasks are concerned. Brody suggests that this can
be interpreted as supporting the often-expressed
view that the elderly wish to avoid becoming burdens
on their families. Brody stresses that attitudes
cannot be taken as simple predictors of actual

behaviour, but the link between the two can be examined by looking at actual care provided by middle-
aged daughters to their mothers. Evidence is beginning to emerge (Brody 1982) that although the
middle-aged daughers may be under considerable
stress, they do not wish to give up what they see as
their responsibilities.

On the basis of this and other studies Brody
recommends income supports for the elderly; increased housing options; financial help for families;
family support by way of respite services, transport
and so on; better information about available provision; systematic programmes to monitor and respond
to changes over time; more flexible conditions of
paid employment to enable people to combine work and
parent care. She argues that if support available
to the women in the middle is not improved, in the
long term the cost to the society may be greatly
increased.

Brody's study is particularly valuable because
it looks simultaneously at the perspectives of
cared-for, the carers and the potential carers, in
parallel with actual care-giving behaviour, and thus
provides the beginnings of a data base on trends
which are relevant to policy development on service
provision. No comparable study is taking place in
this country, although the research I shall discuss
below is attempting to explore both the perspectives
of the cared-for and the carers.
5. As to problems and concerns of the elderly
cared-for, the EOC (1980, 1982) reports, Nissel and
Bonnerjea (1982) and Rossiter and Wicks (1982) do
not set out to analyse these. But by focussing
solely on the concerns of the carers, they relegate
the cared-for to the status of objects - a serious
drawback which Brody avoids by incorporating the
cared-for as participants in the caring and helping
process.

The relegation to object status of the old people whose carers were studied in the U.K. researches
may, wittingly or unwittingly, reflect a real lack
of choices for the old. How far are elderly people
who require help of some kind able to express their
preferences, let alone put them into practice ?
This is a question I hope to explore in my own research. U.K. policy makes much not only of community care but also of client self-determination, and
choices about appropriate care from an array of
services and benefits. These are together sometimes
referred to, particularly in professional journals,
as the 'Continuum of Care', which embraces home-

based care and help at one extreme through sheltered
housing, day care and respite care in part 3 accommodation or hospital, to long term institutional
care. However, such evidence as we have suggests
that choice of service is Hobson's choice, and the
continuum of care forms part of the rhetoric of professional organizations rather than the reality of
services available to the elderly.

My research, a part of which will be discussed
in the following section, derives partly from my
concern to look at the realities of daily life and
support relationships from the micro perspectives of
elderly women and their supporters. The data will
shed further light on the relationships between
community care policy, perceptions of dependency and
its genesis, and choices to be made in the face of
dependency.

DAILY LIVES OF ELDERLY WOMEN LIVING ALONE, AND THEIR EXPERIENCES OF SUPPORT AND SERVICES

My current research aims to explore the views of 50
women over the age of 75 who live alone on their
daily lives and past experiences; in parallel with
the views of people identified by the women as their
prime carers. The women have been identified using
age/sex registers of two general practices in different areas of a large Midlands city. I aim to discover, through interviews, how the women spend their
time, what they see as the most significant - both
positive and negative - features of their daily
lives and how their present circumstances and views
of their worlds have evolved over the years. I am
taking a particular interest in their experiences -
if any - of depending on others for personal care,
instrumental or emotional support and provision of
services. I am interested in how support relationships came about and the part the women played in
any key decisions which were made about help needed.
Where support relationships are identified by the
women, the supporters are also interviewed about
their views on the relationship, how it evolved, its
strengths and problems, and their prognosis for its
future development.

The fieldwork is in its early stages, but the
plan is to re-interview the 50 women and their prime
carers after about 9 months - or earlier if a sudden
change in circumstances takes place - in order to
seek out their perspectives on any changes which
have occurred in the circumstances of the women and/
or their supportive relationships. In particular,

I shall explore reasons for changes and decisions made by any of the parties to relationships. The research may offer a new look at co-ordination among community services and with families who support the women; at how key decisions are made, and by whom.

There have been many surveys of the circumstances and needs of elderly people living at home, and their use of services. By the very nature of their approach to research questions, surveys seldom lend themselves to detailed analysis of the meanings attached by individuals to the 'facts' which they report. Mindful of Beeson's (1975) plea for phencm enological research in order to discover concepts which reflect the reality of people's - especially women's - subjective experience, it is the meanings of dependency, support and service provision to the parties involved which my research seeks to uncover. The subsequent endeavour would be to relate the individual's expressions to aspects of policy and practice of community care. It is, of course, equally important to look at the experiences of elderly men, but the scale of my present research is too small to enable this comparison to be made.

I want to pick up, quite speculatively, two themes which are emerging from the early stages of fieldwork with the elderly women (at present carers' perspectives will not be discussed).

THE 'DOING NOTHING MUCH' SYNDROME

In finding out about how women spend their time it was striking that the almost inevitable answer to a question about what respondents had been doing the day before the interview was 'Oh nothing much', or 'nothing at all'. Taken at face value, one might assume these women's lives to be dull or empty. But through more specific questioning, it often emerged that in fact respondents did a great many things. Activities ranged from personal and household tasks, through various home-based leisure activities, to going out and about and engaging in social exchanges with a few, or even many people. To count as worthy of spontaneous mention, activities and events seemed to be: (a) slightly outside the usual routine (e.g. visiting family or friends, going to the theatre, going to a wedding) and/or (b) of particular import - positive or negative - both for the present and the future (e.g. going to the doctor).

Three speculative explanations offer themselves. First, the 'doing nothing much' syndrome may simply reflect a relative shrinkage in the number and/or

salience of roles, activities and social relationships engaged in with increasing age. That is, the
individual may be experiencing involuntary disengagement (Cumming and Henry, 1961). But this cannot
fully account for those women who are busy for most
of the day with the kind of activities engaged in
over a lifetime, yet still report they are doing
nothing much.

A second possibility is that the 'doing nothing
much' syndrome reflects a generally gloomy outlook
on life. This may have been true for some individuals who seemed to be depressed or fatalistic, having low expectations of quality of life in old age.
But such an explanation could not account for the
majority of cases.

A third explanation is that many of the activities these women engage in are part of what is traditionally 'women's work': keeping body and soul
together, keeping the house, fetching the shopping
and so on. Such work is essentially private, home-
centred, unremarked and unremarkable right across
the lifespan of a majority of women. It has also
been systematically devalued in our society (Oakley,
1981). Why, therefore, should we expect old women
to begin talking about these kinds of tasks in terms
of meaningful activities ? Given that many of the
former beneficiaries of their 'women's work' -
husbands, children - have moved on, and elderly
women have just themselves to care for most of the
time, it seems particularly unlikely that taken-for-
granted activities should be spontaneously remarked
upon.

Taken in conjunction with the next theme, it
will be seen that the 'doing nothing much' syndrome
is of some practical relevance so far as service
provision is concerned.

PASSIVE RESPONDERS AND ACTIVE INITIATORS

The second theme I want to discuss is the passivity
and activity of old women in relation to controlling
their own lives from day to day.

The women interviewed to date fall into one of
two broad groups. One group, the passive responders
(PR), seem to lack positive control over the ordering of their own lives. The other, active initiators (AI), are very much in charge of life. The two
groups do not seem to have discrete characteristics
in terms of health and dependency: some PR women are
fit, and suffer few physical restrictions on their
potential for activity; and some AI women are

extremely frail, face many problems of physical dependency and receive a great deal of support. They
see themselves, however, as being 'in charge' of
their helpers. (None of the women to date appears
to suffer marked loss of intellectual capacity). So
far, there is no obvious emergent link with social
class - whether defined by own or husband's occupation, or by terminal education age - or relative
affluence, present or past. The PR and AI groups
both contain individuals of varying social class and
varying levels of wealth or poverty. Neither is
there any obvious link with current family structure,
in particular contact with surviving children. (As
the research proceeds the possibility of links between class, status and family relationships, and
activity/passivity, will of course be under constant
review).

Some examples may be given by way of illustration, followed by a tentative explanatory hypothesis
which emerges from the data.

1. <u>Active Initiator: Mrs J.</u>, a 95 year old lady,
had had four children, and had been living alone
since her husband's death, at the age of 93, five
years ago. He had died at home after illness over
twelve months. Mrs J. looked after him with a great
deal of help from services: this was as she had
wished. At the time of interview, she was receiving
considerable support from a home help, two neighbours and all her children. She and her husband had
been very keen on the theatre and on travel, and had
been on cycling trips to many parts of the country.
These leisure pursuits - cycling excepted - continued to figure importantly in Mrs J.'s life despite
her considerable frailty; when I first called at her
house she was away on holiday with her daughter.
She reported going on many outings with her children
and grandchildren by car, and visiting the theatre
each saturday night. Mrs J. was a women very much
in control of her own life, who expressed contentment. One comment of hers was "If you moan, people
don't want to know you. As long as you're cheerful
and enjoy a joke, you'll always have plenty of
friends".

2. <u>Active Initiator: Mrs P.</u>, aged 82, had trained
and worked as a teacher, and had been married for a
few years to a man who was also a teacher. Mrs P.
had given up work in order to look after her sick
mother for several years. At the beginning of the
second war she took administrative work in the

Elderly Women and Disadvantage

Ministry of Fuel and Power, and remained in the
Civil Service until reaching retirement age. She
still continues with some social contacts made during her working life, and despite quite severe arthritis manages to get out and about regularly, and
visit her sister in Nottingham. Having lived in the
same house for 40 years in a neighbourhood which has
changed little she retains many friends nearby. Her
lifelong pleasure - from the age of six - has been
playing the piano and singing. This she stills
manages to do, and because of her piano never feels
bored or lonely. Of her present situation she said
"Nothing to grumble about, and a great deal to be
thankful for".

3. <u>Passive Responder: Mrs B.</u>, aged 82, had lived
alone for seven years, since the sudden death of her
husband. He had worked for the gasboard, and Mrs B.
had devoted her married life to caring for her home
and husband. She had had neither children nor work
outside the home. She seemed depressed and with-
drawn, and described herself as waiting to die. She
was receiving no help, and said she required none.
Although relatively physically robust, Mrs B. engaged only in activities to do with personal care and
household tasks. She reported that this had been
true also for much of her married life.

4. <u>Passive Responder: Mrs H.</u>, this woman, aged 86,
had been living alone for 25 years, since her
husband's death. She appeared somewhat frail, walking with a stick, and reported that she had not been
out unaccompanied for many years. Mrs H. spent most
of her waking hours at her married daughter's house,
being collected in the mornings and returned at bed
time. Her daughter was taking care of all Mrs H.'s
household tasks. Mrs H. said "I couldn't even manage to boil an egg without ruining it". This had
been going on for a number of years, and Mrs H.
seemed to take it entirely for granted. She
expressed contentment with her life at present, saying, "I have always spent so much of my time just
waiting for people and keeping myself to myself -
waiting to be talked to, waiting for my husband to
come home, waiting for my daughter to come or my
neighbour to fetch my shopping....". She needed
other people to control her life, and was quite
happy that this should be so.

AI women had in common the fact that they had either
initiated new interests, and/or sustained past

interests and therefore felt a sense of purpose
about life. PR women, in contrast, lacked any definite purpose in life. Clearly, there is a parallel here between AI women and the notion of
'engagement' and between PR women and 'disengagement'. In this sense, what is emerging from research is not new. However, looking at other
characteristics of the women, this research theme
may be important in two particular ways. First, a
new, albeit tentative, hypothesis as to the factors
associated with active initiation and passive response suggests itself; and second, there may be implications for modes of formal service provision if
and when need becomes apparent.

A Hypothesis
The tentative hypothesis which suggests itself - and
will be examined more closely as research proceeds -
is that AI women tend to be those who have created
and maintained space in their lives for investing
energy in activities over and above their involvement in traditional women's work such as looking
after other people (spouse, ageing parent(s),
children) right across the lifespan. AI women are
more likely to have had work outside the home which
they found fulfilling, and to have hobbies or interests pursued over many years. For Mrs J., discussed above, her interests in travel and theatre had
featured all her life. Mrs P., who had found her
paid work fulfilling, had also derived great joy,
lifelong, from her piano. Other examples could be
given.
     In contrast, PR women tend to have engaged in
care-work to the exclusion of all else for a substantial proportion of their lives. Neither Mrs H.
nor Mrs B., the PR women described earlier, had
worked outside the home after marriage; Mrs B. had
never had any hobbies or particular interests.
Mrs H., however, had been very keen on photography,
but said she had no time for it after her daughter's
birth.

EXPLANATIONS AND IMPLICATIONS

There already exist a number of 'typologies' of older women. For example Jacobs (1977) identifies
eleven types of American women; Bart (1975) identifies five types. Typologies can further our understanding, but there is also a danger that categoriz-
ation and labelling becomes an end in itself.
Categorizations are after all social constructions,

and should not be treated as 'objective givens'.

The implications for carers of the two categories of women I have discussed here are drawn from their contrasting self-perceptions. AI women see themselves as people who make their own decisions and control their own lives. They do not see themselves as dependent upon and subordinate to others, despite, in some cases, receiving various kinds of essential support from a number of people. They see themselves as ordering the help they receive. PR women, in contrast, see themselves as circumscribed by and dependent on the routines of their lives, whether or not their lifestyles are influenced and/ or controlled by other people.

A change in health status or usual social network - e.g. death of a family member or close friend - may act as the trigger for initiating or reviewing service provision: whether by lay or official supporters. As part of their response, it is important that service providers should discover something about the woman's self-perception of relative activity or passivity in ordering her life. If, for example, a period of acute illness and high physical and mental dependency in an AI woman is handled by service providers without having knowledge of and regard for the woman's usual self-perception of relative autonomy, there is a danger that she may be treated as if she were a passive responder. She may not be treated as a responsible adult, and thus may become the object, rather than subject, of service provision. Further service providers may be in danger of creating need and demand for services over and above those originally required.

Similarly, service provision to PR women needs to be organized in the light of some knowledge of the women's usual self-perception of relative passivity. Despite their professed aims of sensitive support, service providers may fail to strike the appropriate balance between the inhumane extremes of reinforcing dependence and subordination on the one hand, and enforcing unwelcome independence on the other.

The practical import of the conceptual distinction between AI and PR women is underscored by the fact that the usual notions and indices of dependency commonly applied (often implicitly) by professional services providers, do not necessarily fit in a commonsense and logical fashion with the women's own self-perceptions. Persistence and subtlety may be needed to discover these, bearing in mind (a) the 'doing nothing much' syndrome discussed earlier, which may pose a great challenge to anyone seeking information about usual lifestyle, and (b) the fact that professionals' first encounters are likely to be with women in some kind of crisis or other atypical set of circumstances.

The tentative nature of the hypothesis concerning activity and passivity, and therefore the provisional status of the associated categories, must be re-emphasized. I wish to avoid any suggestion that the categories AI and PR are simple ones, to be associated with simple and obvious service responses: this is clearly not the case. Mere labelling solves no practical problems and may indeed create new ones, by, for example, ascribing stereotyped 'object' status to recipients of services. The research design, following up women and their supporters after initial interviews, should enable these ideas to be explored further. It may also be possible to identify a range of service provisions which are appropriate and effective from the women's point of view and which also avoid the self-generating escalation of service demands.

CONCLUSION

This paper has attempted to summarise some of the evidence that elderly women are relatively disadvantaged as compared with elderly men. By taking as an example policy on community care, the implications for women of some of the assumptions about gender order, incorporated into many aspects of social policy, have been raised.

In-depth analysis of the perceptions which elderly women have of their lives, and of any support relationships in which they are engaged, complements societal-level analyses of the social creation and reinforcement of dependency in old age, e.g. Walker (1980), Phillipson (1982). Work on both levels is necessary as part of the endeavour to expose both ageism and sexism in social policies. Such work should also help to stimulate the development of appropriate and equitable provision of, and access to, services.

ACKNOWLEDGEMENTS

The research described here is supported by the Nuffield Foundation. Thanks are due to Ken Blakemore, Rae Harrison and Meg Stacey for their helpful comments on an earlier draft. And of course thanks are also due to the women I interviewed.

REFERENCES

Abrams, M. (1980) Beyond-three score and ten. A
    second report on a survey of the elderly.
    Micham: Age Concern.
Bart, P. (1975) Emotional and social status of the
    older woman. In P. Bart et al No longer young:
    The older woman in America. Institute of
    Gerontology, University of Michigan, Wayne
    State University.
Beeson, D. (1975) Women in studies of ageing: A
    critique and suggestion. Social Problems 23:
    52-59.
Bond, M. (1980) Women's work in a woman's world.
    M.A. Dissertation, Department of Applied Social
    Studies, University of Warwick.
Bowling, A. & Cartwright, A. (1982) Life after a
    death, London: Tavistock.
Brody, E. (1981) "Women in the middle" and family
    help to older people. The Gerontologist 21 (5):
    471-80.
Brody, E. (1982) The dependent elderly and women's
    changing role: Mimeo. Phidelphia: Philadelphia
    Geriatric Center.
Cartwright, A. & O'Brien, M. (1977) Social class
    variations in health care and the nature of
    general practitioners consultations. In M.
    Stacey (ed) The Sociology of the N.H.S. Keele:
    University of Keele.
Cumming, E. & Henry, W. (1961) Growing Old New York:
    Basic Books.
Delphy, C. (1981) Women's stratification studies. In
    H. Roberts (ed) Doing Feminist Research.
    London: Routledge & Kegan Paul
Department of Health & Social Security (1981)
    Growing Older. London: HMSO
Equal Opportunities Commission (1980) The experience
    of caring for elderly and handicapped dependents
    Survey report Manchester: EOC.
Equal Opportunities Commission (1982) Caring for the
    elderly and handicapped: Community care
    policies and women's lives. Manchester: EOC
Ermisch, J. (1982) Resources of the elderly - Impact
    of present commitments and established trends.
    In M. Fogarty (ed), Retirement Policy: The next
    fifty years. London: Heinemann Educational for
    Policy Studies Institute.
Fairhurst, E. (1982) 'Growing old gracefully' as
    opposed to 'mutton dressed as lamb': The social
    construction of recognising older women. Paper
    presented to B.S.A. Annual Conference,

Manchester.
Fairhurst, E. & Lightup, R. (1981) The menopause: Trauma on road to serenity ? Paper presented to Women in Later Life Conference, London
Finch, J. & Groves, D. (1980) Community Care and the Family: A case for equal opportunities ? Journal of Social Policy 9 (4): 487-511
Jacobs, R. (1977) A typology of older American women. In F. Riessman (ed) Older persons: unused resources for unmet needs. London: Sage.
Jerrome, D. (1981) The significance of friendship for women in later life. Ageing & Society 1 (2) 175-97.
Matthews, S. (1979) The social world of old women. London: Sage.
Nissel, M. and Bonnerjea, L. (1982) Family care of the handicapped elderly: who pays ? London: Policy Studies Institute
Oakley, A. (1981) Subject Women. Oxford: Martin Robertson.
Opit, L.J. (1977) Domiciliary care for the elderly sick: Economy or neglect ? British Medical Journal 1: 30-3.
Phillipson, C. (1981) Women in later life: Patterns of control and subordination. In Bridget Hutter and Gillian Williams (eds) Controlling Women: The normal and the deviant, London: Croom Helm.
Phillipson. C. (1982) Capitalism and the Construction of old age, London: Macmillan.
Preston, C. (1975) An Old Bag: the stereotype of the older woman. In P. Bart et al No longer young: the older woman in America. Institute of Gerontology, University of Michigan, Wayne State University.
Rossiter, C. and Wicks, M. (1982) Crisis or Challenge ? Family care, elderly people and social policy, London: Study Commission on the Family.
Rowlings, C. (1981) Social Work with Elderly People. London: George Allen & Unwin.
Sontag, S. (1972) The double standard of ageing. Saturday Review 23 September: 29-38
Tinker, A. and Brion, M. (1981) Is there equality for women in Housing ? Housing & Planning Review 37 (2): 7-9, 19.
Townsend, P. (1979) Poverty in the United Kingdom Harmonsworth: Penguin.
Ungerson, C. (1981) Women, work and the 'caring capacity of the community': A report of a research review. Unpublished report to Social Services Research Council.

Walker, A. (1980) The Social Creation of Poverty and
    Dependency in Old Age. <u>Journal of Social
    Policy</u> 9 (1): 48-75
Walker, A. (1981) Towards a political economy of old
    age. <u>Ageing & Society</u> 1 (1): 73-94.
Ward, S. (1981) <u>Pensions</u>, London: Pluto.

Chapter Three

CRIME AND THE ELDERLY: EXPERIENCE AND PERCEPTIONS

R. I. Mawby

INTRODUCTION

To many, the heading 'Crime and the elderly' may be
translated unequivocally into 'crime against the
elderly', seen as a self-evident problem in modern
society, and a barrier in the way of a transition
towards a happier old age. Central to the quality
of life debate surrounding the elderly is a concern
that security is under threat from the vandal and
the mugger, symbols of disorder in contemporary
society.
·   Such images are given clarity by a number of
crimes against the elderly which receive prominent
press coverage, and achieve respectability at the
hands of politicians who focus on crime and disorder
as the key problems facing Britain in the 1980s, and
the shift to a 'law and order society'as one solution (Hall et al, 1978). Margaret Thatcher, when
leader of the opposition, confirmed to the Conservative Women's Conference in 1979 that 'hundreds of
elderly people no longer feel safe from assault and
robbery... they fear to leave their homes'.
      Equally, the crime problem may become a major
consideration in assessing the housing needs of the
elderly. For example, Senator Edward Kennedy,
addressing the American Senate Subcommittee on
Housing for the Elderly, asserted in 1972 that 'The
threat of crime and violence against our older
citizens demands a response from all levels of
government... A decent and safe living environment
is an inherent right of all elderly citizens'. (1)
      It is not the aim of this chapter to question
the importance of safety and security for the elderly, or indeed, any other group of citizens. However, before promising solutions, it is necessary to
examine the facts. In the following two sections

the relationship between crime and the elderly is
considered from two perspectives. First, the experiences of the elderly, as both offenders and victims, is assessed. Second, the attitudes towards and
perceptions of crime held by the elderly is afforded
attention. Having demonstrated that the issue is by
no means as straightforward as might have been anticipated, the final section combines explanation
with some practical policy-oriented suggestions.

EXPERIENCE OF CRIME

In considering the experience of crime of the elderly, as either offenders or victims, a number of
methodological difficulties arise. These principally relate to the fact that not all crime is reported to and recorded by the police, and that even
where crimes are recorded, less than half the offenders are subsequently identified. Since with regard
to offending by the elderly, we are dependent upon
data from official statistics, data must be treated
with caution. However, in considering the extent
to which different categories of the population are
victimised, we have access to one other type of
data, in addition to police records, namely the
victim survey. Such surveys have been carried out
on a regular basis in America for some years. In
Britain published data are restricted to our own
and one survey in London by Sparks and his colleagues, (Sparks et al 1977), but a series of national
victim surveys was instigated by the Home Office in
1981. In this chapter, reference will be made to
both police records and the available victim surveys,
but the main emphasis will be on a victim survey
carried out in Sheffield by my colleagues and I in
1975 (Bottoms et al 1981).
    Before concentrating on the elderly as victims
it may be useful to consider briefly details of
elderly offenders. In figure one, offender rates
per 100,000 in each age group have been abstracted
from the Criminal Statistics for 1980, (Home Office
1981) including all offenders either prosecuted or
officially cautioned for offences. As is immediately apparent, the official offender rates for both
elderly males and females are relatively low, and
indeed offender rates appear to peak for boys aged
15 and girls aged 14 and decline thereafter.
    Further detail, for example of the crimes
committed by the elderly, are not available in the
published statistics. It is, however, interesting
that the elderly offender receives distinctive

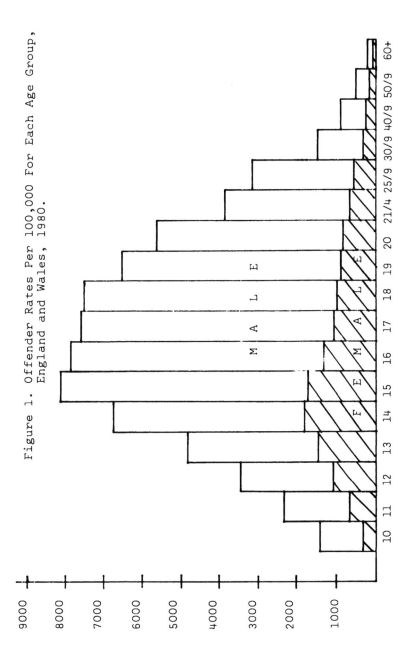

Figure 1. Offender Rates Per 100,000 For Each Age Group, England and Wales, 1980.

47

treatment from the police. Thus, in 1980, for all
known   offenders aged 60 or more, 32% of males
and 53% of females received a caution. The corresponding figures for the 50-59 age group were 3% and
9% (similar to those for the adult population as a
whole), indicating that whatever gerontologists may
say about the variability of the ageing process, for
the police special consideration begins at 60 !
    It is of course possible that elderly offenders
go relatively underrecorded in official statistics,
because of the reluctance of the police and victims
to take official action. Nevertheless, it seems
unlikely that such practices would account for all
the difference, and it is probably safe to conclude
that the elderly are more law-abiding than other
adult age groups, and especially more so than
adolescents.
    Such a conclusion may reflect common-sense, but
if so it scarcely matches findings on the experiences of the elderly as the victims of crime. Data
from our own survey, conducted in seven working class
residential areas of Sheffield in 1975, reveals
clearly that from a total sample of 763 households,
elderly respondents (numbering 147) were statisti-
cally less likely to have been the victims of crimes
than were younger respondents.

Table 1. Number of Different Victimisation Items
          for each Respondent

	Elderly		Other Respondents		Total Sample	
	n	%	n	%	n	%
0	112	76	352	57	464	61
1	30	20	168	27	198	26
2+	5	5	96	16	101	13
Total	147	101	516	100	763	100

This difference was maintained for each type of
crime separately. Moreover this finding is repli-
cated in the London victim survey, (Sparks et al
1977) in a wider range of victim surveys in America,
(Ennis 1967, Reynolds 1973, Hindelang 1976) and in
details abstracted from police statistics (Bell
1982). It is clear that contrary to popular opinion
the elderly are relatively safe from crime.
Before discussing the possible explanations for this
finding, it may be interesting to note the

distinctive features of the elderly who were victim-
ized:
    First, controlling for sex, it was evident that
sex was also related to victimisation, with males
more at risk than females.

Table 2.   Percentage of Elderly and other
            Respondents who were crime victims,
            controlling for sex.

	Elderly (n = 147)	Other Respondents (n = 616)	Total (n = 763)
Males	31.0	48.1	45.4
Females	19.1	37.6	33.4
Total	23.8	42.9	39.2

    Second, we were able to control for whether or
not respondents lived in areas of the city with
particularly high crime rates. Interestingly, while
for younger respondents victimisation rates were
33.7% in low crime rate areas and 55.3% in high rate
areas, the difference was marginal for older respondents (22.4% and 26.5% respectively). That is,
the elderly living in 'problem' areas were hardly
any more likely to be at risk than those living in
other working class areas.
    Third, those who had been employed in unskilled
manual jobs were less likely to have been the
victims of crime than other respondents.
    Finally, while household size was unrelated to
victimisation, there was a tendency for those with
less local friends to be more at risk.
    How then might these findings be explained ?
To answer this, it is appropriate to consider more
generally why some categories are more likely to be
the victims of crime than others (Mawby 1982).
    In some respects, one would anticipate that the
elderly would be more at risk than younger age
groups. For example, age increases frailty and
vulnerability, and so reduces the possibility of
resistance; poverty or absent-mindedness may mean
that the elderly take less protective measures vis
a vis their property.
    On the other hand, three explanations of low
victimisation rates shed some light on the findings.
First, it has been shown that much crime, especially
against the person, is victim-precipitated: at the
extreme, it may be that the 'victim' of violence is

distinguished only by being the one who fared worst
in the exchange (Wolfgang 1958). Thus, if the
elderly are less involved in inter-changes which
may result in an offence being committed, they are
less likely to be victimised. Incidentally, the
finding that serious injury during, say, a robbery,
is most closely associated with victim-resistance,
(Wolfgang 1982) also explains the finding that
violent offences involving the elderly are relatively least likely to result in serious injury
(Hindelang 1976).

Second, we may consider the question of
attractiveness. Where crimes are rationally planned, those targets which appear to offer the most
reward will be more at risk. Thus, while accepting
both that many crimes are unplanned, and that
appearances are often deceptive, the widespread
finding that old-age is associated with poverty
(Townsend 1974) may partially explain the distinction between elderly people and others. Poverty
could also influence the relationship between
victimisation and social class we found for the
elderly, and perhaps the lower relative risk for the
elderly in 'problem' areas.

Finally, it appears that location is associated
with risk. Given that certain locations are especially vulnerable to crime (public houses, city
centres, nearly-empty streets etc.) it follows that
those who spend most time in these locations are
most at risk. Thus, where the life styles of the
elderly differ from those of younger age groups, the
fact that the elderly are less often out of the home
affords them more protection. Returning to the
question of vulnerability, it is perhaps worth
pointing out that crimes against property are more
likely if the property is empty, so those spending
more time at home are doubly protected. Sparks and
his colleagues (Sparks et al 1977) demonstrate
clearly the relationship between age, crime, and
activities. Perhaps the unfortunate irony of this
is that if, in general, policies are pursued which
encourage the elderly to participate more in activities outside the home, their risk from crime
might be expected to rise.

As has been noted, the lower rates of victimisation for the elderly conflict with popular
perceptions. While the above discussion has aimed
at explaining the findings as a reflection of the
wider social circumstances and life styles of the
elderly, it scarcely explains why there should be
so much concern about crimes against the elderly.

Crime and the Elderly: Experience and Perceptions

To   understand this, we need to consider the attitudes held by the elderly towards crime and the crime problem.

ATTITUDES TOWARDS CRIME AND THE CRIME PROBLEM

If the elderly are less at risk from crime than
other sections of the population, one might expect
them to express less concern over the problem of
crime.   In actuality, this is not the case.   In the
Sheffield survey, for example, we included five
statements on the crime situation, responses to
which were scaled to construct a crime problem scale,
where a low score indicated "awareness" of the crime
problem.   On the 21 point scale, the elderly scored
an average 1.8 lower than the mean for the total
sample, and, as is illustrated in table 3, they were
significantly more likely to define crime as a contemporary concern.   Indeed, 24% of the elderly had
a minimum score for each of the items, strongly
agreeing that there was a problem in each case.

Table 3.   Crime Problem Scale

	Percentage	
	Elderly (n = 147)	Total Sample (n = 762)
Agree there is a problem (5 - 11)	85.7	65.1
Neutral (12 - 18)	14.3	31.6
Reject suggestions of a problem (19 - 25)	0	3.3
Total	100.0	100.0

Taking each item separately, the elderly were no
less likely than other respondents to accept that
"crime isn't as serious as many other modern problems".   However, on the other four items, there were
differences of approximately 20%, with older respondents more likely to accept that "our society is in
a state of moral chaos", "criminal gangs run amok in
many cities in Britain" and "it is no longer safe
for women to walk out alone after dark", and refut-
ing the suggestion that there was "no more crime in

51

England now than there was before the war".
Again these findings are paralleled by those
from national opinion polls, (2) and other research.
For example, in America Cook and Cook (1976) showed
that the elderly were most afraid of walking out
alone at night and had become increasingly concerned about crime during the preceding decade, while
Garofalo (1979) used data from the National Victim
Survey to demonstrate that while the rate of personal victimisation fell from 12.5% for the 16-19
year olds to 3.4% for the 65 or more age group, the
proportion who said they felt unsafe in their homes
at night rose from 37% to 63%. In Britain, although
Sparks et al (1977) did not find any age variation
in perceptions of safety in the home, they also
noted a difference in concern over safety in the
streets.
   There are, of course, a number of reasons why
experience and perceptions may not be correlated
with one another. Personal experience is, after
all, only one of a number of factors which may influence attitudes and perceptions. Several explanations have been suggested by previous researchers.
   First, the fact that groups like the elderly
spend more time in their homes may be a result of
their fear of crime (Balkin 1979), rather than
merely a cause of low rates of victimisation. That
is, low rates of victimisation are the result of
protective action, such that freedom from crime is
bought "at the expense of richness of life style,
such as the freedom to visit friends and relatives,
to sit in outdoor locations, to participate in the
free activities of the city, or to traverse the
neighbourhood" (Lawton et al 1976), a condition
Conklin has termed indirect victimisation (Conklin
1971).
   Second, fear may be related to the anticipated
impact of the crime rather than to risk itself.
Thus research (Gay et al 1975, Maguire 1980) has
shown the elderly to be more psychologically affected by crime than younger victims. Thirdly, related
to this, role socialisation may be important, with
groups such as the elderly being encouraged to see
themselves as frail and therefore less able to
"survive" crime (Garofalo 1979). Without wishing
to deny the importance of these factors, two further
issues will be considered in more detail here.
These are the role of the media and the question of
validity.
   Illustrations of the prominence of the elderly
victim in media coverage of crime are common. In

research I myself directed   ·(Mawby et al 1979) on
the handling of social work issues in the press, one
example of this arose, the case of Mrs Willitts,
allegedly battered to death by two children, raising
for some newspapers the wider issue of crime as
committed by the young and a threat to the elderly.
However, although the presentation of the victim has
received some attention by researchers on the media,
(Hall et al 1978) in general research on crime in
the press has focussed on the offender. In a small
study, therefore, we abstracted details of the
characteristics of offenders and victims from a 50%
sample of current crime reports in the national and
local press during one month in 1979.(3) Given the
fact that the survey covered only one month, care
must be taken not to overgeneralise. Nevertheless,
the findings - illustrated in table 4 - were striking. Only 8% of victims were aged sixty or more,
revealing a slight underrepresentation of elderly
victims in press stories. In contrast, while only
3% of offenders were aged sixty or more, a comparison with criminal statistics suggests that the
elderly offender is overrepresented in press
reports.

Table 4.   Crime in the Press
           Age of Offender and Victim

Offender(%)		Victim(%)	
16	7	10	12
17-19	14	10-19	33
20-59	76	20-59	48
60	3	60	8

The reasons for this are by no means clear, but they
partly relate to the concerns of journalism for
stories with entertainment value. Thus violence,
especially murder, and sex offences, or offences
with a sexual motive, were starkly overrepresented,
and reflecting this the victims most commonly cited
were adolescent girls. Whilst crimes involving
elderly victims "scored" less on entertainment
value, the elderly offender was newsworthy, precisely because of his atypicality, on the lines of the
"man bites dog" theme. Thus, the elderly post
office robber described in one story was "good news"
because it was in conflict with commonsense notions
of typical robbers, while the newsworthiness of the
story involving an elderly sex offender and a series

of adolescent partners is evident - the elderly are
seen as rarely offending, and equally rarely sexua-
lly active.

It could be argued that the month in question
was atypical. However, it is also worth noting
that, using an attention score to measure the presentation of stories, those involving elderly victims received no more prominent treatment than other
stories.

Such findings, of course, relate to only one
aspect of media coverage. For example, it is valid
to suggest that press coverage of the elderly victim
should be compared with all other references to the
elderly. Moreover, media images of the elderly may
portray older people as frail and helpless, influ-
encing indirectly their attitudes towards crime.
One American study, for example, has shown that
television presentation of the elderly negatively
affects self-concept and may promote increased
alienation from society (Korzenny & Nevendorf 1980).

Finally, though, the relationship between
attitudes and perceptions and experience may be
considered in terms of the question of validity.
As a number of writers have pointed out (Furstenberg
1971, Lotz 1979, Yin 1980), the extent to which the
elderly express concern about crime varies according
to the precise wording of the questions. The
Sheffield survey allows this point to be considered
in detail, because it included a wide range of
questions related to perceptions of crime. Thus,
in addition to the items on the crime problem scale,
respondents were asked questions relating to:
(i) the advantages and disadvantages of living
in their area. (ii) the extensiveness of local
offence and offender rates relative to other areas.
(iii) changes in crime rates in their area. (iv)
what types of crime were "fairly common" around
where they lived. (v) whether crimes or deviant
acts described in vignettes were common in their
area. (vi) their risk from specific crimes like
burglary and vandalism.

Strikingly, on each of these dimensions, the
elderly either responded in a similar way to other
respondents or gave answers understating the extent
of crime when compared with other respondents. For
example, in response to a check-list, 7.5% of the
elderly, compared with 9.7% of middle aged and 14.9%
of younger respondents felt that violence was a
"fairly common sort of crime" locally (p 0.05), and
19.7% of the elderly compared with 8.5% and 6.5%
respectively (p 0.001) said that none of the items

on the list was common locally.

We are confronted, then, by a second paradox. Not only is there a difference between the experiences of crime of the elderly and their perceptions of the crime problem;   the elderly appear concerned over the crime problem, but do not see actual risk of crime on a local level as severe, compared with younger respondents.   Indeed, it would appear that risk and perceptions of risk are related, and that it is concern over the crime problem which is the most puzzling findings of this research.

Such a conclusion poses the need for further research into the attitudes and perceptions of the elderly.   However, it might be hypothesised that the scale measuring concern over the crime problem may be a measurement, not specifically of the prevalence of crime, but of feelings of impotence and powerlessness.   Thus, it is perhaps significant that women, another relatively powerless group in our society, also scored highly on the scale.   Most especially though, for the elderly, to whom social change - and lack of control over changes - is most evident, the scale may reflect an absence of security and wellbeing on a more general level than one relating merely to crime. If so, it points to a problem for the elderly which receives relatively little attention from academics using more conventional measurements of perceived needs.

DISCUSSION

To accept that the elderly are not especially at risk, and that - when asked specifically about their own situation - old people are not constantly living in fear of crime, is not to dismiss the need for concern.   While our findings are a salutory lesson for those who would seek to dramatise the plight of the elderly victim of crime, and a reassurance to those who are unduly concerned, we should still attempt to focus attention on the elderly victim. Crime can be a traumatic experience, and the needs of all victims have been largely ignored.

Essentially, we can distinguish three levels at which policies might be directed - the attitudes of the elderly towards crime, the prevention of crime against the elderly, and the response to elderly victims.

Considering the first two levels together, a number of American studies (Sherman et al 1976, Newman 1972) have advocated the advantages of segregated housing for the elderly.   The problem

here, however, is that the result may be something
of a cocoon in which the elderly may live, safe from
the threat of intrus ion, but perhaps more afraid of
the untested dangers of the world outside.   Risk,
and perception of risk, may diminish below their
already low levels, but concerns about the world
outside may be magnified.   In direct contrast, we
would argue that attempts should be made to decrease
the distancing process, so that the elderly may be
made more aware of what crimes occur and who commits
them.   We shall return to this when we consider
possible responses to elderly victims.

First though, let us look more closely at how
crimes against the elderly might be prevented.
Referring back to the explanations given for variations in victimisation, we should:

1. Influence vulnerability factors - mount
   crime prevention campaigns, encourage
   neighbour support and minimise isolation
   of the elderly.
2. Affect visible target attractiveness -
   educate the elderly to avoid obvious
   signs of possessions which may attract
   offenders.
3. Address location factors - notify danger
   spots to be avoided; give priority to
   the rehousing of elderly people who feel
   trapped and endangered by the environment
   (especially those who have been victimised).

These suggestions are not new, nor are they restricted to the elderly.   Yet, in the present context
to state them clearly may be a useful stimulus to
action.

If we finally turn to consider the ways in
which those elderly people who have been victims of
crime might be helped, two issues appear as important.   First, considering the likelihood that a
number of elderly people, and also some younger
victims, may suffer stress as a result of the crime,
the extension of schemes on the lines of Victims-
Aid is desirable.   However, given the difficulty of
being able to help all known victims, we would
emphasise two alternatives.   First, it could be
argued that programmes should focus specifically on
the elderly.   Secondly, there is a case for involving the police as a screening agency, (4) where
those (particularly the elderly) who are considered
in special need of help could be identified to other
agencies, including not only voluntary groups but

also statutory services.   The need for Social
Services Departments and the Probation Service to
recognise a role for themselves here (Doerner et al
1976) and for the needs of the victim to be an
integral part of police and social work training,
are crucial.   Related to this, it is important to
consider the part played by the elderly victim at
later stages of the criminal justice system.   Although there is considerable evidence that the victim
is responsible for most crimes being reported to
the police, (Mawby 1979) what little evidence there
is of the later processes (5) indicates that the
role of the victims is a minor one.   As Christie
(Christie 1976) has put it, the State, in assuming
responsibility as complainant, excludes the victim
from any meaningful role in "his" conflict, except
where he is needed as a witness.

But the direct result of this may be that the
victim is victimised for a second time, and in being
so excluded is encouraged to accept a generalised
stereotype of "his" offender.   In contrast, we would
argue that for most crimes a carefully managed con-
frontation of offender with the victim and the results of his action might have positive effects on
both parties.   Whilst the Community Service Order
was introduced as a means by which offenders could
repay "society" for the harm they had done, we would
advocate a more direct focus on the victim.   Thus
C.S. schemes, carefully managed and supervised by
social workers, probation officers and perhaps the
police, could be directed to helping victims whose
property has been damaged, allowing offenders to
see the extent of harm done and victims to view the
offender in a different light.   Actual matching of
offender and victim may be both difficult, and in
some cases undesirable, but it seems important to
encourage reparation, whether this be in a specific
case or on a general level.   The extent to which
offenders may effectively and efficiently compensate
for their crimes could of course be widened to
include more general help for the elderly in need.
Such a move towards emphasising the offender-victim
relationship is especially important where we consider the elderly victims of crimes which are frequently committed by the young.   More generally, the
needs of the victim of crime are as worthy of the
attentions of policy-makers as are needs in other
areas of the Welfare State.

Crime and the Elderly: Experience and Perceptions

SUMMARY

Focussing particularly on research in Sheffield, this chapter has addressed the relationship between crime and the elderly. Whilst the elderly appear underrepresented as offenders, it appears, more surprisingly, that the elderly are also underrepresented as the victims of crime. A number of explanations for this are suggested, relating to the lifestyles of the elderly.

The middle of the chapter then focusses on two paradoxes. The first is that the elderly appear particularly concerned about the crime problem, despite their relatively low rate of victimisation. The second is that perceptions of crime at the local level show a contrary pattern, with the elderly apparently reflecting a lesser awareness of risk.

In the light of this, practical suggestions need to focus on three issues. It is important to try to minimise crime against the elderly, and to help elderly victims, but it is also crucial to allay the fears of the elderly. In this context, we need to consider how far perceptions of the "crime problem" may reflect wider feeling of wellbeing, and the marginal status of elderly people in society.

NOTES

1. As quoted in Cook, F. and Cook, D. (1976)
2. See, for example, The Guardian, 23 November 1982
3. The local newspaper included in this study, which was carried out in collaboration with Judith Brown, was the Bradford Telegraph and Argus
4. Brostoff, P. (1976). In Britain, Victim Support Schemes vary in the extent to which the police play a discretionary role.
5. Currently Joanna Shapland of the Centre for Criminological Research, University of Oxford, is completing a study of the experiences of the victim-complainant in the Criminal Justice System.

REFERENCES

Balkin, S. (1979) "Victimization Rates, Safety and
    Fear of Crime", Social Problems, 26, 343-358.
Bell, D.S. (1982) Action Against Crime: Campaign
    Report. Age Concern, London.
Bottoms, A.E., Mawby, R.I. and Xanthos, P.D. (1981)
    Sheffield Study on Urban Social Structure and
    Crime, Part 3. Report to Home Office.
Brostoff, P. (1976) "The Police Connection: A New
    Way to get Information and Referral Services to
    the Elderly", in Goldsmith J. and Goldsmith S.
    (eds) Crime and the Elderly Lexington,
    Massachusetts.
Christie, N. (1976) "Conflicts as Property",
    British Journal of Criminology, 17.1, 1-15.
Cook, F. and Cook, D. (1976) "Evaluating the Hetroic
    of Crisis: A Case Study of Criminal Victimiza-
    tion of the Elderly", Social Services Review,
    50, 633.
Conklin, J. (1971) "Dimensions of Community Response
    to the Crime Problem", Social Problems, 18,
    373-385.
Doerner, W. et al (1976) "Correspondence Between
    Crime Victim Needs and Available Public
    Services", Social Services Review, 50, 482-490.
Ennis, P. (1967) "Criminal Victimization in the
    United States", in Presidents Commission on
    Law-Enforcement and Administration of Justice,
    Field Surveys III.
Furstenberg, F. (1971) "Public Reaction to Crime in
    the Streets", American Scholar, 40, 601-610.
Garofalo, J. (1979) "Victimization and Fear of
    Crime", Journal of Research in Crime and
    Delinquency, 16, 80-97.
Gay, M., Holton, C. and Thomas, M. (1975) "Helping
    the Victims", International Journal of Offender
    Therapy, 19, 263-269.
Hall, S. et al (1978) Policing the Crisis Macmillan,
    London.
Hindelang, M. (1976) Criminal Victimization in Eight
    American Cities, Ballinger, Massachusetts.
Home Office (1981) Criminal Statistics for England
    and Wales, 1980, HMSO, London.
Korzenny F. and Nevendorf, K. (1980) "Television
    Viewing and Self-Concept of the Elderly",
    Journal of Communication, 30.1, 71-80.
Lawton, M., Mahemow, L., Yaffe, S. and Feldman, S.
    (1976) "Psychological Aspects of Crime and Fear
    of Crime", in Goldsmith, J. and Goldsmith, S.
    (eds) Crime and the Elderly Lexington,

Massachusetts.
Lotz, R. (1979) "Public Anxiety about Crime",
    Pacific Sociological Review, 22, 241-254.
Maguire, M. (1980) "The Impact of Burglary Upon
    Victims", British Journal of Criminology 20,
    261-275.
Mawby, R.I., Fisher, C.J. and Parkin, A. (1979)
    "Press Coverage of Social Work", Policy and
    Politics, 7.4, 357-376.
Mawby, R.I. (1979) Policing the City Saxon House,
    Farnborough.
Mawby, R.I. (1982) "Crime and the Elderly: A Review
    of British and American Research", Current
    Psychological Reviews, 2.
Newman, O. (1972) Defensible Space Macmillan,
    London.
Reynolds, P. (1973) Victimization in a Metropolitan
    Region Minnesota Centre for Sociological
    Research, Minneapolis.
Sherman, E., Newman, E. and Nelson, A. (1976)
    "Patterns of Age Integration in Public Housing
    and the Incidence and Fears of Crime Among the
    Elderly", 67-73 in Goldsmith J. and Goldsmith
    S. Crime and the Elderly Lexington,
    Massachusetts.
Sparks, R., Genn, H. and Dodd, D. (1977) Surveying
    Victims, Wiley, London.
Townsend, P. (1979) Poverty in the United Kingdom
    Penguin, Harmondsworth.
Wolfgang, M. (1958) Patterns in Criminal Homicide
    University of Pennsylvania Press, Philadelphia
Wolfgang, M. (1982) "Victim Intimidation, Resistance
    and Injury", paper to Fourth International
    Symposium on Victimology, Japan.
Yin, P.P. (1980) "Fear of Crime Among the Elderly",
    Social Problems, 27, 492-504.

Chapter Four

ELDERLY VAGRANTS

Martin Blacher

INTRODUCTION

'He was a small, grey man, his face sunken with
age and rough living, his beard an uneven mass
overflowing his wrinkled neck. He was hatless.
His shredded clothes clung to him like a flung
heap of confetti. His lips were curled in to
meet toothless gums, his eyes were hazed
slivers beneath nearly closed lids. And almost
without pause he slavered wordless obscenities'

Charles Ackerman Berry (1978:47)

People still speak of 'an old tramp' or 'an old
dosser'. These familiar, resilient images remain
firmly embedded in the contemporary consciousness,
and the pejorative labels stubbornly persist in
everyday speech. Research carried out at Plymouth
Night Shelter has shown that the average age of
users during the first year of operation (Nov.1980-
Oct.1981) was only 39, and that this fell to 35 in
the second year. Certainly it seems the case that
older homeless men are more likely to be residents
of hostels than to use night shelters, as a recent
survey conducted in a Newcastle hostel confirms
(Burke, 1981). Similarly, in a national survey of
hostels and lodging houses conducted on behalf of
the D.H.S.S., Digby (1976) found an under representation of men under 30, in contrast to which he
notes: '...our sample contained a relative excess of
older men, particularly of those aged 50 to 69'
(page 128).
     In an earlier work Turner (1960) provides a
qualitative account of life in a London lodging
house, which also gives an indication of the wide age
range of the single homeless in the late 1950s.

Recent research funded by the Department of the
Environment   underlines the diversity of the
single homeless, describing them as a 'heterogenous
and ill-defined target population' (Drake et al,
1981). In the research, quantitative data had been
collected over a 3 year period in an interview
survey of 521 individuals in 7 local authority districts and in desk surveys of the clients of a national referral agency and the users of an East
London night shelter over a six months period. The
age structure of all three samples showed a marked
over-representation of young homeless men and women
compared with 1971 Census data. On the other hand,
subjects between the ages of 45 and 64 constituted
19% of the referral agency sample, 30% of the night
shelter sample, and 32% of the survey sample, while
those over the age of retirement comprised 4% of the
referral agency sample 1% of the night shelter sample, and 8% of the survey sample. It was also found
that men were far more likely than women to be long-
term homeless.
     There was a relationship between age and the
number of social and medical problems. Of those
over retirement 21% reported physical handicap, and
46% reported physical illness. When the ages of the
survey respondents were related to the length of
time they had been homeless and to the numbers reporting social and medical problems, it was found
that for the young group there was an increase of
disabilities and other problems with length of time
homeless, for the intermediate age group there was
no perceptible pattern, and for the middle aged and
elderly there was a reduction:

          'There may be a number of explanations for the
          low proportion of older long term homeless with
          problems; only the very hardy survive to old
          age, as people get old they are more likely to
          be picked up by caring agencies, or that the
          end of the road for the homeless with problems
          is an early death' (Drake et al 1981)

Similarly, Coulter (1982) argues that perhaps 'the
long term homeless with social and medical problems
just do not survive to old age', and emphasises that
'harsh conditions endured by thousands of chronically homeless people put at severe risk their health
and welfare'. He also stresses the 'extreme social
isolation of many homeless people'.
     Much of the recent skid row literature has fo-
cussed attention on vagrant alcoholics, the most

conspicuous sub-group of the homeless population.
Wiseman's (1970) interactionist analysis of
American skid row alcoholics and the various agenies
with which they routinely come into contact, and
works by Cook (1975) and by Archard (1979) are all
in this tradition.

The account which follows draws on both ethnographic material and recorded data relating to men
of 60 and over, who constituted a small but significant minority of the users of Plymouth Night Shelter.
The intention is not to account for or to explain
their homelessness, nor is it suggested that the men
who feature in this account are representative of
older homeless men in general. The aim is simply to
evoke distinctive aspects of the lives, perceptions,
and predicaments of some older homeless men who used
a night shelter.

NIGHTSHELTERS

A 'nightshelter' is, as the word implies, somewhere
in which the night can be passed under cover. A
nightshelter is used by those who have nowhere else
to go during the hours of darkness - the majority of
whom would be long-term homeless, those officially
categorised and labelled as 'N.F.A.': of no fixed
abode. Nightshelters generally are the most meagre
form of accommodation: they are, in fact, one step
removed from sleeping out, from 'roughing it' or
'skippering' as it is known by those who are habit-
ually obliged to do so. They are sex-segregated,
and very predominantly male. There is a certain
amount of variation among nightshelters in terms of
their basic characteristics, however. The report on
a recent survey of nightshelters conducted by
C.H.A.R. - the Campaign for the Homeless and Root-
less - highlighted some of these variations, for
instance, size. One of the smallest nightshelters
has eleven places, and the largest in England and
Wales has 108 beds. Some nightshelters are run by
the statutory sector, and some by the voluntary
sector. The oldest nightshelter in the survey
sample opened in 1860, and the most recent, Plymouth
Nightshelter, opened in 1980.

Far more significant are those features which
nightshelters have in common. Sleeping accommodation is usually in open dormitories. Residents are
provided with little more than a bed on which to
sleep, often without sheets, and sometimes without
even blankets. Staffing levels are low, staff pay
is poor and consequently the turnover is high.

Elderly Vagrants

There is a great deal of reliance on Community
Service volunteers or unpaid Volunteers. Access to
the shelter by residents is restricted, and not usually possible at all during the daytime. Washing
and toilet facilities are often inadequate.

The premises themselves are usually located in
non-residential areas, and are, typically, disused
factories, mission halls, schools or even railway
arches.

There are often rules relating to alcohol con-
sumption, smoking, violence, theft, and the payment
of rent. The institutional atmosphere and regime is
further reinforced by regulation times by which to
book in, to leave the following morning, and to have
meals.

Plymouth Nightshelter was first opened in
November of 1980, and came into being as the result
of an initiative by a local voluntary organisation
which was eventually guaranteed financial support
from the D.H.S.S. for the first three years of the
shelter's existence. The premises are an old former
mission hall, circa 1920, located in a distinctly
seedy non-residential area near the City's red light
district.

It had seemed apparent to the project's insti-
gators that although there were two large hostels in
Plymouth, and landladies who catered expressly for
those individuals usually officially described as
"single homeless", a number of men were regularly
sleeping rough around the city. The intention was
that the nightshelter should provide a hitherto
absent initial point of contact at street level for
such men, affording them a bed, meals, access to
medical care, and the possibility of referral to one
of the other available types of accommodation. In
short, the nightshelter was intended as a point of
entry into the realms of more stable accommodation:
in the most enduring image, the nightshelter is "the
bottom rung of the ladder".

In common with other nightshelters, the hours
of operation are limited. Plymouth Nightshelter
opens at 7 p.m. and closes again at 7 a.m. In
addition to a bed and toilet and bathing facilities,
residents are provided with a simple supper and
breakfast, a midday meal being obtainable by arrangement at the local day centre.

Various items of donated clothing are usually
available as required, and there are some old books
and magazines to read, as well as a radio, and now
a television, which are switched on at certain times.
There is always a full time member of staff on hand

to counsel residents when required, and in addition, there are usually voluntary workers, who help in particular with the preparation and serving of meals. Formal rules and regulations are kept to a minimum. Although food is only served until about 9 p.m., men can be admitted at any time during the night, and can come in however intoxicated they might be on arrival. However, drinking is not permitted to continue once men are in the building. It is policy to expect that a man should make arrangements to cover the cost of his accommodation the day after arriving, or after the weekend, should he have arrived on a Friday night. A measure of financial self-sufficiency is being sought in anticipation of much lower funding levels in the near future. Since its inception, 704 different men have made use of the nightshelter. In all, there have been 154 men of 50 or more years old, and of these, 55 were 60 or older. It is to an overview of some of the basic characteristics of these 55 oldest men that I now turn.

Elderly Users of Plymouth Nightshelter

The first annual report on the way in which Plymouth Nightshelter was being used showed that the average age of residents was very low - thirty nine. It had been anticipated that a large proportion of men using the shelter would be 'problem drinkers', although it transpired that less than 40% assessed themselves or were assessed as being such. Twenty five of the fifty five men of 60 or older were problem drinkers. Several of these 25 had received treatment of some sort for their alcoholism, but this had evidently either been to no avail or else had met with success only in the short term. The G.P. who visits the nightshelter regularly has always ensured that there is a plentiful supply of vitamin supplements for heavy drinkers, and has also prescribed Heminevrin to men who were seen to be making a sustained effort to stay dry. But being 'out on the streets' often for a full 12 hours from 7 a.m. until 7 p.m. is hardly conducive to success in overcoming chronic alcoholism. The local hostel for recovering alcoholics, which is in any case now temporarily closed, did not accept older men. Frequently, all that could be provided for such men was support during the hours of the shelter's operation. Thus the rehabilitative goals which the D.H. S.S. has always emphasised have been thwarted through the lack of any appropriate 'next stage' in the case of problem drinkers generally, and older

The Place of Origin by Region of Nightshelter
Residents Aged 60 or More.

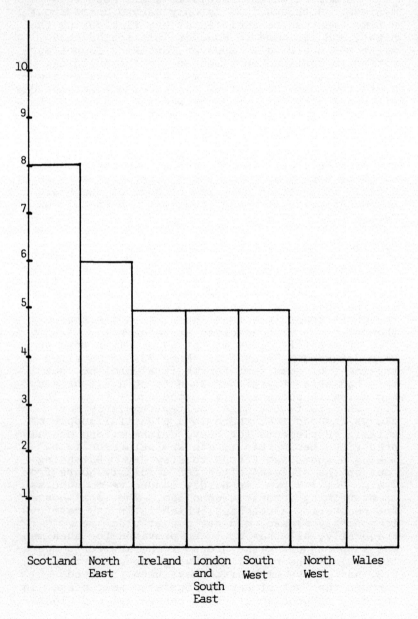

problem drinkers in particular.

The majority of men over 60 using the shelter were found to be suffering from an illness or to be disabled. Bronchitis and arthritis were frequently mentioned, and heart disease, partial blindness, jaundice, and the loss of one or both limbs have also been encountered. Of the older men, 27 had been sleeping rough immediately or shortly before arrival at the nightshelter, and 42 were without any money. In terms of marital status, 24 men said that they were single, 7 were divorced, 3 were still married, 2 were separated, and 2 were widowed.

The place of origin was known for 37 of the older men, and as can be seen on the histogram, almost half of them came originally from Scotland or Northern England. The three married men each gave a home address, one in Leicester, one in Fleetwood, and the other a council house in Manchester. Two other men said that they had lodgings in Plymouth to which they would be returning, and a third man had lodgings in Salford. The remaining 49 men over 60 were all of 'no fixed abode'. The older men first came to the nightshelter by a variety of different means: 12 were referred by the police, 8 were self-referrals and 10 were directed to the shelter by members of the public. The remainder came through the clergy, the probation service, the samaritans, or from other hostels.

Information about previous occupation was obtained for 34 of the older men, and, as might be anticipated, unskilled and semi-skilled work predominated. The men had been kitchen porters or had done similar work in the catering industry. Seven men had been merchant seamen, and five had been labourers.

Length of stay at the nightshelter has varied as widely for the elderly as for any other age group. The general pattern has been that some elderly men have used the shelter on a longterm basis, remaining as residents for several months, whilst others have only spent one or two nights there and then left without giving any hint as to their next intended destination. It is the experience of the long stayers which provides the substance for the following analysis.

Once such men had become established, there was often a noticeable disparity between the stated intention to make a break-out from the stasis and inertia of the routine of life in Plymouth Nightshelter, and the effort to do so. Typically, one man repeatedly remarked that he was fed up with the

nightshelter, and was going to make the journey back
to the London area, although he took no action to
achieve his stated goal. When he eventually left
the nightshelter to live in lodgings to which he had
been referred by the warden, he much resented making
the move. However, as soon as he had sampled the
more flexible routine of living in lodgings, and the
greater degree of comfort and range of amenities, he
quickly settled down.

It is generally true that the older single
homeless men become, and greater the period of time
spent without secure accommodation, the fewer and
meaner are their possessions. In contrast, some of
the younger men travelling in search of employment
have large back-packs or holdalls of clothes and
personal items. To be old on "skid row" frequently
means to be able to carry everything you own in a
faded Tesco carrier bag. There are, of course, exceptions to this. One man in his late 50's, known
to the others as a "magpie", surrounded his bed with
bags and boxes and books. He had a golf club which
he carried with him everywhere, and record sets and
a tea set obtained by mail order from Readers Digest,
none of which were paid for.

One man of 63, who was infested with body lice
when he first arrived, kept a bag of filthy old
clothes under his bed. It was difficult to persuade
him to surrender these items in exchange for new
clean ones, and attempts to get them away so that
they could be disposed of met with a gruff: "That's
my property. Leave it alone".

Policing, Crime, and Elderly Nightshelter Users

As already indicated, the police have been an important referral agent generally since the nightshelter
opened. Of all residents 18% were directed to, or,
in some cases brought to, the nightshelter by the
police. The proportion is slightly higher for men
of sixty or over: about 22%.

What is more difficult to establish is whether
there has been any significant change in police
policy where such matters as public drunkenness are
concerned. It does seem that the police are less
likely to bring charges for drink-related offences
among the elderly, although it is not easy to as-
certain whether this is actually the case, or
whether, since younger street drinkers are more in
evidence, they are more likely to be apprehended.
Certainly elderly men whose drunkenness has brought
them to the attention of the police are sometimes
brought along to the nightshelter rather than being

taken back to the cells.

The attitude of police operating at street level when asked to comment informally on drink-related offences and the elderly has been that such men are routinely "moved on" rather than arrested, but that if a specific complaint has been made, then the police must be seen to be responding accordingly. The arrest of an old man on a petty drunkenness charge is usually seen to be the province of the over-eager young recruit, and as too demeaning for more experienced police personnel. Of the 55 men aged 60 or more who have used the nightshelter, 15 (about 27% of the total) declared that they had a record of previous convictions, usually for drink related offences or for petty theft.

Isolation and the Structure and Routine of Daily Life.

Generally speaking, nightshelter users have a narrow range of social contacts. Interaction seems principally to occur with other single homeless men, and, to a lesser extent, with representatives of the social services, the probation service, and the police. Although nightshelter users are often conspicuous in the city centre, their appearance, and often their intoxicated condition, means that they are avoided by the public.

Within the nightshelter population as a whole, elderly nightshelter users seem to be particularly isolated. Although they are far less geographically mobile than younger men, who often travel extensively in search of employment, it seems that their longer-term location in the Plymouth area has not reduced their isolation. They enter and leave the nightshelter alone, move around the city on their own, and do not form the spontaneous friendships with two or three others in the nightshelters which are frequently observable amongst the younger men. Indeed, one elderly cider drinker asserted: "I've got no friends, I've got no mates, I've only got acquaintances, and that's the way I like it, guy".

However, I would argue that in spite of such assertions, the comparative isolation which is apparent within the confines of the nightshelter is misleading. Beyond the walls of the shelter a sometimes extensive network of associations can be discerned, even if these are often "acquaintanceships", frequently with an instrumental dimension, rather than "friendships" proper. I would further emphasise that as well as there being a much higher degree of social contact than might at first sight appear, such contact is to an unexpected extent contingent on a life structured and ordered by routine. These points are illustrated by three distinctly different individuals. (1)

Harry, the elderly cider-drinker who claimed not to have had any "friends" or "mates", had worked on a casual basis in the kitchens of various restaurants around the city 15 or more years ago. He had in several cases remained on friendly terms with the proprietors of these establishments during the intervening years, and could therefore rely on being regularly given food which had been prepared in excess of the evening's requirements. He also knew a number of individuals in the city with whom he could spend time talking, perhaps over a shared bottle of cider, although he would usually drink alone. After a careful study of the "form" in the Daily Star, a proportion of most of his days would be spent in the betting shop. He also knew those people whom he could engage in a conversation as ·a prelude to a request for a contribution towards the next bottle.

Archie, the oldest nightshelter resident, who is a disabled man of 84, has a somewhat different, but clearly structured routine which he follows each day. After leaving the nightshelter at seven o'clock in the morning, he walks along Bath Street to the taxi office at the junction with Union Street. Here, a chair is kept ready for him by the taxi drivers, and he is given a cup of tea from their vending machine. At the appropriate time each morning he makes his way slowly along to the indoor market so as to arrive soon after it opens, and there he is furnished with another cup of tea and a plate of toast. He then carries out any small errands required by his stallholder friends, who pay him for his trouble. He often combines these tasks with his own personal requirements such as getting his hair cut on the way back to the market. When he is not engaged in this way he will sit and watch the activity in the market, or perhaps go slowly along to the bus station if the weather is fine.

Len is a Londoner by birth, and was 62 years old when he first came to the nightshelter. He has been in the Plymouth area for many years now, and spent several months living in the nightshelter. He too used to spend much of his time in the indoor market. The attraction of the market, apart from the obvious fact that it affords shelter in bad weather, seems to be that it is an excellent meeting place and vantage point from which to keep "tabs" on

other men. (It seems that older men would rather
use the market, and sometimes the bus station, than
the probation-run day centre, which is used to a
much greater extent by younger homeless men). Len
was well-known to many of the stallholders in the
market, one of whom came by car to collect him from
the city centre last Boxing Day morning. He took
Len out to spend a day at his house in Plympton,
where a large party for market traders was being
held.

Before he began his period of residence at the
nightshelter, Len had been sleeping in the shell of
an old car. Cars were his other major preoccupation,
and he was "given" several different M.O.T. failures
by the men who work in the many small lock-up gar-
ages which are located on the opposite side of the
road to the nightshelter. He used to spend hours
proudly sitting in these vehicles which would be
parked for a while on a bomb-site which adjoins the
shelter before being towed away for scrap.

Len used to cover the windows with sheets of
lino or cardboard at night to prevent them from
being smashed by local children. He also used systematically to remove anything which he could find
manufactured from brass or any alloy, and hoard
these articles in boxes. He would augment these
with various other scrap items collected in his
wanderings around dumps and car parks during the
day. He would periodically take his boxes of bits
and pieces to a local scrap metal merchant and sell
them for two or three pounds. Len had four brothers,
and one day he told me that he had recently encountered the wife of one of them in the market, but said
that she had avoided speaking to him.

Although elderly nightshelter users, like the
majority of the younger men, are generally no longer in contact with their families, it does not
follow that there is no family with which contact
might be established. If made, contact might be of
a negative kind anyway (as in the case of Jimmy who
was rejected because of his persistent drinking
problem by his son who lived in Plymouth, and with
whom he literally came to blows after a drinking
bout).

Nevertheless, in some instances at least, there
appears to be the potential for a positive, supportive role to be played by a man's family. For
instance, before Harry died earlier this year as a
result of burns sustained whilst intoxicated in a
Plymouth lodging house one night, he was hospital-
ised for a period of months, and was able to give

staff information which enabled them to trace his numerous brothers and a sister. Several of these close relatives travelled to Plymouth to attend his funeral, and revealed how they had sought Harry for years, and did not know anything about the lifestyle in which he had successfully insulated himself, choosing to roam the city of Plymouth incognito.

But in spite of the fact that elderly night-shelter users have often terminated any contact with their families, or have no surviving relatives any-way, their existences are not as solitary as they might seem at first sight. As I have briefly attempted to show, lives which may appear to be orderless, random and spent in isolation are often in fact quite highly structured and ordered by rou-tine, affording many social contacts outside the immediate milieu of the nightshelter, and of Plymouth's "skid row".

AGE RELATIONS IN THE NIGHTSHELTER

Plymouth Nightshelter does not cater expressly for any specific age group, and the age range of users is very wide - from teenagers to men in their 80's. So on any one night there will usually be a mix of both young and old residents.

Some of the youngest residents are already familiar with the routine of hostel life and with the rigours of sleeping rough, and in many cases they also have a history of court appearances and convictions. Others have only recently left their parental home for the first time - perhaps after an argument, or simply to travel to a different part of the country and look for work, having become dis-affected with unemployment in their home towns. Lack of sufficient money to be able to use the Y.M. C.A. or other hostels often means that the Night-shelter is the only alternative to sleeping rough.

The oldest nightshelter users play a signifi-cant part in the process of the socialization of the youngest. Sometimes this initiation of neophytes takes a passive form, where the keyword would seem to be "emulation". One 18 year old who has made frequent use of the nightshelter, when asked why he keeps returning, gave as one of his reasons that he likes "to watch the old men". Some time later he said that he was spending his money on bottles of cider which he sat on park benches to drink. His street drinking forays were in direct imitation of the older men, rather than being a parody of them.

At other times there are indications of a more

active, albeit unintentional, process in operation
by which the young shelter user is "sponsored" by
one of the old men. Harry was seen to be taking an
18 year old resident "under his wing", as if intent
on protecting him from the harsher realities of
"skid row". Another very hard drinking middle aged
resident offered the youngster some Martini and
whisky. Harry told his protege that he would "break
his neck" if he caught him drinking, and said to the
older man that he would "break his neck twice" if he
caught him giving drink to the youth. Harry also
went to queue at the local D.H.S.S. offices with his
young friend and prevented his watch from being
stolen when he fell asleep while waiting for an
appointment.

However, Harry himself, being a chronic alchol-
ic, was rarely to be seen without a bottle of rough
cider in his hand or bulging from his pocket. While
he was consciously trying to protect the youth he
was at the same time unintentionally socialising him
into the grossest sector of the vagrant world. This
led to the young man saying, when efforts were subsequently being made to find him stable accommodation, "I just want to lead the life of a dosser".

Although this is one of the more extreme
examples, the very presence of the young in the
nightshelter with men inured to the deprivations of
life in hostels, nightshelters and sleeping rough,
frequently tends to reinforce the initiation into a
world which, once entered, is difficult to leave.
Young men pay little attention to the often highly
visible negative aspects of being old and homeless.
Instead they seem more influenced by the adapt-
ability, the resilience, the endurance, and the
capacity to accommodate to a life of homelessness,
all of which are common qualities in the oldest
nightshelter users.

Surprisingly, perhaps, these old men show none
of the self-recrimination and self-pity sometimes
apparent in the middle aged shelter users. Far from
being visible deterrents to the young, their blend
of stoicism and brashness seems to exert a particular appeal.

AGE AND AGGRESSION

In general the oldest men are treated with special
consideration by their younger co-residents. However, the particular attitudes adopted by other
nightshelter users vary somewhat, depending on individual characteristics.

For example, two old men who both used the
shelter for a long time, and whose objective circumstances were quite similar (both were disabled),
elicited markedly different reactions. The majority
of the other residents showed warmth and even defer-
ence towards one of these men, because of his great
age, his acute physical disability, and his pleasant
cheerful personality. The other man in the shelter,
although not quite as old, was almost equally disabled. He evoked a very different reaction because
of his extreme irascibility and generally hostile
and aggressive demeanour. One of the other residents commented: "If I had a flame thrower now, I'd
use it on that filthy old bastard - it makes me itch
just to look at him".

One often gets the impression from the more
colourful literature on nightshelters and from hear-
say that such places are regularly dogged by disputes which escalate to the level of physical violence. This has not been the experience at Plymouth
Nightshelter where, in nearly two years of operation,
there have been few such incidents.

Very occasionally a man will "rear up" and
verbally assail another resident or a member of
staff. Such outbursts usually occur without any
warning and result from incidents which seem trivial
but which, according to one party, amount to intolerable behaviour. It is usually one of the older
residents who feels that these breaches of the norm
cannot be allowed to pass without comment: One such
situation arose when a man of 63, Len, saw another
resident attempting to hide a book inside a newspaper in order to take it out of the building. Len
challenged him, was threatened with violence, and
countered by standing, white with temper, and with
his arms raised in a gesture of imminent attack, as
he screamed a reminder to his adversary, that he had
"been in the marines".

Len also became involved in a similar sort of
flare-up when he judged another resident to be consuming more than his fair share of food. Almost
invariably in such cases, the threatening postures
and the utterances of intent are not acted on and
terminate as, simply <u>displays</u> of threatening

Elderly Vagrants

behaviour.

It is also the older residents who try to
ensure the observance of other aspects of the un-
official code of acceptable behaviour. Although,
verbally, anything goes, anyone using certain exple-
tives within earshot of any of the women volunteer
workers is stringently censured. However, this informal policing of the shelter sometimes takes place
alongside the exercise of self-agrandising of
patriarchal power. Personality plays an important
part in this process.

DOMINANCE AND ASSERTIVENESS

In the twenty-two months that the nightshelter has
been in operation, it has been apparent that at any
phase one particular personality has been ascendant,
that one character assumes or is afforded a position
of dominance. This central figure has invariably
been one of the old residents.

For the whole period of his continued residence,
Harry, the cider drinker, was the undisputed patriarchal figure to whom other residents would quickly
learn to defer. He had carefully cultivated a distinctive style. Although he was only slight, a mass
of grey hair, a grizzled, weatherbeaten and age-worn
face gave him an imposing and sometimes calculatedly
threatening appearance. His odd assortment of
clothing had been carefully blended to constitute
this 'style': on top of the layers of long johns,
shirt, pullover, and jacket would be a large and
baggy overcoat with ample room for one, or more
usually two, litre cider bottles in the pockets. A
tie and a cravat, worn in combination, and always in
lurid pink or red or paisley pattern would decorate
his neck - sometimes complemented by a brightly
coloured scarf. This ensemble would be topped by a
scarlet or green woollen hat, sometimes replaced by
a black astrakhan hat during the winter.

Harry was often verbally aggressive and always
assertive. Last year a portable television had been
brought to the shelter so that the men resident at
that time could watch the League Cup final. The
game was half-way through and six or seven men sat
outside the kitchen facing the television, which had
been placed on a table near the office. At this
juncture Harry thumped on the door, staggered in and
slumped on his bed. A few minutes later he got up
and lurched across to the T.V., exclaiming in a
loud, slurred voice: "There's other people that
want to watch that television too you know", and

turned it 45 degrees so that it faced him alone in
the corner of the room. The group of men continued
to try and watch from what was now an oblique angle,
and not one of them dared to protest, far less restore the set to its original position.

Harry obviously felt himself to be different
from the other men and enjoyed a sense of privilege.
For instance, because he had been barred from using
the hostel where the other men got their midday
meals at weekends, he was given cash with which to
buy food, but he did not want this fact to become
known to the others because he thought they would
all demand the same. He managed to combine a gruff
and assertive exterior with affability and other
likeable qualities. One night another elderly and
similarly seasoned alcoholic, whom Harry had known
for many years, came into the shelter and Harry
immediately busied himself making a bed ready for
this man saying: "George is alright; you're alright
George, you're a man of the road".

Just as the other men had their daily routines,
so did Harry, although his was largely ordered by
the relentless need for alcohol. He spoke once of
feeling physical fear when he realised that the
level in the bottle from which he was drinking had
reached a point where the uncertain quest for the
next one must soon begin. Over the years as fashions changed he had received several different types
of treatment for his chronic alcoholism, none of
which had resulted in more than a brief period of
abstention. Although Harry was sometimes to be
found in the company of another man who was sitting
on a bench drinking cider, he was never encountered
engaging in communal drinking of the "drinking
school" type where resources are pooled and shared.
The same is true for the other older alcoholics.
The "drinking school" is a phenomenon which comes
spontaneously into existence in Plymouth from time
to time, but it is based on the coalescence of a
group of men usually in their thirties or forties.

In addition to assertiveness such as Harry's,
several other factors are important in the pre-
eminence of certain older men. They include duration of residence, extent and visibility of physical
incapacity, style, and quite simply, seniority.
After Harry moved to 'lodgings' and then used the
shelter only on an intermittent basis, Len became
the central dominant individual. He had been using
the shelter for a period of months and had therefore
become established as the most senior resident.

One feature which the dominant older residents

have had in common is a keen interest in what the other men did. On several occasions Len came to the office to enquire whether another man had paid his rent or not. The current central figure, Archie, the disabled 84 year old, spends the majority of his waking hours in the shelter in close scrutiny of the other men, often with a wry expression on his face. From time to time he nods to whoever is in the office saying: "I know him; I know what 'e's like. I know them all, goddit ?"

INDEPENDENCE, ALTERNATIVE PROVISION, AND LIBERTY

Just as elderly nightshelter residents attach great importance to their personal possessions, so are they extremely sensitive about any lessening of independence, and it is as a loss of independence that they generally perceive the suggestion of a move to any form of residential care. The necessity of relying on nightselter accommodation in itself indicates the extent of their lack of real independence, but at the same time there is typically a reluctance to accept any other form of accommodation in which independence might be perceived as threatened or diminished.

There has been much debate in recent years about the loss of basic human dignities involved in the imposition on the disabled elderly of care and treatment in long-stay homes and hospitals. I would argue that the relocation, or, more precisely the "location" of the elderly single homeless is hazardous undertaking. Elderly nightshelter users have often gravitated to the nightshelter because they have been labelled unsuitable for the larger hostels by staff there, or because they themselves do not like communal living on a large scale in what are still Dickensian conditions. Particularly in the case of the disabled elderly, it is difficult to find a landlord or landlady willing to accept the risks and problems involved in having such a resident when there are many able-bodied younger men in need of scarce accommodation. Even if private rented accommodation can be found, it is often the case that three or four men will be required to share one room and this frequently leads to problems. A common reason given for leaving lodgings by men returning to the nightshelter is that they "could not get on with" their room-mates: a man might say "I like to keep myself clean and tidy, but the other blokes living in the room were always filthy". One man in his 70s persistently complained

about the other men in the shelter because, he said,
they were "just dossers", and he was unable to
tolerate living among them there any more. The assertion of an individual's distinctness and separate-
ness from all the others is frequently to be heard,
but on the other hand, as has been seen, elderly
single homeless men are certainly not reclusive by
nature. They are often most content either mingling
amongst the busy crowds of the shopping centre, or
as spectators in high street or market place. It
would in many cases be cruel to remove the men from
their accustomed environment, and residential homes
do not seem to be an appropriate solution anyway.
Archie has twice been taken by nightshelter staff to
spend days at such a home to see whether he liked it
there. On both occasions, although severely disabled he has "voted with his feet" and walked out.
There is often a fear of the loss of self-determination attendant on the surrender of a pension book on
admission to a residential home, a fear which outweighs the advantages of freedom of access and
greater comfort and facilities. At the nightshelter,
Archie is still "his own man" in that he makes his
own arrangements about going and drawing his pension
and handing over his money to pay for his accommodation.

The desire to retain autonomy and dignity, and
not to yield what liberty an old and often disabled
man might still have, is sometimes manifested in an
extreme suspicion and distrust of medical treatment,
even when it is apparent that this is urgently needed, or would be beneficial. The Plymouth Nightshelter project has an honorary G.P. He used to
hold a weekly surgery in the office, where there are
the necessary facilities and supplies, and which was
vacated to ensure a measure of privacy. This was
the procedure for approximately the first eighteen
months of the shelter's existence. He now no longer
holds a regular surgery, but will come at short
notice to visit anyone who wants to see a doctor, or
to issue repeat prescriptions or proceed with long
term courses of treatment. Even though he is therefore regularly available for consultation, some of
the older residents have persistently declined to
see him; others have refused to take any medication
which has been prescribed.

A deep-rooted suspicion or fear of figures of
authority such as doctors and social workers, strong
desire to retain a maximum of dignity, individuality, and autonomy, taken together with an equally
strong desire to remain close to the familiar

environment of the heart of the city, make it difficult to offer any realistic formula for alternative
provision.

Plymouth Nightshelter has been described by
residents as being '4 star' in comparison with other
equivalent establishments elsewhere in the country.
Without any doubt, it provides for many of the requirements of the elderly single homeless men who
use it. It offers warm, dry, secure and clean
accommodation without fear of assault or arrest or
continually being moved on; regular meals; the
provision of any clothing which might be needed; the
use of laundry facilities; the opportunity to bath
or have a shower; television, radio, and books and
magazines for diversion and entertainment; conversation with other residents or with volunteer
helpers; advice and assistance in finding more permanent accommodation from nightshelter staff; and
access to medical advice and treatment, should this
be wanted.

Nevertheless, a more humane alternative to the
still very basic facilities afforded by a nightshelter accessible for only twelve out of twenty
four hours regardless of weather or season, and from
which men must be gone by 7 a.m. every day, is
clearly needed to cater for the elderly user. Such
an alternative would need to retain the positive
aspects of Plymouth Nightshelter, and, in addition
would need to allow complete freedom of access on an
individual basis, to provide more personal furniture
and space, and to offer the opportunity for complete
privacy if this is sought, as opposed to dormitory
style accommodation. Men who are old and alcoholic
should have access to treatment facilities or rehabilitation units regardless of their age, if this
is what they want.

It must finally be emphasised that "liberty" is
the keyword, the most important factor to be considered in relation to these elderly men. This is
so, even though, paradoxically, their circumstances
govern their lives almost entirely, and self-imposed
routine seems an additional strait-jacket.

NOTES

1. In all cases pseudonyms are used to
preserve anonymity.

REFERENCES

Archard, P. (1979) Vagrancy, Alcoholism, and Social Control Macmillan, London.

Berry, C.A. (1978) Gentleman of the Road Constable London

Burke, T. (1981) No Salvation for the Single Homeless S.H.O.T. (Single Homeless on Tyneside)

Cook, T. (1975) Vagrant Alcoholics Routledge and Kegan Paul, London.

Coulter, P. (1982) Singling Out the Elderly Homeless in New Age, Summer 1982, P35.

Digby, P.W. (1976) Hostels and Lodgings for Single People H.M.S.O. London.

Drake, M., O'Brien, M., and Biebuyck, T. (1981) Single and Homeless H.M.S.O. London

Turner, M. (1960) Forgotten Men The National Council of Social Service, London

Wiseman, J. (1970) Stations of the Lost University of Chicago Press

Chapter Five

AGEING IN THE INNER CITY - A COMPARISON OF OLD
BLACKS AND WHITES

K. Blakemore

Introduction

The problematic nature of human attempts to construct and preserve a sense of personal identity is no better illustrated than by the ageing process, just as studies of the impact of unemployment, institutionalisation or being placed in marginal social roles have highlighted the precarious nature of our sense of self.

Studies of ageing have made distinctions between successful and unsuccessful personal adjustments or strategies, either explicitly (Taylor and Ford, 1981) or implicitly - for example, in the many studies of health, morale and life satisfaction in old age.

A key element in deciding whether ageing can be termed successful is the interaction between the environment and the individual. Lawton (1980) has classified different kinds of environmental influence and has outlined a model of individual adaptation and non-adaptation. As he points out, success in maintaining self-esteem and personal identity can depend on the outcome of interactions between levels of competence (which partly refer to health) and the degree to which the environment places demands on the individual. Threats to self-identity and the appearance of maladaptive behaviour can result, according to Lawton, from environments which are intolerable for the individual either because they are too demanding or intrusive, or too limiting and uninteresting. Lawton recognises that neither environments nor individual competences can be straightforwardly measured and admits that "one can rarely be precise about the extent to which a person's perception of the environment reflects the 'objective' physical environment" (Lawton 1980:14).

Therefore, particularly relevant to any

discussion of the relation between old people and
their surroundings are insights into ageing individuals' subjective knowledge and instances in which
this knowledge seems inadequate or cannot make sense
of a changing and personally disturbing environment.
If, as we age, some of us perceive ourselves as
strangers in our own environments, then this poses
interesting questions: for example, about group and
individual differences in perceptions of similar
environments, or about inequalities in ability to
find a satisfactory adjustment to those environments.

Ageing in the Inner City

The object of this chapter is to apply some of the
general ideas on the relation between ageing and
environment to the particular examples of black
(West Indian) and white patterns of ageing in inner
city Birmingham. The aim is to consider:

1. Selected aspects of the objective circum-
    stances in which old blacks and whites find
    themselves - for example, their housing
    conditions, economic resources and occupa-
    tional backgrounds, health and social
    relations. Are old blacks considerably
    more disadvantaged than whites who live in
    the same neighbourhoods, or is it the
    whites who now live in poorer, or more
    isolated, or more stressful conditions than
    blacks ?
2. Old blacks' and whites' subjective percep-
    tions of growing old in their inner city
    environment. Is ageing for either or both
    groups a markedly difficult or anxious
    process ? Is the inner city environment
    seen as particularly stressful and chall-
    enging to their sense of personal identity?

Above all, it is important to qualify general assumptions about the inner city and to ask whether ageing in such an environment is particularly problematic, and if so, for which groups. Enough is known
about the decay, poverty and socially unstable
nature of inner city environments for us to suppose
that they can exert strongly negative influences on
many of the people who live in them, not least the
old. Housing is often sub-standard and some areas
are poorly-maintained or polluted, causing hazards
to health; the inner city might lack the kind of
social institutions in which old people, black or
white, can participate; this environment might also

seem to be physically threatening - for example,
there is indisputable evidence that crime rates are
high (Smith, 1981:35); finally, the inner city can
appear to be aesthetically unsatisfactory. Uncoll-
ected litter, pavements covered with broken glass,
graffiti-covered walls and neglected ugly buildings
could all threaten the aesthetic sense of old people
who may have once hoped to age in a more congenial
environment.

We cannot proceed with these unqualified views
of the inner city environment, however, without
challenging some of them. First, there is a danger
of forgetting that the distinctive peculiarities of
each city and neighbourhood result in varied views
of inner city life. Moving only a few streets to a
"better" neighbourhood may satisfy the aspirations
of some old people; there may be no wish to reject
the inner city environment completely. We should
also beware of imposing outsiders' judgements of
what it is like to live in inner city neighbourhoods
upon people who have spent a good deal of their
lives in them. Even those inner city dwellers who
agree that their environment lacks positive features
may all the same show a surprising tolerance of the
negative aspects; as Lawton points out, it is possible to "tune out" disturbing or irritating elements
of the environment.

It is also possible to overstate the degree of
change to which the physical appearance of inner
city areas has been subjected. In Birmingham, for
example, though much of the central district and
some inner city wards have been extensively rebuilt,
a larger proportion of wards has retained a pre-war,
not to say Edwardian, street layout and architec-
ture. In terms of the basic geography of shops and
other facilities, old people therefore continue to
see much that is familiar to them. This is not to
deny that social, economic and demographic changes
have fundamentally altered life in the inner city
since the turn of the century, but then rural areas
have been subjected to equally profound changes.

Another assumption, that inner city environments are less healthy than others, must also be
questioned. Lawton (1980:27) cites American data to
show that old people living in inner city areas are
significantly more mobile and less hampered by
chronic illnesses than old rural dwellers. These
findings illustrate some positive aspects of living
in densely-populated areas - for example, relatively
easy access to health services - though whether this
rural-urban contrast would be as marked in Britain

is open to question. It should be borne in mind that, relative to suburban dwellers, old people in inner city areas are disadvantaged in health and a lot more besides.

None of these qualifications about the character of inner city environments is meant to override the initial assumption that they are rapidly changing and that they could be destructive of attempts to maintain a sense of personal identity in old age. It now remains to examine this assumption specifically, with reference to a comparative study of old blacks and whites in Birmingham.

Data

The data for the study are drawn from two sources: a survey of 400 people over retirement age living in four Birmingham inner city wards in 1979, and a second set of interviews, carried out three years later, with smaller numbers of West Indians and whites from the original sample. The first survey was commissioned by a Birmingham voluntary agency, AFFOR (All Faiths For One Race) and the aims and methods of this study have been described elsewhere. It is important to note that AFFOR decided to take a random sample in order to gauge the rate of use of social and health services, though this resulted in the selection of black and white groups which are unmatched in terms of age. Over four-fifths of the West Indians are aged sixty to sixty nine, whereas only 35% of the old white group fall into this category. While these proportions reflect reality, a stratified sample of whites including a higher proportion aged sixty to sixty nine could have been taken to make a better comparison with the younger black group. However, some interesting implications follow from this age difference between black and white groups, and these will be referred to below.

The second, follow-up study has been carried out by the author and West Indian interviewers. Names were randomly selected from AFFOR's list of those who had indicated a willingness to be reinterviewed. A total of 62 (12 whites, 25 West Indians and 25 Asians (1)) from the original 400 have been revisited. Semi-structured interviews were arranged and, among a range of topics, respondents were asked to compare their present neighbourhood with the one they first moved to (in the case of West Indians), or grew up in (in the case of whites); they were also asked to talk about their present neighbourhood as they first knew it, to discuss any changes they had observed, and to describe their own personal histories in the context of these changes.

These questions about the environment reflected only one of several concerns of the follow-up study, but it is significant that worries about the neighbourhood and change were the major preoccupation of nearly every one of the whites, whereas most of the blacks did not identify these issues as being particularly important.

OLD BLACKS AND WHITES COMPARED

Objective aspects of the environment in which old blacks and whites live will be described first. The intention is not to provide an exhaustive summary of all types of personal, social and physical environment in the way outlined by Lawton (1980). Only salient aspects of the circumstances in which old blacks and whites live will be presented, chiefly in order to throw light on the way members of each group seem to perceive their environment. It is important, for example, to summarise key aspects of the neighbourhoods in which the old live - their age density and racial composition - and to be aware of the social and occupational backgrounds of old blacks and whites in inner city Birmingham, their housing and living arrangements, patterns of illness and their social relations in the neighbourhoods studied.

Age and Age-Density

Regnier (1976:254) shows that old people living in "age dense" areas tend to express greater satisfaction with their neighbourhoods than those in which old people are relatively few. Where old people are well-represented, socialising with neighbours and friends is enhanced. Shops and services are more likely to meet older residents' requirements than are those in "younger" neighbourhoods.

Table 1 shows that old blacks still form only a tiny minority within their own ethnic groups. This will change substantially over the next two decades as those presently aged 45-59 comprise a much larger proportion of the black population than those now retired. At the moment, however, West Indians who have stayed in Britain have a very few contemporaries to socialise with.

Inner city wards are relatively "young" compared with the city as a whole. They are noticeably different demographically from some of the Birmingham suburbs, where the retired now form as much as a quarter of local populations. As Table 1 shows,

Table 1   Percentages of retired in selected Birmingham wards, by ethnic origins 1971 and 1981

Ward	NCP[a] retired as % of all NCP-origin residents		Other[b] retired as % of all other residents		All retired as % of total population[c]	
	1971	1981	1971	1981	1971	1981
Deritend	1.1	2.5	14	15	10	9
Handsworth	1.5	2.7	20	25	14	13
Soho	1.8	2.7	20	25	11	9
Sparkhill	1.1	2.3	17	21	13	11
Average	1.4	2.5	18	22	12	11
Birmingham	0.9	2.3	16	20	15	17

[a]New Commonwealth and Pakistan: information on Caribbean-origin residents by age is not available for comparison between 1971 and 1981

[b]This category includes all others than New Commonwealth and Pakistan residents and includes, for example, Irish-born as well as UK-born

[c]Paradoxically, the proportions of retired in the NCP and 'other' categories have risen between 1971 and 1981, but the proportion of all retired in the total population has fallen. This is because whites below retirement age have left inner city wards in substantial numbers, while the number of NCP residents (almost all of whom are below retirement age) has increased. The Birmingham statistics demonstrate that these trends have not occurred in the city as a whole and that they are peculiar to inner city wards.

inner city wards have also become "younger" since
1971. The relatively young population of West
Indian and Asian minorities is concentrated in inner
city areas, while over the past two decades many of
the younger whites have moved out of inner city
districts. Thus the white population in certain
inner city neighbourhoods has become increasingly
aged and the old whites who remain are the representatives of a dwindling white group.

Race
None of the four wards studied could conceivably be
called entirely "black" areas. Though the population of one ward, Soho, is three-quarters New Commonwealth and Pakistan origin (OPCS, 1982), the proportion in the other three is about half. Nevertheless, old whites who have remained in the inner city
have experienced a lot of change recently in the
racial composition of their local environments particularly when it is realised that, in the four wards
as a whole, the proportion of black residents has
increased from an average of 33% to 57% over the
past ten years (OPCS, 1972 and 1982). Moreover,
ward-level statistics do not show that some neighbourhoods within wards have remained almost exclus-
ively white, whereas others are now mostly West
Indian or Asian. Black neighbourhoods inside such
wards as Handsworth or Sparkhill therefore stand out
as being markedly different from the rest of the
city, in which the proportion of New Commonwealth
and Pakistan - origin people to all residents as a
whole is only 15%. In some inner city streets,
specialised foodstores, travel agencies, restaurants
and cafes, and religious centres vividly display the
ethnic heterogeneity of the concentrated minority
populations they serve.

Socio-economic Status
Old whites are more likely to have earned more
throughout their working lives than blacks, to have
benefited from an occupational pension, insurance
scheme or interest on savings and to have, in retirement, a higher weekly income (AFFOR, 1981). As
almost half of the old whites had worked in skilled,
semi-professional or professional occupations whereas very few blacks had done so, such economic dis-
parities in retirement might be expected.
     The retired whites represent a generation of
workers among whom were many trying to "better
themselves" in the 1930s. Coming from skilled and
"respectable" working class families, those who had

chosen to live in Handsworth and similar areas had
done so precisely because they were more prestigious
wards than more solidly working class ones. Over
four-fifths of old blacks, on the other hand, have
spent all their British working lives in semi- or
unskilled jobs. In retirement, they are more dependent than whites on means-tested benefits because
their national insurance contributions may fall
short of entitling them to a full pension.

Some qualifying remarks should be made about
these broad comparisons between old blacks and
whites. First, we should not forget that just over
half of the whites also once worked in semi- or
unskilled jobs and that some share a low level of
income with blacks. The majority of the old white
population is composed of women, a substantial proportion of whom are widows whose occupational backgrounds are usually in factory work and who now live
simply on a state pension. It is, after all, the
younger and better-off whites who have been able to
move away, leaving behind the older and poorer whites in the inner city.

It should also be pointed out that, though the
average black weekly income was found to be lower
than the whites', there was a slightly higher proportion of West Indians (9%) than whites (4%)
receiving over £41 per week in 1979 (AFFOR, 1981:
18). There is a small minority of better-off West
Indians either preferring to remain in inner city
neighbourhoods or finding it difficult to move out,
and though their numbers are small their presence
in the local West Indian community is significant,
especially for other old people.

Housing and Living Arrangements
Most retired West Indians have been living in Britain for between 16 and 25 years. Almost all those
interviewed by AFFOR had spent all their time in
Birmingham itself, usually in the same neighbourhood
or an adjoining one. Old blacks have not moved
around much in Britain and, though most have been
settled in their neighbourhoods for a larger period
than Asian migrants, most came to Britain after
half their working lives were over. This contrasts
with the old white population, which is intensely
local in origin. Three-quarters of the whites have
lived in their present neighbourhoods for thirty or
more years; some are still living in the houses in
which they were born or grew up. Old whites therefore have clear memories of the neighbourhoods as
they were in pre-war days; their identification with

the past character of their communities is very strong indeed.

There are also differences between blacks and whites as far as home ownership is concerned. The AFFOR survey showed that West Indian pensioners have not become owner-occupiers to the same extent as Asians or whites. Less than a third of old West Indians own their accommodation; a half rent from the city council or a housing association; the remainder rent from private landlords. Among whites, on the other hand, there is a considerable proportion of owner-occupiers (56%), a much lower proportion renting from the the council or housing association (12%), but a relatively high number renting from private landlords (32%).

These findings indicate a mixture of advantages and disadvantages for each group. The blacks are evidently disadvantaged in that few enjoy the security of home ownership. Not many West Indians have much to show for their labours in Britain. However, 99% of all old blacks are at least provided with standard amenities in their homes, whereas a significant minority of old whites is not. AFFOR found that 17% of whites do not have an inside W.C., 12% lack a fixed bath and 15% are not provided with piped hot water.

Such discrepancies can partly be explained by the fact that fewer old blacks than whites rent from private landlords. Council-owned accommodation, though sometimes in disrepair, nevertheless usually contains the facilities mentioned above. The whites, on the other hand, either live in houses they have bought after renting privately for some years - typically, landlords failed to modernise such property and their present owners may be disinclined now to make changes or cannot afford them - or they are continuing to rent from private landlords, again finding in some cases that standard domestic facilities are not provided.

Thus, as a group, old whites are clearly advantaged in terms of property ownership, but we should not forget that a minority is more disadvantaged than blacks as far as important features of their domestic environment are concerned. Even owning a house is a mixed blessing from the point of view of the inner city resident: the low value of inner city houses, worries about property maintenance and security, and desire for smaller, more manageable homes may cancel some of the supposed advantages of house ownership.

Old blacks, who tend to live in smaller units

of accommodation than whites, are not necessarily more disadvantaged in every case. Some old blacks living in very small flats are having to tolerate cramped or restricted domestic environments. A fifth of old blacks live in one- or two-roomed(2) flats, whereas no whites do so. But probably as many West Indians as not are living in a size of flat they find suitable, while some old whites would actually prefer a small flat to a house in which half the rooms are unused.

Health and Illness

There is evidence to show that ethnic minority groups and particularly West Indians and Asians, are disadvantaged as far as enjoyment of good health is concerned. In Birmingham, for example, a study of hospital admissions over a five-year period revealed higher-than-expected rates of stroke, hypertension and diabetes among Asians and West Indians aged 30-59 (Cruickshank, 1980), though the rate of heart attack appears to be lower than among whites of the same age.

The AFFOR survey indicates that the generally poorer health of West Indians and Asians in Britain is reflected in the retired group. Use of hospital services and rate of medical consultations are both significantly greater among West Indians than among the old whites living in the same inner city environment; it is likely that this difference can be partly explained by cultural differences in perception of illness and medical services (Blakemore, 1982), but there is no doubt that there is also an objectively higher rate of disease among old West Indians. AFFOR's data show that the proportions of West Indians reporting problems with dental health and hearing and, more seriously, with walking and sight, are no less than among whites whose average age is significantly higher and who might therefore have been expected to report a higher rate of illness. In fact, these findings demonstrate the impact of racial inequalities in determining susceptibility to illness among old people, and confirm American evidence (Lawton, 1980:36) of poor health among members of black and migrant groups.

Social Interaction

The social relationships in which the old engage are clearly as important a part of their environment as physical and economic conditions. Some ideas of the density of the social networks in which old blacks and whites live can be gained from observing their

living arrangements and frequency of contact with
friends, neighbours and others.

Approximately the same proportion of old blacks
and whites live alone - about two-fifths in each
case. This might be expected among the whites, who
form the older group and include a higher proportion
of widows. But the white group also has a relatively high proportion (50%) of members living as couples; very few whites live in households of three or
more.

The number of old blacks living alone seems
high for a comparatively "young" group. However, at
least three factors explain this: first, as migrants
the West Indians sometimes came to Britain alone,
never to marry or revive former marriages; second,
divorces and separations have been more common among
blacks; third, old West Indians tend not to live in
three-generation households, as do many Asians, and
neither are they surrounded by such dense networks
of kin (though even as far as old Asians are concerned, the strength of such ties can be overestimated).

It is almost certain that higher proportion of
old blacks will be living alone in the near future,
as the average age of the retired black group begins
to match that of the whites. But there are other
points of comparison: fewer blacks than whites live
in couples - only 37% compared to the whites' 50% -
but more blacks (23%) live in households of three or
more than whites (10%). The difference is not a
very large one, but it highlights the fact that more
blacks than whites still have younger relatives
staying with them. The AFFOR survey showed that the
frequency of contact old blacks and whites had with
their friends was roughly comparable.

More blacks than whites see neighbours more
than once a week, though old white men are more
gregarious than their black counterparts and old
white women significantly less so. A comparably
small proportion of black men and women and white
men (only about 7%) rarely speak to their neighbours
- but the incidence of social isolation in old white
women is more than double this figure.

The significance of these basic findings on
social interaction should be weighed with caution.
These data are presented simply to sketch some aspects of the social environment of old blacks and
whites and they say nothing of the meaning or quality of the relationships referred to. It should not
be assumed that frequency of visits from relatives,
for example, is always associated with morale. In
conclusion, the significance of the patterns of

social life surrounding old blacks and whites, as
with all the other characteristics of their environment already referred to, can only be assessed in
relation to subjective interpretations of ageing in
the inner city.

THE SUBJECTIVE EXPERIENCE OF AGEING

Though old blacks and whites share the same environment in the sense of living in the same neighbourhoods, the preceding discussion has shown that the
circumstances in which they live are different in
important respects. Old blacks are not always more
disadvantaged than whites - for example, in terms of
housing or frequency of social contact with neighbours, friends and relatives - but they often differ
from them in important respects such as health,
income and availability of others of similar age as
well as cultural background to mix with.

The way in which these objective differences
between old blacks and whites relate to subjective
views of ageing and of the inner city environment is
problematic. American evidence (Cantor, 1976)
suggests that old blacks worry less and express more
satisfaction with their lives than old whites who
live in similar inner city areas, despite extremely
low income levels among blacks, histories of job
discrimination and forced early retirement, poor
health and below-average life-expectancy. It is a
common finding that the least well-off have low expectations and adjust to deprivation and poor environments, though there are difficulties in assuming
that American evidence can be applied to old West
Indians in Britain, who have a different history of
migration and possibly different sorts of expectations. There is another, more fundamental question:
can expressions of satisfaction or dissatisfaction
with growing old in a particular environment be
taken at face value ? How should such attitudes be
interpreted ?

It is also important to ask these questions
about the attitudes of old whites to inner city
life. The whites expressed much anxiety about their
futures in the neighbourhoods in which they live;
they deeply regret the ways in which their communities have changed and appear to feel that the environment which surrounds them undermines their sense of
security, continuity and identity. Just as the subjective views of old West Indians must be interpreted in relation to their personal circumstances and
biographies, so must those of the old whites.

Ageing and Identity Among the West Indians

It will be recalled that one of the main aims of
this chapter is to ask whether ageing among inner
city blacks is a particularly anxious process and
whether, in comparison with old whites, the inner
city environment threatens their sense of personal
identity. In some respects the evidence of the
AFFOR and follow-up surveys does confirm the American finding that old blacks are not particularly
concerned about the stresses of their environment
but, as will be demonstrated below, this apparent
satisfaction hides some deeper concerns.

To begin with, it is certainly true that few
old blacks spontaneously expressed the anxieties
about the inner city environment which preoccupy the
whites. Old West Indians did identify certain things - notably crime, fear of violence among young
people, and a decline in neighbourliness - as negative features of the environment, but their attitudes towards these things are more fatalistic and passive than among old whites.

Such fatalism or passive acceptance is illustrated by the West Indians' views about moving away
from their present neighbourhoods. Only a quarter
expressed any desire to move, whereas a half of the
whites wish to do so. When those West Indians who
wish to move were asked about desired destinations,
most mentioned another inner city neighbourbood or
a street in the same neighbourhood. In fact, hardly
any West Indians identified neighbourhood problems
as cause to move; dissatisfaction with accommodation
accounted for nearly all responses.

The finding that three-quarters of West Indians
wish to stay where they are in their old age reflects feelings of resignation and passive acceptance
rather than happy adjustment to inner city life.
The idea of moving into "white" suburbs is unthink-
able for most old blacks, mainly for practical
reasons such as inability to purchase housing, fear
of racial harassment or the lack, in other areas, of
the kinds of shops, churches and other services
appropriate to their needs. The follow-up interviews confirmed that old West Indians' expectations
are very modest. Most have lived locally and worked
in the same inner part of Birmingham since migrating; their British horizons have not been raised
much during this time and they have either been
socialised into accepting the inner city or have
been forced into this position by racial and economic factors.

Moving, for most old blacks, means a journey

93

back to the West Indies, either to visit or stay
permanently, rather than an attempt to find a better
British environment. Thoughts of going "home" act
as a channel for some old blacks' dissatisfactions,
diverting negative feelings about immediate surroundings into hopes of return - plans which never amount to much, but which make old age in Britain a
little more tolerable. Over a third of old West
Indians have a considerable yearning to return
"home", though only a very small proportion at any
one time appear to make definite plans to return
(AFFOR, 1981:33). Thus despite the fact that nearly
all West Indians will grow old and die in Britain, a
sense of detachment from this country and of not
fully belonging to the neighbourhood does affect
blacks to varying degrees. This is not to deny that
some have made satisfactory adjustments to their
local environments and to growing old in Britain.
For example, some of the oldest members of the West
Indian community could be described as pioneers who,
having been among the first to find accommodation
and jobs, have developed a strong sense of self-
sufficiency and independence.

Nevertheless, many old blacks experience a
particular sense of loss in their old age: a gradual
realisation that, though vague intentions to return
"home" have provided some comfort, they will not
after all be put into practice. For migrants, to
the personal realisation of ageing and mortality is
added a realisation that one may, after all, age
and die in a foreign land. And though this realisation may be gradual, it can nonetheless constitute
a form of surprise or shock. Paul Scott's novel,
Staying On, explores such feelings of regret about
never having returned "home" and of losing opportunities to grow old in a way one once expected, as
experienced by an ageing white couple in modern
India. With some adaptation, Scott's observations
apply, ironically enough, to ageing blacks in
Britain. In particular, there are parallels in the
marital stress that can be caused by the conflicting
wishes of one spouse to stay and of the other to
return.

Does the inner city environment compensate for
any feelings of loss of "home" or loneliness which
old West Indians might have ? There is agreement
among some old blacks that the growth of the local
black community has brought some advantages for
them. Local shops provide food they like; there are
local Pentecostal, Seventh Day Adventist, Baptist
and Methodist churches which have black

congregations and social groups (mostly for women);
a few local public houses and clubs are seen by the
men as congenial places to spend time. One West
Indian woman commented:

> "I lived for many years in Gloucester. It's
> more or less a village. The people there are
> very friendly, but you can't get the right
> food there. I prefer the company of my (black)
> neighbours here".

However, it would be wrong to conclude that the
inner city environment does very much to sustain
older blacks' sense of identity or feelings of West
Indian-ness. The realities of older blacks' lifestyles and views of the environment suggests the
opposite. Low income means that it is not possible
to take full advantage of nearby shops which sell
foods used in West Indian cooking, particularly as
such foods - including staples - are much more expensive than their British or European equivalents.
The high expense of life in Britain was remarked on
by most old blacks, and was mentioned by men as the
chief reason for not going out. Men and women often
talked of patterns of socialising in the West Indies,
where much life is lived in the open air and where
it seemed possible to meet people in a leisurely and
unplanned way, without necessarily incurring financial cost. As Foner (1979:166) points out, older
men in rural Jamaica are often able to accumulate
some land, build up a small business or trade, or
play leadership roles in local voluntary associations, though even in the West Indies prestige is not
conferred uniformly on the old, but mainly on those
who have proved reasonably successful. In Britain,
Foner concludes, there are fewer opportunities for
old blacks to achieve successful or prestigious
roles.
     Rapid social change has accentuated the differ-
ence between West Indian and British society. It
also means that most old blacks have noticed considerable changes, since their arrival, in the inner
city neighbourhoods they have lived in. Most of
those interviewed in the follow-up survey felt that
neighbourhoods were "friendlier" in the 1950s and
early 1960s than now. Stories of racial prejudice
and difficulties in finding jobs and accommodation
are common; there are also memories of communities
much less polarised than they seem to older blacks
now. Selective memory could account for some of
these observations, but old age for many blacks is

accompanied by feelings of considerable alienation
from an industrial society which, though it provided
work for most of them, now appears impersonal and
unfriendly.

Not only has the proportion of young to old increased recently in inner city wards, but also unemployment, despair and anger have become more prevalent among the young. While old blacks may understand these problems, they are at the same time
often frightened by these additional signs of change
and uncertainty. Therefore the contemporary inner
city environment does not even begin to compare with
the sort of community in which many old blacks might
once have imagined they would age: that is, either
in a half-remembered, probably rural West Indian
setting, or in the kind of urban environment which
they recollect from their earlier days in Britain.

These generalisations do not apply equally to
all old blacks. First, there is the minority noted
earlier who are somewhat better-off financially than
the average. As Foner notes, these people may enjoy
relatively high status and, being able to return to
the West Indies if they wish, do not necessarily
feel trapped by a retirement in Britain. Second,
there are noticeable differences between those who
have ties with relatives and those who live more
isolated lives, cut off from people who once knew
them in the West Indies and without any strong relationships in Britain. Sometimes such people find
relatively little to enjoy in their social lives in
Britain, but feel they could not survive now in the
West Indies, or that they must stay in Britain because medical services are free here. As the AFFOR
data showed, there is already a considerable proportion of old blacks living alone and, though not
all of these are socially isolated, there will inevitably be a growing pool of old disengaged blacks.

Differences in adjustment to growing old in the
inner city are perhaps most noticeable in the comparison between male and female attitudes and patterns of activity. The Birmingham evidence provides
some confirmation for Foner's belief that "the
situation of old women in England appears to differ
less radically from what it was in Jamaica than the
situation of old men" (Foner, 1979:171). Old black
women are less likely to be cut off from relatives
and friends than men, and church activities provide
a very strong focus for the social lives of nearly
all black women. The men, while they are more likely than old women to go out daily, attend church
less regularly (about half go every week) and do not

enjoy the multiplicity of church-related activities
engaged in by some of the old women during the week.
For women without immediate family in Britain, the
churches often provide social support and can be a
source of psychological strength; but for old men,
these benefits are less meaningful or less appropriate. In general, old black men are ready to
accept retirement as a period of declining activity
and of leisure at home. While women are more fear-
ful than men of the dangers of the local environment
- most are reluctant to go out alone in the evenings - they are, on the whole, enmeshed in wider
circles of activities, friends and relatives than
old black men.

Ageing and identity Among Old Inner City Whites
While the hallmark of most old blacks' attitudes and
expectations is an apparent satisfaction or, more
likely, a resigned acceptance of the inner city
environment, old whites show strong feelings of dissatisfaction with it. Twice as many whites as
blacks wish to leave home, not for a nearby neighbourhood, but usually for a suburban location.
Given the higher average age of the whites and the
common dislike of older people for the idea of moving, this is a particularly significant finding.
    The local environment, as it appears to most
old whites, now offers them relatively little,
either as far as neighbourly or friendly social ties
and leisure activities are concerned, or as the kind
of place which provides feelings of rootedness. In
general, they deprecated day centres, lunch clubs
and "things set up for old folks", as one respondent
put it. Most prefer social activities which include
younger, if not young, people: drinking at the local
club or public house, or playing bowls, cards or
darts. However, it is precisely these leisure out-
lets which old whites feel are being closed to
them; not wishing to mix with blacks in the neighbourhood and finding that old friends have died or
moved away, they begin to feel deprived of suitable
social contacts. The lack of people to go out with,
or call on, is particularly remarked on by women
who, in any case, go out less often than the men.
    Nearly all the strong feelings of dissatisfact-
ion expressed by the old whites are centred on
racial differences; other issues, such as the economic decline of the inner city, were mentioned very
rarely. To understand their attitudes, it might be
salutary to imagine the response of white middle
class people to the sudden settlement of, say, a

large number of Asians in an English country village.
It is, to the old whites in the inner city, the
weird combination of unfamiliar languages and cultural ways in a basically familiar setting which
seems to heighten their sense of dislocation from
the environment and their past in it. Moreover, the
speed with which these changes are occurring needs
to be appreciated: as the demographic data discussed
above indicate, the race and age balance of inner
city wards has changed greatly within the past ten
years. Interestingly, most of the old whites seem
to have noticed that the previous decade has been
one of particularly rapid change; they view the next
decade with apprehension.

Unfortunately, therefore, feelings of lack of
control over one's environment or a lack of identification with it, not uncommon in old age, are ex-
aggerated among old inner city whites by the perceived strangeness and unpredictability of the
society around them. Such feelings are typified by
quite ordinary instances, such as not knowing the
names of more than one or two others living in the
same street, finding that carefully-grown garden
flowers have been senselessly uprooted by young
people, hearing loud music and raucous laughter in
the early hours of the morning, or finding that a
well-known shopkeeper has closed a family business
that can be remembered from pre-war days. The old
whites often contrasted this lack of familiarity
with the present-day neighbourhood with what they
recalled of the past, when "we knew the names of
everyone who lived in this street" and "when people
were so polite and kind", or when "the street and
doorsteps were so clean you'd almost have to take
your shoes off to walk down our road".

There are more serious examples of the perceived unpredictability and unfriendliness of the
environment. In the follow-up interviews, experiences of hostile encounters between respondents and
young blacks were usually mentioned. Reported experiences of street crimes and house burglary are
too frequent and serious to be discounted as exagg-
erated rumours, and do pose a threat to old blacks
and whites alike. But whereas old blacks did not
often mention crime as a negative feature of their
environment, the whites did. As neither the AFFOR
nor follow-up surveys set out specifically to discover old whites' attitudes towards race and crime
in their neighbourhoods, the re-direction of the
interviews along these lines by respondents themselves - particularly in the follow-up survey -

indicates their strength of feeling on such matters.
However, the undoubtedly racist attitudes of
most old whites should not be viewed out of the context of their past and present experiences. As a
particular cohort of white people, they have witnes-
sed a bewildering amount of change to "their"
communities. It should also be noted that their
racism is not completely indiscriminate. Though, as
with old blacks, most of the social ties and friendships of old whites have remained firmly on their
own side of the racial divide, there are exceptions
as far as some old whites' next-door neighbours are
concerned. As often as not, West Indian or Asian
neighbours would be described as kindly and helpful
- "They couldn't do enough for me" was the most
common statement. One old man mentioned striking up
an acquaintance with some old West Indians who shared nearby allotments, where mutual gardening interests can evidently override racial prejudice.

However, it is noticeable that nearly all the
comments on relationships with blacks referred to
receiving help; there was little or no sense of
meeting black neighbours for their own sake, or of
wishing to find out more about their lives and
beliefs. This lack of knowledge was aptly summed up
by the vague description by one man of his
(Pakistani, Muslim) neighbour as "a vicar, I think,
in their synagogue, like..." Old whites' encounters
with blacks are mostly incidental and short-lived;
they do not seek company irrespective of race and
there are few institutional settings locally where
old blacks and whites could mix.

Though most old whites feel angry or threatened
by the changes which have happened around them, and
have experienced an erosion of their morale and
sense of security, these feelings do not entirely
circumscribe their use of the environment. Many
regretted that they no longer felt safe enough to
walk in the local park or go out in the evenings,
but apart from that nearly all men went out every
day. In fact their rate of activity, in this sense,
is significantly higher than among West Indian men.
Among old white women, however, there is a lower
proportion going out daily - about half - and a
higher proportion (about a third) who go out only
once a week, or less than that. This is as much an
age as a sex difference, though most women fear
street attacks more than men and might be staying
indoors partly for this reason. Whatever the cause,
the implications in terms of perception of the environment are very important: men still see the

neighbourhood as "theirs" and continue to lead social lives outside the home more often than white women, and certainly more than old blacks. Old white women, on the other hand, are more home-centred - particularly in very old age, when a considerable proportion live alone. For them, the environment outside the home can become increasingly strange and hard to understand. Though relatives may visit, such women may be forced to call on help from neighbours who may not speak the same language or who may not behave in expected ways. Thus, for old white women in particular, problems of adjustment to their environment can be exacerbated by both the real hazards and changes of inner city life, and the fears and subjective feelings they have about the people who now live around them.

DISCUSSION AND CONCLUSION

This chapter has explored the relationship between an inner city environment and two distinct groups of old people. It has attempted to show that, while old whites tend to be objectively better off in their personal circumstances than old blacks, their expression of a sense of deprivation is much stronger. Most old blacks seem to have a fatalistic, accepting attitude towards their environment.

This does not mean, however, that West Indians' experience of old age in Britain is unproblematic. The incidence of poverty and ill health among them appears to higher than among old whites and, in addition, they must cope with the potentially lonely role of the ageing migrant. But it is precisely because they are migrants that old West Indians seem to divert angry or resentful feelings they may have about their environment towards an acceptance that, if conditions in old age are unsatisfactory then the individual has in a sense brought this about by migrating in the first place. Poverty, isolation and a sense of not being very welcome in British society can all too readily be interpreted by old blacks as evidence of personal failings, bad luck, or God's will. The migrant, by leaving "home", has set in motion a chain of events which have led either to personal success or failure. Perhaps the particularly high rate of consultations of GPs by old blacks (Blakemore, 1982) reflects not just an objectively higher rate of morbidity in this group, but also a need to discuss personal anxieties and insecurities with doctors; it is well-known that patients often seek reassurance, sympathy or

explanations of their fate from medical practitioners. It is possible that, for old blacks, this is
especially true.

Therefore the findings of previous American
studies, that old inner city blacks are relatively
satisfied and adjusted to their environment, must be
applied with caution. This study shows that the
experience of growing old in British inner city
neighbourhoods is more often accepted with resignation or fatalism than with satisfaction by old
blacks. Though these neighbourhoods' populations
have become increasingly black, they actually do
little to enhance old blacks' sense of identity,
security or engagement.

Old whites also find that their environment
does little to support their morale or sense of
identity - in fact, for many, the environment is a
permanent reminder of their marginal role as strangers in their own land. Unlike old blacks, however,
the whites do not blame their predicament on the
results of their own actions. They sense, in the
social transformation of their environment, the loss
of a valued community. But this loss, and with the
growth of the local black population, are together
seen as changes beyond their control. Their feelings are projected on to what seem to be disturbing
elements in the environment - the "strange" ways of
black neighbours, the threat of burglary, the un-
collected garbage which lies in the street. Old
whites discuss and blame their environment much more
than old blacks do; their sense of deprivation in
old age is much keener.

There is, finally, a parallel between the subjective experiences of old age by blacks and whites,
despite the objective differences between each
group's background and present circumstances. Both
West Indians and whites are experiencing the loss of
anticipated and possibly hoped-for patterns of ageing. We all carry in our minds, however vaguely
formed, a model of what it will be like when we are
older; modern western culture may not encourage us
to analyse or elicit these images, but they are
there nonetheless. Old whites, it could be argued,
are having to come to terms with the loss of a way
of growing old which they had anticipated when they
were middle-aged, before rapid changes in the ethnic
composition of inner city neighbourhoods had set in.
Though some familiar reference points remain, they
are to varying degrees experiencing grief and shock
caused by the loss of their images of community and
of satisfactory ageing. Old blacks, on the other

hand, may vaguely remember a pattern of ageing as it used to be in the West Indies; they experience some discontinuity between these memories and the reality of old age in Britain.

While old West Indians and whites share a sense of loss in old age, however, it should not be forgotten that each group has its distinctive cultural background, and, to a lesser extent, different living conditions and personal circumstances. Any attempt to find common solutions to the problem of isolation, loneliness or anxiety experienced by old people in inner city neighbourhoods, irrespective of cultural background or a sense of what the most appropriate services might be, should therefore be viewed with scepticism.

NOTES

1. The results of interviews with old Asians will not be discussed in this paper.
2. Not counting kitchens and bathrooms.

REFERENCES

All Faiths For One Race (1981) Elders of the Minority Ethnic Groups, published by AFFOR, Lozells, Birmingham.

Blakemore, K. (1982) "Health and illness among the elderly of minority ethnic groups living in Birmingham", Health Trends, Vol.14, 2, 1982: 69-72.

Cantor, M.H. (1976) "Effect of ethnicity on the life-styles of the inner-city elderly", in Lawton, M.P., Newcomer, R.J., and Byerts, T.O., Community Planning for an Ageing Society, Dowden, Hutchinson and Ross.

Cruickshank, J.K., et al, (1980) "Heart attack, stroke, diabetes, and hypertension in West Indians, Asians, and whites in Birmingham, England", British Medical Journal 281:1108.

Foner N. (1979) Jamaica Farewell Routledge and Kegan Paul, London

Lawton, M.P. (1980) Environment and Ageing, Brooks/Cole.

Office of Population Censuses and Surveys (1972 and 1982), Census 1971 and Census 1981 (County Reports and Small Area Statistics relating to Birmingham).

Regnier, V. (1976) "Neighbourhoods as Service Systems", in Lawton, M.P., et.al., Community Planning for an Ageing Society, Dowden

Scott, P. (1977) _Staying On_, Panther Books
Smith, S.J. (1981) "Negative interaction: crime in
    the inner city", in Jackson, P. and Smith, S.J.
    (eds.) _Social Interaction and Ethnic Segregat-
    ion_, Academic Press.
Taylor, R. and Ford, G. (1981) "Lifestyle and age-
    ing", _Ageing and Society_, Vol.1, 3, 329-45.

Chapter Six

STEREOTYPES OF OLD-AGE: THE CASE OF YUGOSLAVIA

Dianne Willcocks

INTRODUCTION

In studies of social deviance (eg. Young 1971) it
has been suggested that when society defines a group
of people as deviant in some respect it tends to
react against them in ways which can isolate them
from the company of 'normal' people. A social
stereotype is constructed which influences subsequent behaviour patterns of the 'deviant' group and
this creates a self-fulfilling prophecy. In this
chapter consideration is given to the image of old
people held by different groups in society and the
extent to which stereotypes of old age represent a
form of "deviance" which may influence social
interactions.

At a recent international seminar in Dubrovnik
a group of social gerontologists conducted an investigation which explored such issues in relation to
the situation of old people in Yugoslavian society.
A wealth of descriptive material was generated
through an interesting mix of field trips to health
and social services facilities provided for old
people plus meetings with old people in community
and residential settings. In addition an attitude
survey of four different respondent groups was used
to construct and contrast profiles of old people (1);
the groups interviewed were old people, young people,
care staff and "experts".

The evidence that was collected will be used to
illustrate social divisions between old and young.
For society tends to act in ways which marginalise
the situation of old people by emphasising and
exacerbating their dependent status and denying them
opportunities to achieve a viable and acceptable
role. A social stereotype is created which may
cause negative shifts in self-perception amongst the

elderly. The paper ends by suggesting strategies
whereby the notion of stereotypes can be used to
generate positive changes in the social reality of
old age.

IMAGES OF OLD AGE

In the summer of 1982 an international seminar for
some forty social gerontologists was held in
Dubrovnik, Yugoslavia (2). In addition to the formal programme of conference papers and workshop
meetings the delegates were offered a fascinating
mix of field-trips to various agencies concerned
with social provision for elderly people; these
visits evoked a series of images of old-age in
Yugoslavia society which provide a backcloth for
this discussion of social stereotypes.

Residential Care
An obvious starting point for examining social·care
was the local old people's home. A first impression
of Dom Umirovljenika is that it offers an attractive
picture to the outside world. It is a modern unit
constructed from natural stone and built on three
floors, blending in with the traditional form of
surrounding buildings; there is a pleasant approach
along a gently contoured pathway set among colourful
shrubs and foliage. A bright cheerful entrance hall
greets the visitor.
        This 114 bed home is run in accordance with the
hotel model-of-care. It offers a comparatively
structured life: a list of rules and regulations
appears in the entrance hall and staff generally
wear uniform. But within that basic framework residents are in control of key areas of their daily
activities. For these old people community integration is a reality: ·it is an accepted principle in
such institutions that the local residential home
will provide the venue for the local old people's
club and that there will be reciprocal social visiting arrangements between residents and non-residents.
        Thus old people living alone might choose to
spend part of their day in the home much as any
group of outsiders might colonise a hotel lounge.
More important the dining room offers restaurant
facilities which provide good quality food at a
reasonable price to any would-be diner and this en-
courages many visitors - both old and young. When
the head-of-home was asked about resident participation in the organisation of home-life her complaint
was that although a residents' committee does exist

and operates to fulfil certain defined functions the old people are generally too pre-occupied with their community interests to devote sufficient time and energy to it.

Admissions to residential care were said to result from the breakdown in the provision of family care coupled with the inability of elderly people to live independently within the community as a result of failing health. Thus, this first visit focussed on the need of the elderly for social care as a response to increasing dependency.

Elderly People in a Rural Community
An alternative image of ageing was presented by the population of a tiny hamlet in a mountainous region some thirty miles north of Dubrovnik.

Three elderly families were visited in Majkogi-Podosojnik, a community numbering some 300 people. In the first household, a young son and his wife lived with an elderly mother farming the land together and providing mutual services and support. Inter-generational support and care remain rigidly bound into Yugoslavian value-systems.

In the second household two female cousins lived in adjacent cottages, eking out a subsistance living from their few remaining sheep and a small vegetable garden. At 73 and 70 years old, they remained fiercely independent in the face of diminished resources and uncertain health which reduced further their capacity for productive labour. Each was supported financially, in part, by family in Dubrovnik. Their rooms were spartan and had an aura of decay about them. Yet their hospitality was warm and friendly as they talked with pride of their occasional sorties to village shops or the local church some mile and a half distant.

A third household comprised two elderly brothers and their wives. The elder couple were 83 and 82 years old and the husband was visually impaired, an ex-mason who expressed profound regret at his declining strength and ability, yet claimed to enjoy his family life to the full. In this joint household situation it was the younger couple who carried out the heavy tasks in the fields and performed major household duties. They had younger family members whom they visited in the local town and they made two trips to a son in New York. They still produced olives and grapes as well as a range of fruit and vegetables and they maintained twelve sheep, two goats and a horse. This continued active economic participation combined with support from

extended kin assured a relatively comfortable existence for the family within the traditional rural
setting.
    Despite the optimistic approach to ageing em-
braced by these different families they are regarded
as problematic by the providers of public health and
social services whose resources are stretched to
encompass the various requirements of the elderly in
such a remote community. The population of the
villages is ageing as young people leave to seek
employment in the towns and the possibility of
practical family care, other than financial support,
becomes impeded by geographical barriers. Thus, a
positive image of old-age appears to be under
threat.

Rehabilitation Facilities
Visits were also organised to establishments which
cater for the assessment of needs and the rehabilitation of elderly and other persons. These were
situated along the coastal region surrounding
Dubrovnik, in an area of outstanding natural beauty.
Prirodno, at Petrovac, specialises in respiratory
diseases and offers a range of therapies including
individual treatments in atmospherically controlled
exercise chambers; underwater massage in sea-water;
and a waveless swimming pool with a hydraulic lift
for the less mobile to enter the water independently. The world-renowned Igalo Rehabilitation Centre
provides similar treatments but in addition offers
the unique mud bath treatment for rheumatic conditions. This strictly controlled method uses organically radio-active mud extracted directly from the
sea-bed.
    Such centres operate as medical establishments
yet provide a hotel-style of accommodation and
service. They aim to promote the positive aspects
of ageing by fostering the ability of their clients
to lead independent lives.
    These examples of the way in which the seminar
organisers developed a fascinating mix of visits for
conference delegates suggest that social gerontologists may, themselves, acquiesce to the "social
problem" stereotype of old-age and tend to focus
interest on the difficulties encountered by service-
providers in meeting needs associated with abnormal
features in the ageing process. This raises questions about how we perceive the characteristics,
relations and problems of elderly people, and the
extent to which such perceptions may account for the
way society responds to their needs.

SOCIAL STEREOTYPES AND SOCIAL PROBLEMS

Acccrding to Lippman (1922) stereotypes exist as
"pictures in our heads" which outline the social
world that surrounds us and largely determine the
way in which we, as social actors, will perform.
Furthermore, our actions towards other people may
determine the way in which they respond to us and so
we can influence social reality by encouraging others to act in accordance with our expectations and
stereotypes.
    Thus, through social interaction, stable and
relatively enduring changes in behaviour may occur
where a social actor starts to behave in accordance
with a social stereotype and thereby surrenders his
autonomy to the process of stereotypical confirmation.

Figure 1. Social Stereotypes: A Process of Social
           Perception and Behavioural Confirmation
           through Social Interaction

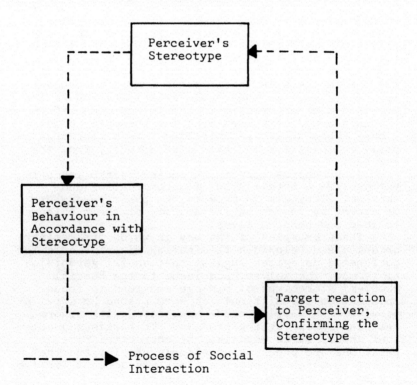

Stereotypes of Old-Age: The Case of Yugoslavia

Jock Young (1971), in his study of marihuana users, refers to a deviancy amplification spiral whereby the stereotype created by society for those labelled as drug-takers obliges them to interact with others in constrained ways determined by the stereotype. Erving Goffman (1968) charts the moral career of mental patients, outlining the manner in which particular images the hospital holds of the mentally ill are internalised and acted out by the patient. The advantage of this model in explaining outcomes is that it does not limit explanation to the notion of linear causality but stresses the mutual interaction and feedback between relevant variables.

But what is the nature of the social stereotype ? Where is it generated, and how can the phenomenon of stereotypical confirmation be applied to the elderly ?

A stereotype links more familiar concepts such as role and status. Tessa Perkins (1979) has argued that social status refers to a position in society which entails certain rights and duties whilst social role involves the performance of those rights and duties. Social stereotype is an evaluative conflation of these two. Thus "a stereotype brings to the surface and makes explicit and central what is concealed in the concept of status or role".

The elderly are a low-status category in Western society for whom only a diminished social role is generally permitted. Dependency, which is associated with failing physical and/or mental ability, together with a withdrawal from active participation in the labour force, presents an image of old-age as a non-productive and burdensome phase of the lifespan. In such a situation socially and economically valued roles become unattainable and the loss of an acceptable role contingent upon the state of retirement may influence the way in which elderly people perceive themselves - as a social problem.

Thus, where a stereotype abstracts the negative elements within the definition of social status and social role for a given group such as the elderly it will produce negative self-images for members of that group and a process of stereotypical confirmation will be established.

But what is the basis of a societal reaction which enables those who occupy powerful positions within the social structure to exclude or marginalise certain groups such as the elderly ? One might describe a scenario in which there is a direct conflict of interests between 'opposing' groups. In this case one could suggest that the elderly are regarded in terms of a financial imposition on society at large. This may be coupled with a sense of moral indignation whereby the existence of elderly people divorced from the work ethic and no longer controlled by a value system based on deferred gratification might appear threatening to the dominant group. However, the basis for our concern would normally be presented as humanitarian. Thus, we mask any moral or material conflicts by defining the group as socially problematic and instigating action "in their interests". A stereotype label is then attached to the object of our concern and this one-dimensional image will determine all other perceptions of that person.

It is important to note that just because a stereotype may be perjorative it does not necessarily entail that it will be inaccurate. Perkins (1979) has argued that the strength of any given stereotype will be dependent upon the particular configuration of validity and distortion that is achieved - were they totally inaccurate stereotypes could not function in the manner described above for they would be rejected by the 'target' group.

It is more likely that the stereotype presents an interpretation of events which conceals the 'real' cause of the group's attributes. Thus reduced economic activity of older workers is a function of changes in the nature of work and the labour market, not necessarily in indication of the declining willingness or capacity of elderly people to work. Furthermore, stereotypes are selective descriptions of certain problematic areas and to that extent they exaggerate. For example, the image of old people as prone to institutionalisation is somewhat erroneous in that this applies to just one in twenty of the elderly population.

A PRELIMINARY INVESTIGATION OF OLD AGE STEREOTYPES

In order to extend our understanding of the way in which stereotypes of old-age may be held by different social groups an empirical investigation was designed to explore images of ageing. It was argued that social intervention to compensate for negative stereotypes of ageing and generate more positive attitudes towards elderly people would have a beneficial effect on the self-esteem and ultimately on the quality of life to which old people might aspire.

A pilot study (3) was therefore designed "to compare the social perceptions of old-age among available samples of old people, staff experts and young people".

It was anticipated that any stereotypes would contain both positive and negative elements but that the distribution of elements might vary for different social groups. A second aim then was "to compare the frequency of some selected features of stereotypes in the sample of old people, staff, experts and young people".

Selecting a Sample

In all, some 117 individuals participated in the study: 46 old people (36 from a residential home, 10 from the rural community); 17 care staff; 44 young people (from high school) and 10 experts (delegates to the social gerontology conference). Mean age was 80 years for the old people; 16 for the young; 45 for the experts and 40 for staff. All participants were local inhabitants of the Dubrovnik area, apart from the experts who comprised an international group. An imbalance between sub-samples was undesirable but unavoidable.

Collecting the Data

All respondents were questioned - either alone or in groups, using a structured interview. Following a brief introduction the respondent was asked to do two things: (1) to write down a list of problems (up to a maximum of 10) experienced by older people, as it appeared to the respondent, and (2) to express agreement or disagreement with a series of stereotype statements Standard prompts were used to clarify any misunderstandings. Young people and experts were interviewed in groups and recorded their own responses. Individual interviews were held with old people and staff, and the interviewer wrote down responses.

Analysing the Results

A series of categories was developed by several "judges", according to the Guttman technique, in order to deal with the lists of problems. Significant differences between the frequencies for the different samples were determined using chi-square tests both for the problem frequencies and for the responses to stereotype statements.

RESULTS AND DISCUSSIONS

Problems of Old Age

According to the elderly, LONELINESS and ILL-HEALTH present the major problems of old-age. 97% of "old people" cite loneliness as compared with 88% of "staff"; 75% of "experts"; and 49% of "young people". A smiliar profile exists for illness whereby 96% of "old people" perceive it as problematic compared with 77% of "staff"; 75% of experts, and 43% of "young people".

The largest discrepancy occurs between old and young and whilst for old people the level of homogeneity is very high, for others loneliness and illness appear slightly less important in comparison with other problems. Interesting differences occurred within the "old" sample insofar as those living in the community in a rural environment see loneliness as peripheral whereas those living in residential care all quoted loneliness as one of the two most important problems they face, despite the fact that the latter group may be exposed to a greater number of social contacts than the former.

This confirms the early American work of Lowenthal (1964) on the importance of the quality of social interactions in maintaining morale, which was also demonstrated more recently in a British study of residential homes (Willcocks et al, 1982). Attempts to reduce the scale of institutional arrangements (i.e. small homes and homes with group-living arrangements) were seen to enhance rates of new friendship formation and the social integration of new residents.

Thus, a more explicit recognition of health problems of old people together with a more critical approach to the nature of loneliness offers scope for social intervention.

FINANCIAL PROBLEMS are regarded as a source of difficulty in old age by only 7% of "young people" but from 35% to 63% of the remaining sample. It is possible that this difference results from limited contact between young and old with the exception of the grandparent-grandchild relationship. It is interesting to note that experts are most concerned at the potential financial burden presented by old people.

Perceptions regarding SOCIAL RELATIONSHIPS differ widely and significantly. Staff and experts generally agree (82% and 87% respectively) that this poses problems in old age and this may well reflect their own difficulties in working with old people which they project onto their elderly clients, of whom only 46% agree. For young people there was often difficulty in understanding the term "relationship problems of the old" and they would tend to interpret this as a failure on the part of older people to understand the young.

UNHAPPINESS is a problem which is apparent to staff more than other members of the sample. However, this achieves a relatively low frequency overall. A similar pattern exists for BOREDOM since staff are exposed on a daily basis to what may by their criteria appear as a meaningless and uneventful life-style for old people. Furthermore, they are obliged to modify their own behaviour to counteract this problem i.e. they are encouraged to increase their social interaction with clients and spend more time in friendly conversation.

Additional problems referred to by different groups of respondents were IMMOBILITY, HELPLESSNESS, FEAR OF DEATH and LOSS OF FREEDOM. For all these problems group variation failed to produce a significant difference and the frequencies are generally low. Nevertheless, they may represent important elements within the stereotype which support key variables and influence social interaction between old people and others. Insofar as problems such as fear of death and loss of freedom may be somewhat intangible as compared with practical matters such as financial affairs and ill-health, it is important that we consider the more complex social interventions necessary to cope with these former problems and do not limit ourselves to the organisation of services to deal with the latter.

An overall ranking of problem perceptions for each group is shown in table 1. These were developed from response frequencies, and illustrate the difference in interpretation of problems noted above. As Turcinovic et al (1982) suggest "it seems that each sample looks at the elderly people's problems through the eye-glasses of their own life situation so that the final pictures of the same phenomenon are different". However, if the model of stereotype confirmation holds it seems reasonable to suggest that it will be the abstracted ideas of the dominant group that produce the stereotype and deny the validity of the target group's own definition. Thus, experts may start to influence self-perception of the elderly.

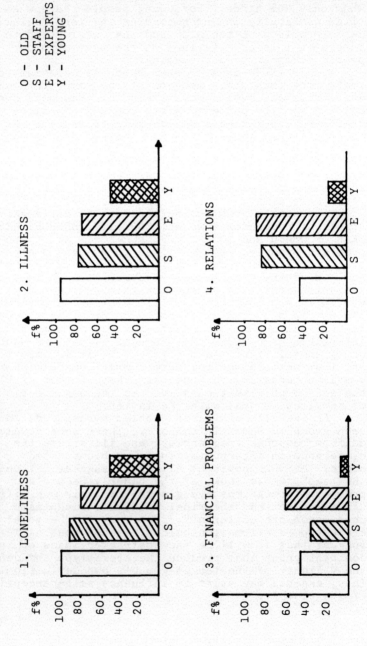

Chart 1. Proportion of Groups Referring to Each Social Problem of Old-Age

1. LONELINESS

2. ILLNESS

3. FINANCIAL PROBLEMS

4. RELATIONS

O – OLD
S – STAFF
E – EXPERTS
Y – YOUNG

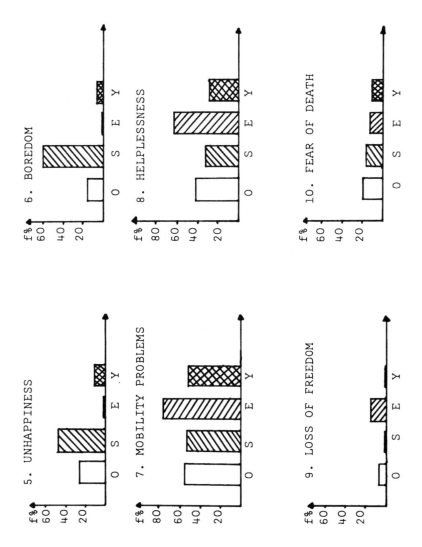

Response to Social Stereotype

In order to explore this possibility further respondents were asked to agree/disagree with a series of seven stereotype statements:

<u>Old People like Children</u> Substantial agreement on this issue was shared by young people (91%) who appeared to identify with grandparent figures and old people (85%). But only 71% of experts, and 59% of staff concur. This lower figure for staff may relate to earlier findings regarding negative staff perceptions of the social relationships of old people.

<u>Old Age is the Hardest Period of Life</u> The elderly, staff and young people tended to agree (68% to 82%) compared with only 29% of experts. This may be an indication of professional optimism divorced from the everyday reality of life as an old person.

<u>Old People are Kind and Tender</u> Old and young are in relatively high agreement at 55% and 50% respectively compared with the lower agreement shown by experts (28%) and the least by staff (7%). If this negative image held by staff is permitted to feed into the self-perception of the client group it may well have adverse consequences for future behaviour patterns and self-esteem.

<u>Old People are a Burden to Society</u> It must be of some concern to us that the highest level of agreement to this statement was found amongst old people themselves (58%): other samples ranged from 0 to 13%. The old are conscious of discrimination against them and attribute it to their failure to remain independent. It appears to old people that society treats them as a strain on the productive capacity of the dominant groups and hence they internalise this negative stereotype to their own further detriment.

With the remaining three statements there was a high level of agreement with the stereotype and a similar response from each group of respondents. The statements were: <u>Old people respect tradition</u>; <u>Old people are proud of their age</u>; <u>A man is as young as he feels</u>. This confirms the argument discussed earlier that stereotypes must contain certain accurate elements within them which achieve a relatively broad measure of consensus if they are to operate effectively.

Stereotypes of Old-Age: The Case of Yugoslavia

Table 1. Ranking of Perceived Social Problems in
         Old Age for each Group

OLD PEOPLE

1. Loneliness
2. Ill-health
3. Mobility problems
4. Financial problems
5. Relationships
6. Helplessness
7. Unhappiness
8. Fear of death
9. Boredom
10. Loss of freedom

STAFF

1. Loneliness
2. Relationships
3. Ill-health
4. Boredom
5. Mobility problems
6. Unhappiness
7. Financial problems
8. Helplessness
9. Fear of death
10. Loss of freedom

EXPERTS

1. Relationships
2. Mobility problems
2. Loneliness
2. Ill-health
5. Financial problems
5. Helplessness
7. Fear of death
7. Loss of freedom
9. Unhappiness
9. Boredom

YOUNG PEOPLE

1. Mobility problems
2. Loneliness
3. Ill-health
4. Helplessness
5. Relationships
6. Unhappiness
6. Fear of death
8. Financial problems
8. Boredom
10. Loss of freedom

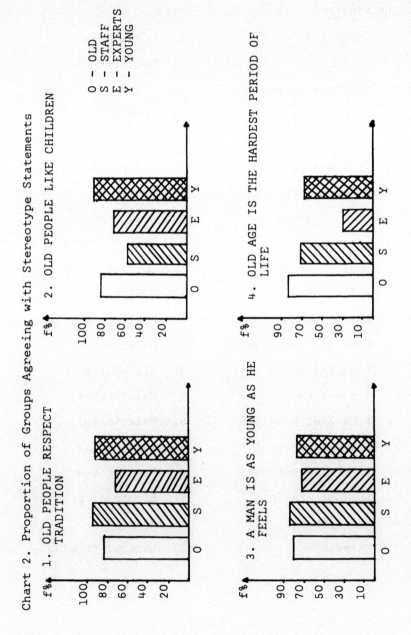

Chart 2. Proportion of Groups Agreeing with Stereotype Statements

O — OLD
S — STAFF
E — EXPERTS
Y — YOUNG

1. OLD PEOPLE RESPECT TRADITION

2. OLD PEOPLE LIKE CHILDREN

3. A MAN IS AS YOUNG AS HE FEELS

4. OLD AGE IS THE HARDEST PERIOD OF LIFE

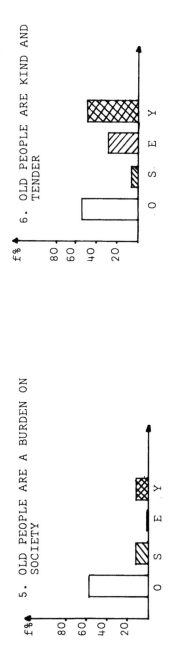

5. OLD PEOPLE ARE A BURDEN ON SOCIETY

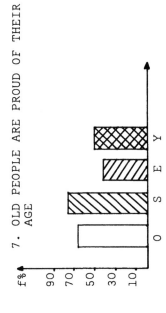

6. OLD PEOPLE ARE KIND AND TENDER

7. OLD PEOPLE ARE PROUD OF THEIR AGE

SUMMARY AND CONCLUDING REMARKS

In this paper selective descriptions of the social
world of elderly people in Yugoslavia have been
presented in association with the findings of an
attitude study of old-age. It has been argued that
stereotypes of old-age are an important element in
"shared cultural meanings" and that a dynamic relationship exists between the images society holds of
old people and the subjective experiences of the old
themselves. A process referred to as "stereotype
confirmation" illustrates the way in which old
people respond to such images. It is argued that
the balance between negative elements and positive
elements within the stereotype will be a key deter-
minent of the quality of life experienced by the
elderly in society.

The life-style achieved by residents in a
Dubrovnik old-age home was to all external appearances materially adequate and old people are able to
retain autonomy and exercise free-choice in many
activities of daily living. Yet institutional
arrangements for the care of the elderly are not regarded favourably within the society. In many respects residential care represents an option of last
resort which occurs by default where alternative
arrangements have proved inadequate.

Thus, the stereotype of an elderly resident is
constructed around notions of social isolation and/
or physical dependency often combined with unsatisfactory social relationships. This has important
consequences for the way in which staff perceive residents and ultimately for the way residents see themselves. An important contribution to this discussion is offered by Helen Evers (1982) who has identified three categories of female patients in long-
stay geriatric wards. She demonstrates the way in
which ward staff shape their social relationships
with patients in accordance with the label that has
been ascribed and how these social stereotypes may
represent a denial of the individual's experiential
world.

An alternative image of ageing was presented in
the rural community of Dubrovnik where old people
retain independence and avoid isolation by remaining
integrated within traditional social networks represented by family and neighbourhood groupings.
Unlike the elderly living in institutions whom Evers
(1982) has described as "divorced from their own
biographies" old people living a dignified life in
the community can successfully resist the negative

label to which residents succumb. Thus the positive
elements of the stereotype will determine the nature
of social interactions and this will have a beneficial effect on quality of life.

The attitude survey - even at this pilot stage
- has provided a vivid illustration of the range of
social problems different groups in society may
associate with old-age and the extent to which these
may determine the nature of stereotypes. It is
argued that social behaviour of the non-elderly derived from a belief in the stereotype will influence
the self-perception and self-esteem of the elderly,
together with subsequent behaviour patterns which
incorporate an acceptance of the stereotype by old
people.

The transmission of deviant stereotypes by the
mass media has been well documented by Young (1971).
He suggests that in order to create news-worthy
items the media "select events which are atypical
and present them in a stereotypical fashion". In a
sense, old-age and dependence are held by society to
be a deviation from the norm of youth and independence. It is possible that this is reflected by the
way in which aspects of ageing are dealt with by the
media. Further investigation of the role of the
media in generating and perpetuating stereotypes of
old age is required if we are to understand fully
the mechanisms of stereotype confirmation.

The evidence collected for this paper supports
an argument that images of ageing derived from social stereotypes are a significant factor in explaining the subjective meaning of old age for the elderly, irrespective of their objective social conditions. This points to certain practical consequences
and actions that could be instigated to improve subjective quality of life.

First, measures could be introduced to bring
into prominence the factors which are common to the
perception of old-age problems among different
social groups. This would reduce the possibility of
misunderstandings and ill-conceived or inappropriate
social interactions. In order to achieve this correspondence in the social perceptions of different
populations it would be necessary to disseminate
factual information about the situation of old
people in society and the role of social relationships in promoting their subjective well-being.

Secondly, social intervention in the circular
process of stereotypical confirmation could be implemented. The aim would be to develop revised
social stereotypes by shifting the balance between

121

the positive and negative elements contained in the concept. Thus one could stress the resources older people offer to society rather than focussing on aspects of dependency. It is argued that this would influence the behaviour of the perceiver to the old person who would then respond in accordance with a positive self-image.

In order for these changes to be effective it would be important to ensure their acceptance and incorporation within major social institutions. Specifically, they must form part of the socialisation process for young people and they must form the basis of training programmes for those who work with elderly people.

Such proposals are not intended to present an alternative to measures which address themselves to the material interests of old people. It is acknowledged that the social relationships of the elderly are mediated by social structure. Furthermore, the process of stereotypical abstraction is but a reflection of the norms and values of society, as determined by dominant groups. Nevertheless, it is argued that a focus on social interaction can offer us strategies for introducing ameliorative programmes in specific areas of social life which will improve the social reality of old-age.

NOTES

1. This attitude survey was designed and carried out by a group of social psychologists from U. of Rijeka, Yugoslavia. The material was discussed in depth with the international seminar group following which a written paper was produced by Turcinovic et al (1982). The present author is much indebted to the Yugoslavian team for their generosity in permitting the findings to be reproduced in the context of this extended discussion of stereotypes.

2. Social Gerontology in International and Cross-Cultural Perspectives III May 31st - June 11th 1982; held at the Inter-University Centre of Post Graduate Studies, Dubrovnik.

3. This investigation was devised and conducted during the two week seminar referred to earlier; as such the methodology was subject to constraints of time, space and finance. Nevertheless, it is argued that this exploratory probe with an available sample might produce results which could assist in the reformulation of the problem on a more adequate basis.

REFERENCES

Evers H. (1981) "Care or Custody ? The Experience of
    Women Patients in Long-Stay Geriatric Wards" in
    Controlling Women: the Normal and the Deviant.
    ed. Bridget Hutter. Croom Helm, London
Goffman E. (1968) Asylums Penguin, London
Lippman W. (1922) Public Opinion. Free Press, New
    York
Lowenthal M.F. (1964) "Social Isolation and Mental
    Illness in Old Age" American Sociological
    Review 29; 54-70.
Perkins T. (1979) "Rethinking Stereotypes" in Ideo-
    logy and Cultural Production ed. Michele
    Barratt et al, Crocm Helm, London
Turcinovic P, Vehovec, J, Brdar I, Milic I. (1982)
    Stereotypes and Social Perceptions of Elderly
    People's Problems conference paper for Inter-
    national and Cross-Cultural Perspectives in
    Social Gerontology III. Dubrovnik, June 1982.
Willcocks D.M. Peace S.M. Kellaher L.A. (1982)
    The Residential Life of Old People: a study in
    100 Local Authority Homes Research Reports 12
    and 13. Survey Research Unit, Polytechnic of
    North London.
Young J. (1971) The Drug Takers. Paladin

Chapter Seven

ACCOUNTS OF ONITSHA MARKET LITERATURE: PERCEPTIONS
OF AGE AND WISDOM

Pamela Shakespeare

Many academic studies of modernisation in Africa and
the third world concentrate on the population movement towards urban areas, the social structure generated in occupation-based communities of migrant
workers and on the culture which develops with
rapid urbanisation.

A complementary area of concern is what happens
in the traditional communities whence the urban migrant population is drawn. Migratory work patterns
necessarily affect the demography of formerly traditional villages. The population distribution is
severely affected. In some cases the only males
remaining in the villages are old men and young boys.

What connects these two populations ? Each of
them obviously has perceptions about the way of
life, beliefs and values that they see as character-
istic of the other. And there are certainly tensions between traditional value systems and the value
systems that prevail where modernisation is taking
place. Non-academic literature provides one medium
where the tensions are reported. It includes accounts of events which demonstrate a clash between
cultures, and carries different value judgements of
the social scene, which serve the same purpose.

This chapter discusses some aspects of popular
market literature from South Eastern Nigeria. It
provides a description of some of the types of literature available and comments on perceptions about
older people and their values and beliefs. These
perceptions are largely those of members of a young
urban population about traditional concepts of age
and wisdom. In some cases they are descriptions of
the attributes of old people; in other cases they
are reflexive statements commenting on what older
people think about younger people and their mores
at the present time.

124

Two implications which seem to be apparent in the market literature have particular relevance. The first of these is much in the mould of "the dog that didn't bark". There is comparatively little reference to the sagacity of older people. They no longer appear to be a reference point for younger people. Secondly there is the implication that the elders who knew "the olden days" and who still live and uphold a traditional lifestyle are stranded: left behind in more senses than the merely geographical.

It is difficult in a short space to do justice to the vitality and exuberance of the market literature or to explore the idiosyncracies of the style of writing which is often flamboyant and fanciful. However I have reproduced the quotations as they were printed, and this may help to give a flavour of the material.

BACKGROUND

The main source of market literature in Nigeria is the Eastern town of Onitsha. Before the Nigerian Civil War Onitsha had the most famous market in the whole of Nigeria. In order to appreciate the content of Onitsha Market Literature it is necessary to place it in context. The following description of the context of the market literature draws heavily on the work of Emanuel Obiechina (1971, 1972)

In the drift from rural to urban areas which has characterised settlement patterns of many parts of Africa in this century a town such as Onitsha would have had many attractions for people moving from a rural to an urban environment. As well as becoming a highly developed commercial centre, by virtue of its location as a gateway to the east from the west of the country, it acquired numerous educational institutions. And as certification and literacy became increasingly important pre-requisites for jobs, education came to be seen more and more as a key to success.

After the second world war many of the soldiers who returned from abroad, with the assistance of financial bonuses they received, were able to set up new businesses. Often the businesses were partially staffed by relatives invited to move from rural areas. There was an increase on literate and semi-literate urban dwellers not familiar with the mores of urban life, and hence a potential audience for a new indigenous literature which could educate people to their new roles. Education was turned into a business to satisfy a demand that far outstripped what orthodox educational institutions could provide.

Some of the businessmen began to set up printing presses that had lain dormant during the war and to print the work of aspiring authors. Although most authors were paid very little if anything at all, having one's name in print was seen as being prestigious. A large volume of material thus came on to the market in the forties, fifties and early sixties.

THE LITERATURE

In its many forms the literature reflects the complexities, pitfalls and pleasures of modern life. For the most part it is explicitly instructive, although some is devoted to entertainment. Much of it is aimed at a young audience and is devoted to love, the etiquette associated with it, and its ascendancy as a criterion for marriage over economics and family ties.

A second category of booklets concerns careers and organisations. Again, it deals with etiquette and useful skills, and much of the content is concerned with advancement from a youthful point of view. The third category is essentially informative. Some examples include, The Last Days of Lumumba; The British Political Shooting of the Nigerian Coalminers in November 18, 1949; Dr. Nkrumah and the Struggle for Freedom. A fourth category is basically moral. As with the other categories, the titles are often lengthy: How to Avoid Dangerous Ladies and Modern Harlots; and No Condition is Permanent. A fifth category is a hybrid of the third and fourth: perhaps the best way to describe it is as knowledge and things worth knowing. It has more explicit moral allusions than the informational category, but is less evangelical than the moral category. Typical titles include: Complete Riddles and Jokes and Things Worth Knowing in Questions and Answers; and How to Know Proverbs and Many Things in Questions and Answers.

AGE, WISDOM AND THE OLDEN DAYS

It is in the last two categories that the most interesting allusions to age and wisdom occur. Their general purport is that although wisdom, age and the olden days still receive lip service they no longer have any real efficacy. They have become reduced to states of passivity.

In 'How to Avoid Dangerous Ladies and Modern Harlots' there are several revealing statements on the theme of passivity in the face of moral decline:

> Even today men and women who are between sixty and eighty years and who were brought up in an unadulterated way and culture feel sad to what today's younsters and matured men and women are doing without shame.

> Gone are the days when a married woman knew only her husband. In those glorious past women regarded unfaithfulness as a great toboo-ill-attitude which cried to God for vengeance.

> It was in those days that women and men lived for well over eighty to a hundred years because they respected not only God's commandments but also the great traditions of their fatherland.

> A girl of 13 who should have been an absolute virgin if it were about 60 years ago is an addicted harlot today.

Thus the wisdom and morals of the olden days no longer stand and this is a cause for regret. In the booklet "How to Become Rich and Avoid Poverty", traditional wisdom helps a man to acquire wealth without the benefit of modern knowledge:

> About A Court Messenger.
> The name of this man is Ben. He is a court messenger, he is not educated but he is very wise. People call him 'No Leave, No Transfer'. He became a court messenger since 1929 but no promotion.

Despite the virtues of the old ways wisdom is being redefined. In Money Hard to Get But Easy to Spend the biline is Read and become Wise. Knowledge and wisdom have become almost synonymous with literacy and wisdom. Quite a lot of the booklets point to the acquisition of wisdom through proverbs and things worth knowing. Thus, there seems to be some kind of bridge between old ideas of wisdom and the new emphasis on knowledge. In one of the books the following question and answer occur.

> What do you understand by proverbs ?
> Answer: proverbs are the law quotations of
> the ancient people and are also known as the
> oil with which words are eaten.

Many of the traditional proverbs reinforce the conclusion that wisdom is a passive state rather than
an active strategy, whereas knowledge is an operational way of proceeding.

All the categories of booklets I have described
encompass areas of experience in which the elders or
traditional holders of knowledge and wisdom can no
longer have access to the type of wisdom required.
It has been pointed out by Obiechina (1972) that
many young Nigerians - encouraged perhaps at school
by literary encounters with Jane Austen, Emily
Bronte et al - have enthusiastically taken up the
European ideal of romantic love, whose ideals are
well beyond the scope of traditional knowledge,
wisdom and protocol. Similarly, the formal business
procedures in the contemporary world are not the
formal procedures of traditional society. On the
etiquette of business letters the elders have nothing to offer. Literacy is power.

The booklets are for the most part national and
international in their focus. Leaving aside the
question of factual accuracy, much of the inform-
tion is based on the speeches of famous leaders, on
public statistics, and so on, culled from sources
which depart from traditional ways of storing knowledge.

Wisdom, frequently accompanied by accounts of
the olden days, does then make an appearance in
Onitsha market literature. It is however seen as
comparatively passive. Descriptions of old people
portray them as looking on helplessly and with regret at what has come to pass. What it once meant
to be wise is juxtaposed with current wisdom, which
seems to be synonymous with knowledge and skills.
In the market literature at least, the complexity
and ebullliance of the new order wins - though
whether art reflects life is   another matter.

REFERENCE

Obiechina, E. (1972) <u>Onitsha Market Literature</u>
    Heinemann, London
Obiechina, E. (1971) <u>Literature for the Masses: An
    Analytical Study of Popular Pamphleteering in
    Nigeria</u> Nwamife Books, Enugu, Nigeria.

Chapter Eight

JUST A SONG AT TWILIGHT: RESIDENTS' COPING
STRATEGIES EXPRESSED IN MUSICAL FORM

Jennifer Hockey

The focus of this chapter, as the title indicates,
is a song created and intended for performance by
the residents of a Local Authority home for the
elderly in the North East. I will be discussing it
in order to demonstrate the usefulness of material
of this kind for the researcher seeking access to
the experience of elderly people living in care.
Though it is not possible, here, to pursue its
significance exhaustively, to discuss in depth the
issues which are raised, I offer an interpretation
of this song as a case-study which casts light upon
both the concerns and the preoccupations of those
who generated it and also upon the methodological
approach particular to anthropology.

BACKGROUND

My research interests are the concepts or systems of
meaning intrinsic to our own culture through which
death is perceived and encountered. A residential
home for the elderly offered me a context within
which to explore such concepts or cultural frameworks as they are expressed in the life of a community closely in touch with one specific kind of
death; that is in extreme old age, often long after
the deaths of former contemporaries, and always
after some degree of physical decline and deterioration.
        During nine months fieldwork which began in
October 1980 and ended in July 1981 I adopted the
role of a voluntary care worker. Three months were
spent working six hours a day, five days a week in
the home. A further six months involved two or
three day's work every week, choosing a more varied
range of shifts than previously. Though I worked
predominantly alongside staff I was, as an unpaid

helper, free to spend time with residents whenever conversations developed and to conduct pre-arranged interviews when I chose.

In this way I acquired a knowledge of the workings of the entire community. I needed to understand the significance of everyday events for both the cared-for and also for the carers. The latter, the carers, are in many respects more accessible to the researcher willing to participate unobtrusively in their work for an extended period. The very elderly, by contrast, are encountering events and experiences from which the researcher, however willing, is precluded by virtu e of age. Barbara Myerhoff (1978), in her account of a day-centre for elderly Jewish people in Los Angeles, writes,

> 'At various times, I consciously tried to
> heighten my awareness of the physical feeling
> state of the elderly by wearing stiff garden
> gloves to perform ordinary tasks, taking off
> my glasses and plugging my ears, slowing down
> my movements and sometimes by wearing the
> heaviest shoes I could find to the Center'.

Similar attemps have been made during training weekends for those employed in residential care using techniques such as fastening thick foam pads to the soles of shoes. Though simulation of this kind goes some way towards placing the researcher, quite literally, in the shoes of the elderly it does not, of itself, fulfill one's aim which is not so much the sharing of experience as the understanding of the concepts or mode of thought through which very elderly people seek to make sense of what is happening to them. To furnish oneself with their viewpoint is not the same as being able to understand and explain their mode of thought.

The song I propose to discuss is the kind of material which can reveal the way in which the elderly think about and seek to manage their experience. It is a statement chosen deliberately and offered in a public setting by the residents about the meaning of ageing and dying for them. When set alongside careful observation of behaviour, recordings of conversation and taped interviews, it represents a valuable clue to the way in which its singers think about themselves and their situation.

Just a Song at Twilight

THE SONG

HOPE !

There's always a <u>hope</u> - though it may be quite
small   1
There's always a <u>star</u> - though the darkness may
fall -   2
There's always a <u>gleaming of gold</u> in the grey,   3
There's always a <u>flower</u> growing wild by the way.   4

There's always a <u>song</u> floating out on the air,   5
There's always a <u>dawn</u> to the night of despair -   6
There's always a <u>path</u> for the faithful to
tread,   7
There's always a <u>bend</u> in the <u>roadway ahead</u>.   8

There's <u>always</u> a <u>hope</u> - but we've got to
<u>believe</u>   9
We've got to be ready to <u>see</u> and <u>receive</u>   10
The hints and the signs   11
Although faint they appear -   12
To <u>wait</u> and to <u>trust</u> till the meaning grows
clear.   13

And when through the murk of the shadows we
grope   14

<u>We've got to remember</u>,   15

<u>We've got to remember</u>,   16

<u>There's always a hope</u> !   17

(underlined in this way by the resident, Arthur
Grant, to show which words were to be stressed in
the singing).

INTERPRETATION

(To ensure confidentiality, all proper names used
are fictitious.) To understand what is implicitly
being expressed in a song of this kind, one must
begin by asking what kind of social context it occu-
pies; who was responsible for its inception and how
did it come about ?
     Its social context is Highfield House, a modern
purpose-built Local Authority home offering Part III
accomodation for up to 45 elderly people. The
home's teak-furnished bed-sitting-rooms and airy
communal dining-hall resemble those of a number of

other institutions. Like many unwaged people, its
residents pass their time reading newspapers, watch-
ing television, eating, washing and sleeping. What
distinguishes Highfield House from other such social
contexts is that each of its residents has experienced a permanent separation from his or her previous domestic and professional contexts and will
remain thus separated until progressive physical
deterioration culminates in death. This very particular circumstance underlies each and every event,
action and conversation within the home. It is
intrinsic to our exploration of the meaning of the
song.

Those responsible for the song's inception are
a small group of relatively fit, less dependent
residents whose friendship with one another in many
cases stems from childhood residence in the former
village, now a city suburb, adjoining the home. As
representatives of a common memory of significant
events and experiences within the former village,
the members of this group offer a reference point of
some kind, both to each other, and to those whose
withdrawal into the deterioration of the present
belies a former awareness and involvement with the
affairs of the locality.

Staff too are not unfamiliar with the biographies of those associated with this group. Their
relationship with these individuals arises not so
much from the close physical contact used in the
care of the very dependent as from the complex
verbal inter action needed to ensure co-operation
from those accustomed to independence and respect.

Thus the distinguishing features of those associated with the offering of the song can be summarised as relative fitness and independence, significant associations with the former life of the
immediate locality and a continuing capacity for
sociability. Encompassing all of these features,
they come to represent an acceptable model of ageing
for both staff and residents.

Nonetheless, each member of the group has
experienced loss of family and of fitness and all
face the forms of dependency and deterioration represented by those who surround them in the home.
Although they share a common lot with those bereft
of a social role in the wider society, the assets
accruing from relative fitness and a less dependent
relationship with staff make it possible for the
members of this group to articulate the concerns and
pre-occupations of their fellows.

Thus the song has arisen out of the shared

values and continuing friendship of a very specific
group within the home. To those who joined them in
rehearsing the song, this group retain, in memory,
their former position and status within the local
community.

As to the way in which the song came about:
its career had begun the previous spring when an
Easter card bearing the verses had been sent to
Henry Johnson, a member of the group we have been
describing. 'We liked the words so much', Henry
told me, 'that we asked Arthur to set them to
music'. Arthur Grant was a lifelong friend, former
schoolteacher and chapel organist, now resident in
the home. The 'we' is a reference to Henry's associates in the home. The intention was to prepare the
song for performance at the Christmas concert held
every year in the home. Previous concerts had
attracted the attention of local television, thereby
making it very much a public performance.

Thus we can approach the text itself in the
knowledge that it is a fragment selected by a particular group of residents from their external environment and appropriated for a specific purpose within the home. It becomes meaningful to the extent
that it absorbs and embraces that which is critical
within the bounded social context of its performance. It is filled with meaning through its deliberate adoption into the lives of its singers.

THE TEXT

From its imprecise, inspirational sentiments this
text is readily identifiable as an example of a
particular genre of quasi-religious texts and poems,
often to be found on calendars and greetings cards.
The genre is perhaps best exemplified in the work of
'Patience Strong'. Like magazine horoscopes, it is
the vagueness of this form of writing which is particularly important in that it allows the reader to
impute his or her own specific meaning to its
imagery.

The example of the genre we are dealing with
here was originally printed on an Easter card. Its
theme is Hope, that which was given to the world
through the resurrection of Jesus Christ, and is
central to the Christian concept of Easter. Written
in the characteristically imprecise style of their
genre, the verses were found to be appropriate to a
quite different point on the Christian calendar when
detached from an original context of chicks, rabbits
and budding flowers. Sung by the very elderly in

the dark November afternoons leading up to Christmas, the words which had previously lent vague Christian undertones to Easter's associations with spring, fine weather and fresh hopes now took on a more profound and urgent 'religious' significance.
    It is that more profound and urgent significance which is revealed if we examine the relationship between the images used in the verses and the comments and conversations which pattern the daily round within the home. Familiarity with the texture and the quality of residents' daily lives enlightens us as to why these particular verses spoke to them with such clarity. Such was the energy generated in the appropriation, transformation and rehearsal of these verses that we may infer that those residents concerned recognised a number of very crucial themes traced in the simple images of these lines. I will now go on to discuss the resonance of these simple images - of old age, of the world of nature and of the afterlife - and so   · describe the three themes which are of particular significance for those who age in residential care.

IMAGES OF OLD AGE

Line 6 is perhaps the most immediate point of identification with the verses for residents encountering the bodily experiences of extreme old age. 'There's always a <u>dawn</u> to the night of despair' readily articulates the experiences of those condemned by too many daylight hours of dozing to suffer the persistent aches and pains of an ageing body through long wakeful nights. Line 14, 'And when through the murk of the shadows we grope', is similarly resonant for those whose failing limbs and eyesight are tried by the unceasing requirement to edge their way back and forth along the corridors which lie between bedrooms and dining-hall. Such experiences are also alluded to in the phrases, 'though the darkness may fall' (line 2) and, 'the bend in the roadway ahead' (line 8), a bend which may appear at times unattainable when a zimmer frame compensates so poorly for the limbs' lost vigour. The word 'grey' in line 3 has multiple reference points in a bland physical environment where extreme old age and lack of fresh air are everywhere reflected in greying hair and flesh, and all movement is made across monochrome lino and carpet tiles. Any gleaming of gold to be found in these grey surroundings arises from such chance events as a joke, a visitor or a burst of spring weather.

In drawing out the imagery of bodily discomfort we
find the concept of a journey implicitly traced in
line 7, the 'path for the faithful to tread' and
line 14, 'when through the murk of the shadows we
grope'. Suggested through the imagery of physical
suffering, the motif of a journey is implicitly lent
additional associations with the Christian ideology
of life as pilgrimage. As they grope through the
murk of the shadows, it is the faithful, the belie-
vers, who find a path and a bend in the roadway
ahead. It is a journey of suffering, a night of
despair, which not only has an ending or a dawn, but
also leads towards meaning.

If we consider that in one form or another many
of these residents have experienced a dramatic
change in their domestic and social circumstances
brought about by deterioration in their physical
state, we begin to see the significance of a journey
motif within the chosen song. In many cases changes
in personal circumstance have occured at a time in
life when the uncertainties and upheavals of youth
have long since given way to the stability and pre-
dictability of a long-established marriage within a
familiar and well-ordered domestic environment.
Bereft of reference points, previously taken for
granted, the resident confronts a solitary one-way
journey into the indeterminacy of the future. This
period of up to thirty years following retirement is
singular in its lack of classificatory markers comparable with the various rites of transition whereby
the individual has negotiated his or her passage
through the earlier years of life. As Haim Hazan
(1980) asserts in 'The Limbo People', a study of a
Jewish day-centre for the elderly, 'the elderly are
confronted with two conflicting demensions of time.
Their position in society consists of static elements whereas the unavoidable process of disintegra-
tion changes conditions and abilities'.

The conflict between two very different dimensions of time is particularly marked for those who
age in residential care. While the rigidly repetitive routine of the institution creates a sense of
timelessness, the individual's subjective experience
is of a personal time dimension characterised by
progressive physical decline. Remarks from residents such as,

'You never know what to expect when you're
getting old. You never know what's coming
next'

135

'You never think about old age, do you,
you never think. You ought to prepare for
it'

and most commonly of all,

'I never thought I'd come to this'

attest to the fact that the unprecedented bodily
experiences of ageing in the unfamiliar environment
of residential care may bring with them an acute
sense of disorientation or discontinuity between
past and present. As changes in the body multiply,
the experience of an unanticipated rupture in one's
path through life breeds a growing sense of uncertainty and insecurity with respect to the future.
     For example, Mrs Dent, an 84 year-old resident,
would talk at length about the deterioration in her
condition which she had observed during her first
eight months in the home. 'I know I'm getting old
but I never expected this kind of deterioration',
she told me, going on to refer to residents who had
been in the home for up to eleven years. She con-
fided her fears of the unpredictable range of suffering she faces during the indeterminate period of
time remaining to her.
     Uncertainty about the unknown course of future
deterioration is compounded by the awareness that
any one of the physical impairments which arise may
lead rapidly to death. Mrs Williams, another resident, had had a mastectomy during late middle age
and the illnesses of her eighties sustained her fear
of the recurrence of cancer. As each aspect of
ageing manifested itself she would ask staff, 'Do
you think this is the end ?', seeking out the
Catholic priest to make her funeral requirements
quite explicit. Gran McCardle, also a Catholic and
in her mid-nineties, was known to have requested the
last rites on several occasions and was wont to re-
mind staff that, 'you can be struck down in a moment'. Another resident, Mrs Porter, received an
unprecedented number of cards and presents during
the week leading up to her 91st birthday. She con-
fided her appreciation of these gifts to a staff
member and added a query as to why people had been
so kind to her this year. Was it to be the last ?
     Thus to those whose passage through physical
deterioration is contained and constrained within
the static and repetitive routine of the institution, the motif of a journey which is traced in the
imagery of physical suffering has a very personal

significance. The song acknowledges the fact that
though staff may manage a repetitive cycle of admissions and exits to and from the institution, the
resident encounters a solitary, one-way journey into
unknown and uncertain personal territory. The acknowledgement is couched in a form which not only
offers comfort by asserting an end to suffering, but
also lends purpose, meaning and therefore dignity to
that suffering by implicit reference to the Christian concept of life as pilgrimage. Though a present
of discomfort and constraint continues to replicate
itself day after day, as the residents move back and
forth between the same bed, armchair and mealtable,
their sense of uncertainty about the nature of their
fate as individuals is both acknowledged and trans-
cended through the image of a painful journey which
leads towards a meaningful destination.

IMAGES OF THE NATURAL WORLD

In common with many poems and texts of this kind,
images of the world of nature are used extensively
in these verses. Thus we find the star, the wild
flower, the dawn, the gleaming of gold in the grey,
the song floating out in the air and the bend in the
roadway ahead. These images are used to fulfill two
different purposes in the verses.
     Firstly they use the external world of nature
to give metaphoric form to the hopes and fears associated with human hardship and struggle. In line
2 we read that, 'There's always a star - though the
darkness may fall - ' and in line 4 we are told
that, 'There's always a flower growing wild by the
way'. Thus the uncertainties of human life are
placed within the broader context of the cycle of
nature and the message to the reader is that present
hardships or discomforts can be accepted as part of
a larger pattern. Comforts and relief will come in
their own good time, just as spring follows winter
and sunshine follows the rain. In other words, it
is not for the individual to strive for or to seek
to possess, happiness. It will come like the flower
growing wild by the way and the song floating out on
the air.
     Secondly, the images are used to endorse and
validate the Christian message by drawing on that
separate body of folk wisdom, the Lore of Nature.
For example, in line 1 we are offered the rash and
contestable assertion that, however small, there is
always a hope. The form of this line is echoed in
the following seven, all of them variations on the

adage, 'Every Cloud has a Silver Lining', all of
them referring to that which by the Lore of Nature
we know to be true. By the eighth line the validity
of the first line is well established and we are
open to the injunction of the third verse.

Thus images of the world of nature are used,
a) to suggest that both suffering and its relief are
inevitable, each to be accepted in its turn, that
'into every life a little rain must fall', and b) to
invoke a body of folk wisdom which lends further
weight to the message of Christianity. These roles
are essentially overlapping or mutually reinforcing.
The presentation of suffering as something to be
accepted as part of nature's cycle underscores the
song's Christian injunctions that the individual
should be humble, patient and trusting.

What can we infer from the fact that residents
chose verses bearing messages of this kind for their
public performance ? Private comments suggests that
the uses to which images of the natural world are
being put in these verses correspond to many of the
strategies through which residents seek to come to
terms with their present situation.

If we consider that residential care is made
available only to those 'in need of care and attention not otherwise available' we realise that no
matter what form of response residents offer, their
continued and inevitable presence within the home
ultimately represents passive acceptance of care.
The active seeking of alternatives is no longer an
option for them. And indeed, when new residents are
asked how they are settling in, they offer replies
such as,

> 'I'm beginning to but it will take time.
> It takes a while to get used to it but I'll
> just have to'.

> 'I'll never be happy here but I'll have to
> stick it, 'cos I won't live that long, much
> longer'.

> 'I accept things the way they are here. I
> have to, there's nothing else for it'.

> 'I'm not happy here but I'll just have to
> make myself happy'.

> 'You never know what's coming next. You just
> have to accept it'.

To express acceptance in words such as these is to
betray the helplessness and desperation from which
it stems. It is the one strategy open to all who
encounter hardship and loss of power yet it inevitably implies personal failure and loss of integrity.
    Here we see the significance of the use to
which natural imagery is put in the verses. As we
saw, the verses describe a present condition of
darkness, despair and greyness. All that remains to
the faithful is hope. Only by 'waiting' and
'trusting' can they hope to stumble upon the 'wild
flower', the 'song' and the 'bend in the roadway
ahead'. Couched in religious terms which are validated by references to the natural world, the acceptance of hardship assumes a dignity and stature
which distinguishes it clearly from resignation,
apathy or passivity. In their singing, residents
are implicitly invoking the authority of two traditional sources of truth, Christianity and the Lore
of Nature. Thus they validate their one remaining
option, acceptance, and allay any notion that it may
be little more than a giving up.
    As the comments of new residents testify, they
keenly feel the loss of alternatives and accept
residential care because they have no choice. We
can compare them with more settled residents such as
Henry Johnson, Arthur Grant and others associated
with the song's creation, who have retained their
health and been able to create a role for themselves
within the home. Arthur Grant summed up his life
story and personal philosophy with the following
words,

> 'You never know how things change in the world.
> Where you get to. How things link up or break
> up. That's life, you take it as it comes.
> Sometimes its good, sometimes bad'.

What we find among residents such as Arthur is that
acceptance has been elaborated, through reference to
cultural values rooted in their past lives, into a
system through which dignity and status may be acquired. Proverbs, aphorisms, systems of authority
rooted in former professional lives and religious
texts are all cited in support of residents' acceptance of present circumstances.
    Thus Mr Bradbrook, complaining that care assis-
tants had hurt his back by dropping him hard onto a
chair after his bath, curtailed his resentment with
the opening line of a hymn,

'Well .... We are but little children, frail and
helpless all ......' He expresses acceptance of his
present helplessness and interprets it in terms of
the Christian metaphor of man as child and God as
father. Ethel Halliwell also ended a series of
complaints with the biblical text, 'We must learn
not to kick against the pricks'. Mrs Porter invokes
professional rather than religious values. Formerly
associated with one of the city's most thriving
businesses, she said it was important to accept
rules and regulations. There was someone at the top
and what she said had to go. Mrs Porter had been at
the top herself and she knew that this was how it
had to be.

In these and many other examples, as in the
chosen verses, we see the invocation of traditional
sources of authority to validate a patient, trustful
and accepting response to hardship. By drawing on
such traditional values as discipline, hierarchy,
and Christian humility and trust, residents are able
to impute meaning and therefore grace and dignity to
an otherwise demeaning acceptance of failing health
and lost independence.

IMAGES OF AN AFTERLIFE

Though we have dwelt so far on the relevance of the
song's images for the present circumstances of
residents' lives, we must not overlook the original
significance of its metaphors. Thus the 'dawn to
the night of despair', the 'flower' and the 'song'
are all faint hints or foretastes of that much
happier life which lies beyond death.

I suggested that the appropriation of the verses by the residents lent them a more profound and
urgent religious significance than was originally
intended on the greetings card. Sung by those for
whom death is an everpresent possibility, the Easter
message of the gift of hope for the resurrection to
eternal life has a very immediate personal relevance. The resurrection ceases to be an intangible
precept of the Christian religion and instead assumes the pressing reality of an imminent event.
Closing a 'choir practice' Arthur Grant, in his role
of choir master, sought to encourage the more faint-
hearted by promising a growing repertoire by that
time next year. Awareness of what the future held
le d him to add the proviso, '....... if we're all
still alive by then'. His own death came within six
months.

Thus underlying the significance of verses for

a here-and-now which is centred around the management of the contraints of ageing in residential care
is a more fundamental layer of meaning associated
with the immediacy of dying.
 Set to music, the image of a pretty landscape
with wild flower, song and star constitutes a
vehicle whereby residents may implicitly affirm that
their bodies are failing, that they stand very close
to personal annihilation or transformation to an
unimagined state. The preparation of this statement
for expression in a public setting is an acknowledgement of all the private statements which are being
made in bedrooms and bathrooms throughout the home.
Talking with Mrs Heslop, resting in her room after
a period of ill-health, the subject of her daughter's family, living in the north of Scotland, arose.
Stressing their remoteness she told me that in the
past she had had to fly up there.

 'I'll fly there again', she added, 'either
 here or here'

Her hand, raised from one level to the next revealed the meaning of her words. Little distinction
remained between plane flights and heavenly flights.
My suggestion that a few day's rest would help restore her strength brought the reply, 'If not in this
life, then in the next. I'll be 93 next month, you
know'.
 Comments such as those made by Arthur Grant and
Mrs Heslop suggest that the Christian concept of the
resurrection to eternal life, alluded to throughout
the verses, constitutes a public acknowledgement of
residents' private pre-occupations with the nature
of their own death. It is upon this pre-occupation
that the overall sense of the verses bears most
directly. The slender hopes and the faint hints and
signs, apparent only to the trusting as they grope
for a path through the murk of the shadows, all
refer to that most critical but elusive of goals,
the discovery of meaning. Pre-occupation with the
approach of death inevitably presages reflection
upon the long life that has gone before.
 Those who care for the residents are aware of,
and skillfully avoid, the rambling repetitivness
which periodically comes to the fore in conversations with the elderly. The young are locked within
the linear flow of a time dimension directed towards
the next days off and the forthcoming summer holiday. They lack the telescopic vision of the elderly, for whom meaning lies not in the foreseeable

achievements of the future but rather in the coll-
apsing, condensing and integration of the decades
which separate past from present experience.

This aspect of ageing, the search for meaning
through repetition and reminiscence, has been discussed by many writers on the subject of ageing.
Barbara Myerhoff (1978), writing of the members of
the Los Angeles Jewish day center, says,

> 'their histories were not devoted to marking
> their successes or unusual merits. Rather they
> were efforts at ordering, sorting, explaining,
> rendering coherent their long life, finding
> integrating ideas and characteristics that
> helped them know themselves as the same person
> over time, despite great ruptures and shifts'.

The search for coherence, the creation of life history which transcends the changes and losses of the
recent past, represents a major if unacknowledged
pre-occupation of the residents of Highfield House.
Faced with the certainty that one's past life is
one's whole life, that admission to care has brought
with it social death in one form or another, the
achievements and the regrets of the past assume
their ultimate dimensions. Nothing further promises
to dwarf, diminish or erase them and it is to these
events and experiences that the memory returns during the vacant hours which remain. As lines 15 and
16 of the song repetitively assert, 'We've got to
remember, We've got to remember,'.

Detailed examples of the ways in which residents seek to discover and express all that is most
valued and most regretted in their past lives are
too numerous to present here. Briefly one can call
attention to those women who became increasingly
pre-occupied with the deaths of their children often
more than twenty or thirty years previously; to the
men whose scrapbooks and medals became an ever more
vital aide-memoire in the telling and re-telling of
their professional, social and domestic autobiogra-
phies. Jewellery and photographs serve a similar
function. A significant illustration is given by
an otherwise unobtrusive postcard pinned up next to
a religious text above a resident's bed. It showed
a Lancashire churchyard with graves prominently
framed in the foreground. After many years of family life in the North East, this particular resident, Elsie Crawford, had travelled back to her
birthplace in Lancashire in her old age to find her
mother's grave. Her purpose satisfied, Elsie said

she felt 'easier'. Moreover she said she'd 'found' some of her old schoolfriends by picking out their names on headstones. Her journey had served to give form and order to a long distant past and her black and white postcard recorded its permanence.

Like Elsie Crawford who pinned an image of her origins firmly above her bed, the fixing of a dissolving past is crucial to many residents in their search for meaning and coherence. When placed on a bedside locker, such small personal objects as postcards, traycloths, candlesticks and clocks assume a new power or sentimental value. The whole of the intimately familiar domestic surroundings of the past is now condensed into these small icons or reminders. The very disparate range of avenues offering access to meaning attests to the individuality of those who search. But in each case we find that the need to repair and to re-assess, and the desire to sustain and to re-create constitute the essence of the process. The persistence and determination exhibited in the mulling over and the displaying of that which was lost and that which was achieved reveal the urgency of the task.

SUMMARY

There are a number of different areas of experience for which the images of the song have very resonant implications for residents. Though our discussion has been brief and far from exhaustive, we begin to see the way in which a somewhat banal and sentimental set of verses takes on meanings which transform them into a heavily loaded symbolic statement. The more carefully we listen to the background noises within the home, the more we become aware that something of more profound significance than just a song at twilight is being rehearsed.

In the simple images of these verses, residents recognised metaphors for the bodily experiences of old age, the world of nature and the afterlife. They appropriated them for a specific purpose, transforming them into a new musical form. The three themes we have discussed are, a) the significance of a journey motif traced through images of physical suffering for those whose passage through physical deterioration is contained within the repetitive routine of the institution; b) the aptness of the Christian ideology of trusting acceptance, validated through images of the natural world, for those who seek to come to terms with present difficulties in a dignified rather than resigned fashion; c) the

powerful immediacy of images of the afterlife and
the stress on discovering meaning for those who
approach death.

   As we have noted, the song takes on these meanings in relation to its social context and to those
who chose and created it. What is distinctive about
both its singers and their context is that an independent social identity within the wider society no
longer exists for them. They have moved away into
a physical, cultural and therefore conceptual space
which is peripheral both spatially and temporally
to the wider society and to their past lives. This
last period of life is singular in its lack of
classificatory markers as compared with the various
rites of transition through which individuals negotiated their passage during earlier years. The
space between entry to and exit from the home is,
in many ways, uncharted personal territory. It is
within this territory that residents have set their
song. It is a symbolic statement which implicitly
condenses the lost independence of the past, the
pressing needs of the present and the imminent event
of the future. In making this statement the singers
orient themselves within the otherwise very disor-
ienting concerns and pre-occupations of their past,
present and future circumstances. Form, order and
meaning are given to the otherwise unstructured
descent into physical decline and death. Thus in
the last verse, those who presently grope through
the murk of the shadows are exhorted to remember
and to hope, to look back and also to look forward.

   The residents used this song as a coping strategy. It gave coherence and clarity to their
perception of themselves and their circumstances.
I suggest that as researchers, we too can use this
and other such material to achieve the same ends.

REFERENCES

Hazan, H. (1980) The Limbo People. A study of the
     constitution of the time universe among the
     aged. Routledge and Kegan Paul, London
Myerhoff, B. (1978) Number Our Days Dutton, New
     York.

Chapter Nine

LONELINESS: A PROBLEM OF MEASUREMENT

Clare Wenger

Loneliness has assumed a prominent place in the
image of old age (Wilkes, 1978).   It is perhaps
significant that younger people are more likely to
think of loneliness as a problem of ageing than old
people themselves (Harris, 1975; Havighurst, 1978).
On self-report, the incidence of loneliness is very
little different between age groups and in fact lack
of friends, which we can assume is a related problem, is perceived more frequently by the middle-aged
(Tornstam, 1981).
    In this chapter, I want to look at the problems
involved in the measurement of loneliness: but before loneliness can be measured, it must be identified, and before it is identified it must be defined.   This chapter therefore looks first at some of
the definitions of loneliness, goes on to discuss
some of the conceptual and operational problems involved in measurement, and describes and evaluates
some of the methods of measurement which have been
employed.   A more recent attempt at measurement
based on an aggregate measure, which attempts to
overcome some of the problems encountered, will then
be discussed and evaluated and the relationship between methodology and findings examined.   Finally
some implications for social gerontology will be
suggested.
    An exploration of the literature on loneliness
reveals two related aspects.   Firstly, it is evident
that while the concept is much referred to, research
on the topic itself is scant.   (Fromm-Reichmann,
1959; Weiss, 1973).   Secondly, many who have written
about loneliness comment on the fear of loneliness
and suggest that avoidance and reluctance, on the
part of both sufferers and researchers, to discuss
the topic is partly responsible for our lack of
understanding.   'Loneliness is a subject surrounded

by prohibitions and embarrassments', says Seabrook
(1973), and Fromm-Reichmann suggests that 'all adults are afraid of loneliness' (1959). Weiss (1973)
goes so far as to suggest that very little research
has been done on loneliness because it is difficult
to recall and sufferers are not only reluctant to
discuss it but engage in denial. All of this he
feels had led ('even among professionals') to a lack
of understanding of persons experiencing loneliness.
This fear of loneliness has been linked by the more
philosophical commentators (e.g. Berblinger, 1968;
Moustakas, 1961), to the fear of death.

Perhaps the widespread assumption that the
elderly are more prone to loneliness than other
groups has something to do with our awareness of
this fear. Old people are, after all, closer to
death. Moustakas (1961) writes, 'Our elder citizens
so often have feelings of uselessness, so often experience life as utterly futile. Old-age is fertile
soil for loneliness and the fear of a lonely old age
far outweighs the fear of death in the thinking of
many people'.

Studies of loneliness among cross-sections of
the population (Tornstam, 1981) and among groups
indentified or assumed to be particularly vulnerable
to loneliness - such as those living alone; the unmarried; college students; young mothers; the widowed; the divorced and separated; those who have just
moved; prisoners and their families - suggest that
loneliness among the elerly is not especially prevalent (Weiss, 1973). Lake (1980) found that the
loneliest sub-set are in fact single parents. A
minority are lonely in all sub-sets and the proportion who are very lonely demonstrates a certain consistency. The same can be said for the elderly over
time and in different countries (Shanas et al.
1965; Hunt, 1978; Goldberg, 1970; Sheldon, 1948;
Townsend, 1965; Karn, 1977; Wenger, 1981).

Since we have a shared concern with social gerontology, however, our concern is with the manifes-
tation of loneliness amongst the elderly. It is a
problem with which the helping professions have yet
to get to grips (Wenger, 1979) and one which is perceived as a contributory presenting problem amongst
elderly people seeking help from social services
(G. Grant, 1981; Hazan, 1980). Loneliness is also
closely linked with depression (Brown et al. 1978),
the most common mental illness of old age and one
which can lead to self-neglect, sickness and the
need for help from the various statutory services.
Loneliness has been shown to be a predictor of need

for residential care (Wager, 1972), medical care
(Grad, 1971; Isaacs et al, 1972) and domiciliary
services (Townsend, 1965; Tunstall, 1966; Shanas et
al, 1968). For these reasons, and because the fear
of loneliness lurks within us all, a need exists for
a better understanding of loneliness. Without such
understanding, it is more difficult to prevent or
ameliorate the pain with which it is associated.
First, however, it is necessary to try to arrive at
a more precise definition of the concept.

DEFINITION

Even in a book called <u>Loneliness</u>, Seabrook (1973)
admits, 'Loneliness is a vague term' and presents no
definition. Fromm-Reichmann (1959) suggests that
real loneliness defies description. At a basic
level, Moustakas (1961) has described it as 'longing
to be with others and to be loved', while Weiss
(1973) suggests that loneliness is 'caused not by
being alone but by being without some definite needed relationship or relationships', which refines
Moustakas' definition by introducing the idea of a
specified <u>type</u> of relationship. While both
Moustakas' and Weiss' definitions do not deny potential amelioration, Hazan (1980) has defined loneliness as 'an acute feeling of deprivation accompanied by the realization that the balance between
the desired and the controllable will never be re-
dressed'. This suggests that it is somehow incur-
able, but most researchers imply that loneliness is
not irreversible.
      Psychology appears to be primarily concerned
with existential loneliness. Berblinger (1968) defines loneliness as 'an unhappy compound of having
lost one's points of reference, of suffering the
fate of individual and collective discontinuity, and
of living through or dying from a crisis of identity
to the point of alienation from oneself'. This definition seems rather opaque and he himself admitted
that 'the very meaning of this state, its symptoms,
signs and treatment are not too well understood'.
Presumably, there are those who have not lost points
of reference but who have never gained them. Another psychiatrist, Witzleben (1968), while stating
that there is no clear definition of loneliness,
identifies two types: (1) loneliness caused by loss
of an object, which he calls <u>secondary</u> loneliness,
and (2) a loneliness 'inborn in everyone' character-
ized by the feeling of being alone and helpless in
the world, which he calls <u>primary</u> loneliness.

Loneliness: A Problem of Measurement

Primary loneliness has been referred to by others as
a universal human experience or as existential loneliness. Witzleben seems to consider primary loneliness as 'real' loneliness but secondary loneliness
as more common. Loneliness has been identified by
some as uniformly painful (Berblinger, 1968;
Sullivan, 1953), while others find redeeming features in it as necessary for creativity (Fromm-
Reichmann, 1959, Moustakas, 1972). The latter view
however may be the rationalisation of the lonely
intellectual !
    Writing in 1959, Fromm-Reichmann considered
that different types of loneliness had not been delineated, and Weiss in 1973 claimed, 'We still lack
a secure taxonomy of types of loneliness'. However,
Witzleben's dichotomy has not been the only such
attempt to grapple with the problems of definition.
While isolation has been found to have no clear correlation with loneliness (Tunstall, 1966; Sheldon,
1948; Townsend and Turnstall 1973; Abrams, 1978),
Weiss (1973) distinguishes between emotional and
social isolation as forms of loneliness. The first
he suggests seeks amelioration in a close one-to-one
relationship and the second in a supportive network.
    Several writers have suggested that loneliness
can be either situational/circumstantial or temper-
amental/characterological (Weiss, 1973; M. Grant,
1979). Situational loneliness may occur because a
person is separated from his or her family or from
the other partner in a particularly close relationship. It is common after bereavement, especially
the loss of a spouse. It may also result from the
absence of someone in whom to confide. Temperamental loneliness, on the other hand, has been linked to
feelings of rejection or loss as a child (Bowlby,
1973) and is thus related to depression (Brown et al
1978).
    Certainly, Seabrook's (1973) case studies of
lonely people, one-third of whom were over sixty,
support the contention of the relationship with an
unhappy childhood, although Weiss (1973) has specu-
lated whether early loss necessarily makes one more
susceptible to loneliness as an adult. Situational
loneliness may, it would seem, be more amenable to
amelioration than temperamental loneliness.
    On the whole, sociologists have adopted simpler
definitions of loneliness. Lopata (1969) has defined it as 'a sentiment felt by a person when he defines his experienced level or form of interaction
as inadequate' and suggests that 'Loneliness is
dependent on a social self wishing to be involved in

meaningful interaction with significant others'.
This definition was paraphrased by a respondent in
my own research who said of her loneliness, 'It's
mainly a longing for my own kind'. Townsend and
Turnstall(1973) state 'to be lonely is to have an
unwelcome feeling of lack or loss or companionship'
and B. Power (1980) uses almost the same words defining it as 'an unwelcome or painful feeling caused
by lack of companionship'. Neither of these definitions however seems to go far enough, omitting as
they do the explicit notion of intimacy.
    Many who have written about loneliness in old
age do not define the term at all (Abrams, 1978;
Blau, 1973; Sheldon, 1948; Karn, 1977). Its meaning
is taken for granted as part of the commonsense
knowledge of a member of society. In this they appear to agree with Tunstall (1965) who states that,
'In practice the definition has to be accepted that
an old person is lonely only if he says he feels
lonely, and not otherwise'. While admitting to some
problems with this approach, he suggests that the
concept of loneliness has the advantage of being
familiar to the informant, who can thus be asked
further questions about it'. This leaves in question, of course, which concept is being discussed.

PROBLEMS OF MEASUREMENT

As we have seen, loneliness is ill-defined even by
those who have taken a professional interest. But
there are other problems which complicate this elu-
siveness further. As Hadley et al. (1975) point
out, 'the term may have different meanings for different individuals; some people may experience loneliness but be unwilling to acknowledge it'. Fromm-
Reichmann (1959) made a similar point more forcefully, 'Those who are in the grips of severe loneliness cannot talk about it and those who have been
seldom do not either'. It has even been suggested
that loneliness is 'an experience which has been so
terrible that it practically baffles recall'
(Sullivan, 1953). There are however other reasons
for a reluctance to talk about being lonely.
    'There is an assumption that anyone admitting
to loneliness has something wrong with them' notes
Lopata (1969). Lake (1980) has also commented on
the stigmatizing effect of loneliness, while
Seabrook (1973) observes that it makes people feel
'unloved, unworthy and ashamed'. 'Moustakas (1961)
attributes this phenomenon to the fear of loneliness, which everyone is subject to, so that the

lonely are either avoided or provided with company.
Those who experience loneliness, however, are not
unaware of the stigma and this together with the
reluctance to re-experience pain·cause one to question the adequacy of self-reports as a measure of
loneliness.

Another aspect of self-reported loneliness,
which may lead to distortion, has been alluded to by
both Tunstall (1966) and Townsend (1965). What do
we do about the old woman who tells her daughter she
is lonely but tells the researcher she is not lon-
ly ? Since loneliness is an emotive subject, it is
a choice area for manipulation and emotional black-
mail. As Seabrook (1973) suggests, 'There are no
criteria to assess the prevalence or intensity of
the loneliness people admit to. It is often used as
a synonym for lack of fulfillment, unhappiness or
failure in many areas of experience'. Another researcher (Clifford, personal communication) has
found that among the elderly it is difficult to distinguish between loneliness and boredom. In other
words, even if people admit to loneliness they may
be talking about something else'.

MEASUREMENT

There is of course an interaction between academic
discipline, definition and methodology. Loosely
stated, this can be glossed as the positivist/inter-
pretive dichotomy, which like most dichotomies is in
reality a continuum. Theories and methodologies are
affected by the subjects, sample sizes and milieux
of study as appropriate to various disciplines.
They are also affected by the aims and demands of
funding bodies inasmuch as researchers often conduct
that research which they can get funded rather than
that which they may feel is scientifically most
valid. In order to be convinced about the repre-
sentativeness of results, large sample studies have
been favoured by many funding agencies. This means
that positivist methodologies need to be employed
even where researchers might feel that time-consum-
ing in-depth study might be more fruitful. The
difficulties of studying attitudes and other states
of mind using large sample techniques are known to
most of us and need not be enumerated here. Some of
the problems vis-a-vis loneliness have already been
discussed. Psychological theories of loneliness are generalisations based on clinical practice and theory
reinforced by observation. Scales which have been

devised have treated loneliness as one component of
broader scales designed to evaluate morale, life-
satisfaction or depression (Challis, 1979).
     Most studies of the elderly at home have relied
upon a self-assessment scale (Townsend, 1965; Power,
1980; Sheldon, 1948; Karn, 1977; Shanas et al. 1968;
Tunstall, 1966). The usual question asks: 'Do you
ever feel rather lonely ?' and is coded: 'Never,
rarely, sometimes, often, always'. Assessments consistently indicate that two-thirds of the elderly
claim never to suffer loneliness. This means that
for one-third loneliness is an occasional or frequent problem. How serious being lonely 'sometimes'
is, is difficult to estimate. Perhaps we are all
lonely at least sometimes if we are honest with ourselves. On the other hand, might respondents claim
to be lonely sometimes because they cannot bring
themselves to face the fact or to admit that they
are lonely all the time ?
     Some researchers have had misgivings about the
reliability or validity of self-assessment measures.
Hadley et al (1975) studied elderly people already
identified to them as lonely. While using a self-
assessment scale they felt that 'if a connection can
be established between the subjective feelings of
loneliness and the old person's pattern of social
relationships, the meaning of loneliness may be
better understood. In other words, self-assessment
was not enough. They point out however, that the
mere enumeration of contacts tells us nothing about
the length of visits or intensity and satisfaction
of the relationship and hence their potential to
alleviate loneliness. Abrams (1978) devised a range
of measures picked out from various life-satisfact-
ion scales included in his questionnaire, which
'carry a meaning of either loneliness or non-loneli-
ness'. These measures are listed below:

1.   Compared with other people, I get down in
     the dumps too often. (Agree)
2.   I feel just miserable most of the time.
     (Agree)
3.   I never dreamed that I could be as lonely
     as I am now. (Agree)
4.   I have no-one to talk to about personal
     things. (Agree)
5.   I no longer do anything that is of real use
     to other people. (Agree)
6.   During the past few weeks did you ever feel
     very lonely or remote from other people ?
     (Yes)

7.   During the past few weeks did you ever
feel depressed or very unhappy ? (Yes)

Responses were analysed separately with each item
being evaluated as a measure of loneliness although
only two items refer to loneliness directly. This
approach has the advantage that it may reduce the
risk of denials or stigmatising effects amongst respondents. Since no definition of loneliness was
given in this study we must infer from the items
what is being measured. At the same time, while
these items are referred to as 'measures of loneliness' they are not used in an aggregate way to refer
to loneliness and may better be interpreted as in-
dicators or possible correlates of loneliness. However, most of them appear to measure morale rather
than loneliness.
     In summary, non-clinical attempts to measure
loneliness have for the most part relied on a personal self-assessment of experience. As discussed,
many factors affect the reliability of such measures, including reluctance to recall loneliness,
stigma and denial. At the same time, attempts to
overcome some of these problems have so far been
unconvincing, either because they have linked self-
assessed loneliness with frequencies of contact
which tell us little about intimacy (Hadley et al.
1975) or because they appear to be only peripherally
or intuitively concerned with loneliness (M. Abrams
1978). These measures also tell us little about the
intensity, pervasiveness or prevalence of the feeling.
     In an attempt to arrive at some measure of the
pervasiveness and intensity of loneliness, without
triggering avoidance or denial by respondents as a
result of the question, I introduced a similar form
of measurement in a study of about 600 elderly people at home in North Wales. In this case, loneliness was defined (implicitly it must be admitted) as
a feeling of inadequacy of social contacts. Com-
parablywith Abrams, these 'loneliness responses'
were dispersed throughout a more general questionnaire, but in contrast they were also used to form a
crude aggregate or cumulative measure. Responses
considered to indicate loneliness were as follows:

1.   Do you feel lonely much ? (Yes)
2.   Do you see enough of your friends and
     relatives ? (No)
3.   Do you meet as many people as you would
     like to ? (No)

4.   Is there anyone in particular you can
     confide in or talk to about yourself and
     your problems ? (No)
5.   Do you wish you had more friends ? (Yes)
6.   Are there people around from whom you can
     ask small favours ? (No)
7.   Are there people in this area who you can
     call real friends ? (No)
8.   Could you tell me how you spent last
     Christmas ?
     (Alone and lonely - interviewer assessment)

On the basis of these responses, respondents were
classified as not lonely if they scored zero, moderately lonely if they scored one or two, and very
lonely if they scored three or more. The highest
score was six and the mode zero. While this scale
attemps to improve on previous measures it still
needs refinement. All items have at this stage been
weighted equally and the boundaries between low,
moderate and high loneliness were determined arbitrarily. More work needs to be done to refine an
aggregate measure. In the interests of replication,
respondents were also asked the standard self-perception of loneliness question and subsequently
these responses were compared.

FINDINGS

Other research has demonstrated that loneliness has
a high correlation with living alone, widowhood
(and, as a result, with being female), singleness,
early loss and poor health or infirmity (Havighurst,
1978; Hunt, 1978; Lopata, 1969; B. Power, 1979;
Seabrook, 1973; Townsend and Turnstall, 1973 and
Weiss, 1973). While several writers have shown that
loneliness increases with age, Tornstam (1981) has
demonstrated that when the above factors are controlled, age is not significant. The incidence of
loneliness does increase with age but it is not ageing that causes loneliness; rather that the old are
more likely to be beset by situations which may
cause loneliness at any age, for example: bereavement; living alone; lack of friends or ill health.
     In my study, more than three-quarters reported
that they were never or rarely lonely, a fifth admitted to being lonely sometimes and only 5 per cent
said they were lonely often or most of the time.
These findings are comparable with Shanas et al
(1968) for Britain as a whole and with Karn's (1977)
findings for retirement migrants. The fact that

Table 1. Loneliness (%)

	N=	Self-perceived Loneliness			Loneliness Measure		
		Never or rarely	Some-times	Often/most of time	Low	Medium	High
Total	(683)	76	19	5	63	29	9
Shanas[1]		72	21	7	*	*	*
Age:							
65-69	(176)	78	19	3	69	24	7
70-74	(221)	80	16	5	61	32	8
75-79	(148)	71	20	10	66	27	8
80-84	(79)	75	22	4	65	25	10
85-89	(34)	59	29	12	47	37	17
90+	(25)	84	16	0	39	50	12
Age at Arrival:							
Under 40	(306)	78	17	5	70	27	4
40-60	(133)	79	12	9	62	28	11
Retirement movers	(45)	58	35	6	59	26	15
Retirement migrants	(170)	77	19	4	54	33	13

Household Composition:							
Lives alone	(226)	58	33	9	53	37	10
With Spouse only	(266)	87	8	5	65	25	10
With younger relative(s)	(130)	78	20	2	70	23	7
With elderly relative(s)	(56)	91	9	0	74	26	0
Marital Status:							
Single	(106)	85	10	5	59	36	6
Married	(326)	87	9	5	68	23	9
Widowed	(246)	58	35	7	57	33	9
Health:							
Good/excellent	(297)	88	10	1	73	24	4
Alright for age	(243)	73	21	5	61	31	9
Fair/poor	(137)	55	32	13	45	36	18

1. E. Shanas et al. Old People in Three Industrial Societies, London, Routledge and Kegan Paul, 1968, p.271, Table II.

these figures also correspond very nearly with
Sheldon's study of old people in Wolverhampton in
1945 demonstrates that the incidence of loneliness
amongst the elderly has remained stable and not
deteriorated as is often suggested. However, the
aggregate loneliness measure does appear to have
revealed feelings of loneliness which were not admitted in answer to the self-perception question.
Only 63 per cent were not lonely, while 29 per cent
were moderately lonely and 9 per cent very lonely.
Because divisions between the categories were defined arbitrarily these differences should be treated
cautiously. However, when the findings for different sub-sets of the elderly population are compared
some interesting differences show up.

There are indications that where loneliness
might be seen as acceptable - among those who live
alone and the widowed - it will be admitted; but
where a need exists to rationalise or conceal loneliness - migrants, the single, the married and those
living with others - it will not be admitted or perhaps not recognised. As Table 1 shows, it was, for
instance, surprising to find that loneliness among
retirement migrants based on self-assessment was
comparable with that of those who had lived in the
region all their lives. The aggregate measure,
however, shows that both for those who moved in
middle-age and for retirement migrants loneliness is
higher than admitted, while figures from both measures are comparable for long-term residents. And
while the aggregate and self-perceived figures for
those who live alone are comparable, the levels of
loneliness among those living with a spouse only and
those living with elderly relatives are higher using
the aggregate measure. By the same token, while the
aggregate and self-perceived levels for widows are
equivalent the single and married show higher levels
of loneliness using the aggregate measure.

Using the aggregate measure, men overall appear
to experience less than women (Table 2). Loneliness
increases with age but more women than men are lonely in all age groups. After eighty-five more than
half are lonely to some extent. However, more single men are lonely than single women and more widowed men are lonely than widowed women. What is surprising is that loneliness among married women exhibits a higher level than among other groups. More
married women are very lonely than are widowed women
(or single women) and more than twice as many are
lonely as are married men. Visits from other relatives are less frequent to married couples than to

Table 2. Loneliness by Sex and Marital Status. (%)

	MALES				FEMALES		
	N=	Low	Moderate	High	N=	Low	Moderate	High
Single	(35)	49	46	6	(69)	64	30	6
Married	(185)	79	19	2	(128)	52	30	18
Widowed	(57)	49	37	14	(180)	60	32	8
All[1]	(278)	69	26	5	(382)	58	31	11

[1] Includes a small number of divorced/separated.

those living alone and couples who spent Christmas
without other company also experienced loneliness.
There is some indication here that relatives under-
estimate the social needs of elderly couples.   In
rank order, the group most prone to loneliness are
widowed men, closely followed by single men, then
married women, widowed women, single women and
married men.   However, married women are the group
most likely to be very lonely.

Compared with the total sample the very lonely
are less likely to have been born in the country in
which they now live, and more likely to have come to
the country within the last ten years.   As a result,
they are twice as likely to have moved after the age
of sixty.   They are almost twice as likely to be
women and more than twice as likely to be living in
a child's household.   They are less likely to have
been living alone for more than twenty years and
less likely to be childless.   They are more than
five times as likely to have low morale and twice as
likely to have small support networks.

Those who are very lonely are, as we have seen,
a small minority of the elderly so it is difficult
to look at the separate components of the loneliness
measure.   However, it is possible to make some tentative observations.   Among those who are married,
loneliness is expressed in terms of a lack of friendship.   Lonely married men are not likely to admit
to loneliness but tend to want more friends, and to
feel that they have no real friends nearby, do not
meet enough people and do not see enough of their
friends and relatives.   Since all very lonely married men saw a relative at least weekly it is presumably friends to whom the latter refers.   The most
frequently mentioned loneliness factors in nine out
of ten very lonely married women are that they do
not meet enough people and wish they had more friends.   Two-thirds of these very lonely women feel
that they do not see enough of friends and relatives
and admit to feeling lonely much of the time.   In
contrast to lonely married men, more than half of
the lonely married women see a relative less often
than once a week.   Retirement migrants are overrepresented among the very lonely marrieds.

Widowed and single people are frequently identified as prone to loneliness.   Widowed men are
seven times more likely to be very lonely than
married men but less than half as many widowed wom-
en as married women are very lonely.   One explanation for the higher incidence of loneliness amongst
married women may be that widowed women are more

likely to form mutually supportive friendships when
they are alone (Jerrome, 1981) and may thus receive
more expressive support than married women (Lipman,
1981). Amongst widowed men and women loneliness is
most common amongst the recently widowed. The most
common component of loneliness among widowed men is
that they do not see enough of friends and relatives. Three-quarters of them consider that they do
not meet enough people and admit to feeling lonely
much of the time, even though three-fifths see a
relative weekly compared with approximately a quarter of other widowed men. Here again women are more
inclined to admit to loneliness. Friendship appears
to be more important to widowed women who are more
likely to say they do not meet enough people and
that they wish for more friends than that they do
not see enough of friends and relatives.

Widows may experience intense loneliness on
bereavement but appear to overcome this in time.
Women seem to cope better with widowhood perhaps because female longevity has prepared them to face
this loneliness. More widowed men than women are
very lonely, but while women seem more likely to
seek alleviation in friendship men more frequently
turn to the family.

Among the single, equal proportions of men and
women are very lonely. However, we are here speaking of very small numbers so there is a need for
caution. Loneliness amongst the single is more likely to be associated with social isolation. Again
men are less likely to admit to loneliness than are
women. For both single men and women the most
common cause for concern is that they do not meet
enough people. The very lonely single are more likely to spend a lonely Christmas than other groups.
Three-quarters of very lonely single women see a
relative less than weekly.

Looking at the very lonely as a whole, it becomes apparent that friendship is more important
than family in terms of loneliness (as has been documented elsewhere: Blau, 1973; Arling, 1980; Hadley
et al 1975). This may explain the lack of correlation with social isolation (Challis, 1979) which is
usually measured predominantly in terms of family
contacts. Four out of five very lonely people say
they do not meet enough people and seven out of ten
wish for more friends. Two out of three admit they
feel lonely much of the time and do not see enough
of friends or relatives; one in two has no real friends in the area. It could be claimed that this is
due to the choice of loneliness measures, three of

which specifically refer to friends. However, less
than one in five is without a confidant and even
fewer have no-one of whom to ask favours and it was
found to be relatives who usually fill these roles.
Among the elderly living in a child's household more
than twice as many (22 per cent) are very lonely
than in any other form of household. (See also Hunt
1978).

DISCUSSION

It is inevitable that the results of any study of
loneliness will refer to the way in which loneliness
is defined and measured by the researcher; in this
case by subjective attitudes to the social environment and available contacts. Both definition and
methodology can be affected by the funding context
in which research is conducted. In this instance,
being funded by the DHSS, I was concerned to measure
loneliness in terms which were relevant to potential
amelioration. I was less taken up with existential
loneliness than with feelings of unsatisfactory
social linkages. In this context, the findings seem
to have important implications both for increased
reliance on family care for the elderly and for the
enhancement of neighbourly and community involvement
by social and health services (National Institute
for Social Work, 1982).
     At the same time, for the reasons already dis-
cussed, I was disconcerted by the acceptance of the
single question self-assessment of loneliness as a
reliable measure of such unhappiness. It is usually
assumed that it is more difficult to acquire funding
for small sample intensive studies and as a result
the large sample survey method has been most widely
used in policy related research. The composite
measure used here is a compromise between a conventional survey and a more detailed longitudinal exploration of the problem. It attempts to overcome
the effects of denial and at the same time unravel
some of the underlying complexities.
     There are, however, dangers involved both in
studying loneliness as an isolated phenomenon and in
regarding the elderly as a separate group. While
loneliness may be experienced at any stage of the
life cycle, it can only be adequately understood
within the context of a person's life history. The
same may be said of adaptation to ageing.
     What all the aforementioned surveys demonstrate
is that the majority of people are not lonely. Even
within groups predisposed to loneliness such as the

recently widowed, those who say they are lonely and
those whom my scale identifies as lonely are a minority. Studies of the survey type cannot begin to
grapple with the essential understanding of what
predisposes an individual to loneliness. In my own
study, in-depth interviews were subsequently conducted with those who were indentified as very lonely. Unfortunately, shortage of time and manpower
meant that these were limited. Control interviews
with similarly situated people were also attempted.
     From these interviews it was possible to iden-
tify recurrent situations. The very old, particularly those living in an adult child's household,
often said they were lonely primarily because they
saw less of their contemporaries. In many cases,
they had outlived all their friends. One old man,
when asked if there was any special time when he
felt lonely said, 'Yes, whenever I hear that another
of my old friends has died. I feel more alone.
There's no-one left that remembers the old days'.
Women who have raised large families are also prone
to loneliness in old age. Often they say that their
earlier lives were too full and too busy to make
many friends, 'The family was all I needed then;
when they all left it was too late'. The same may
be true for those who have worked all their lives in
demanding occupations, particularly where hierarch-
ical structures reinforced social distance in the
workplace.
     Women nursing housebound husbands and widows
who did so for long periods before widowhood are also prone to loneliness. In the last case, self-
imposed isolation during a terminal illness of a
spouse is more likely to lead to loneliness if the
onset follows soon after retirement migration.
Childless couples whose marital relationship has
been particularly close and exclusive, especially
where a move has been made on retirement, are also
more likely to be lonely. Research in the United
States (Lipman and Longino, 1981) has shown that in
most marriages elderly men receive expressive support from wives but many elderly women turn mainly to
daughters or friends for such support. Lehr (1981)
has shown that relations with spouses affect relationships with children in a dynamic way. All of
these factors have implications for the understanding of loneliness.
     If we want to understand and seek to ameliorate
the loneliness of old age, my contention is that we
must look at old people's lives as a culmination,
and take a life course perspective. How elderly

people cope with the demands of ageing depends on
what has gone before and what resources they have.
Brown and Harris (1978) have shown that depression
is more likely among women (young and old) who have
had previous bouts of depression. The same is probably true of loneliness: in fact there is a high
correlation between the two conditions, loneliness
being a frequent component of depression. Elder and
Rockwell (1979) suggest that the stressfulness of
change depends on three factors: (1) how drastic the
change is; (2) the individual's personal history,
expectations and adaptive skills and (3) the stage
in the life course at which the change (or loss)
occurs. They consistently rank the death of a
spouse as the highest magnitude of life change: it
is, of course, that loss which is most likely to be
experienced by the elderly. How the latter adapt
can be predicted, they suggest, only in the context
of their individual life histories. Life history
affects the resources of the individual-material,
social and emotional (Cibulski, 1981).

     This biographical perspective has been adopted
by the Bonn Longitudinal Studies in Ageing. Amongst
their findings a common theme is the need to adopt a
differentiated view of patterns of adaptation in old
age (Fooken, 1981). They find that outlook on life
and inter-generational relationships are affected by
a combination of life history, present situation and
future time perspective (Lehr, 1981). Other studies
suggest that patterns of adaptation are formed early
in the life cycle and tend to be consistently dependent or consistantly independent (Goldfarb, 1965;
Harel, 1979).

     A life course approach to loneliness would not
of course be exempt from problems. Any such study
of loneliness in the elderly could presumably integrate both retrospective and longitudinal aspects.
It might then be possible to relate loneliness, its
onset and recurrence, to critical incidents in a
person's life. But although loneliness may be related to major biographical events, it may also
occur at times when or even because nothing remark-
able is taking place. A longitudinal approach to
loneliness must therefore seek to identify tempera-
ment or conditioning which predisposes to loneliness
as well as the types of life events or adaptations
most likely to result in loneliness.

     A consistent outcome of all the reported long-
itudinal studies is that an independent extra-
amilial orientation of life leads to a healthier
adjustment to old age. Approaches of this type,

which take a life perspective, appear to have more
potential explanatory power in determining why some
people are more prone to loneliness (depression, low
morale, etc.) than others. As the earlier discussion has shown, loneliness may persist even when frequent regular contact with family exists. In many
cases familial relationships may provide instrumental help, but intimacy may for numerous reasons be
absent. It is significant that more than half of
the elderly persons in my study sought support from
a friend or neighbour when they felt 'down and needed someone to talk to'. It seems likely that this
reflects the importance of age homogeneity in close
relationships (Rosow, 1967) and the importance of
empathy as well as intimacy. In general the findings of researchers concerned with loneliness and
morale have indicated that while family may provide
instrumental support, friends assume a far greater
importance where emotional and expressive backing is
needed. Of these two aspects of caring, it is
perhaps instrumental support which can be more easily substituted. This raises important questions
about the locus of social support for the elderly.
   Neither the fact that loneliness is difficult
to define, measure and understand nor the fact that
it is not restricted to the elderly, should suggest
that it is a problem which social gerontologists can
afford to ignore. Given the greater propensity for
the aged to suffer losses and to experience the
resulting stress, we may be surprised that it is not
a more common problem. As it is, we found that both
loneliness and low morale are twice as common amongst elderly clients of social services as among the
elderly as a whole. In our desire to improve the
experience of ageing we must consider the management
of this painful experience as we do any other. Much
policy emphasis is placed on the role of the family.
If old people are lonely, it is usually the family
network which is seen to be at fault or lacking.
Those who experience loneliness, however, seem more
likely to complain of lack of friendship - and indeed friendship has been demonstrated to be more
important than familial support for morale and self-
esteem (Blau, 1973). Perhaps, therefore, caring
professionals working with the dependent elderly may
need to pay additional attention to the larger social networks of their clients, for whom friends may
prove to be the most important emotional resources.
Perhaps, too, more emphasis needs to be placed on
education for ageing - our own and that of others -
so that those who are not yet elderly may look ahead

now and plan their lives accordingly, and may in the
process come to see today's elderly as having needs
which are recognisably similar to their own.

REFERENCES

Abrams, M. (1979) Beyond three-score and ten: a
    first report on a survey of the elderly.
    London: Age Concern
Arling, G. (1980) "The elderly widow and her family,
    neighbours and friends" in Fuller and Martin,
    The Older Woman, Springfield, Ill., Charles C.
    Thomas
Berblinger, K.W. (1968) "A psychiatrist looks at
    loneliness". Psychosomatics, Vol.9., No.2. 96-
    102.
Blau, Z.S. (1973) Old Age in Changing Society New
    York: Franklin Watts Inc.
Bowlby, J. (1973) "Affectional bonds: their nature
    and origin" in Loneliness: the experience of
    emotional and social isolation. Robert S.
    Weiss (ed) Boston, Mit. pp.38-52.
Brown, G.W. and Harris, T. (1978) Social Origins of
    Depression: a study of psychiatric disorder in
    women. London: Tavistock
Challis, D.J. (1979) "The measurement of outcome in
    social care of the elderly". Kent Community
    Care Project Paper 31/2. Personal Social Servi-
    ces Research Unit, University of Kent.
Cibulski, O. (1981) "Instrumental support networks
    of the elderly". Paper presented to the XIIth
    International Congress of Gerontology, Hamburg
    11th-17th July.
Clifford, D. (1982) Personal communications. Killar-
    ney: Bishop's House.
Elder, G.H. & Rockwell, R.C. (1979) "The life course
    and human development: an ecological perspect-
    ive" International Journal of Behavioural
    Development, 2, pp.1-21.
Fooken, I. (1981) "Women in Old Age: the need for a
    differentiated view". Paper presented Xllth
    International Congress of Gerontology in Ham-
    burg, 11th-17th July.
Fromm-Reichmann, F. (1959) "On Loneliness" in D.M.
    Bullard (ed) Psychoanalysis and Psychotherapy.
    Chicago: University of Chicago Press. pp.325-
    336.
Goldberg,E.M. (1980) Helping the Aged Allen and
    Unwin
Goldfarb, A.I. (1965) " Psychodynamics and the three
    generational family" in Shanas & Streib (eds)

Social Structure and the Family: generational relations. New Jersey, Prentice-Hall

Grad de Alarcon, J. (1971) "Social causes and consequences of mental illness in old age". In Kay, D.W.K. & Walk, A. (eds). Recent developments in psychogeriatrics Ashford: Headley Bros.

Grant, G. (1981) Monitoring social services delivery in rural areas: intake cases in two contrasting area teams. Working Paper No.14, Social Services in Rural Areas Research Project, Dept. Social Theory & Institutions, University College of North Wales, Bangor

Grant, M. (1979) "How to make friends: and article for lonely people". Woman's Own.

Hadley, R. & Webb, A. (1974) Loneliness, Social Isolation and Old People: some implications for social policy. London, Age Concern

Hadley, R. & Webb, A. (1975) Across the Generations. London: George Allen & Unwin

Harel, Z. (1979) "Discriminators between survivors and non-survivors among working class aged living in the community". The Gerontologist. Vol.19, No.1. pp83-89

Harris, L. (1975) The myth and reality of ageing in America. The National Council on Ageing, Inc. Washington, D.C.

Havighurst, R. (1978) "Ageing in western society" in David Hobman (ed) The Social Challenge of Ageing, London: Croom Helm.

Hazan, H. (1980) The Limbo People: a study of the constitution of the time universe among the aged. London: Routledge & Kegan Paul

Hunt, A. (1978) The elderly at home: a study of people aged sixty five and over living in the community in England in 1976. Social Survey Division, OPCS.

Isaacs, B., Livingstone, M. & Neville, Y. (1972) Survival of the Unfittest: a study of geriatric patients in Glasgow, London: Routledge & Kegan Paul.

Jerrome, D. (1981) "The significance of friendship for women in later life". Ageing and Society, Vol.1, part 2, pp.175-197

Karn, V. (1977) Retiring to the seaside. London: Routledge & Kegan Paul

Lake, T. (1980) Loneliness: Why it happens and how to overcome it. London: Sheldon Press.

Lehr, U.M. (1981) "Consistency and change in family role activity and satisfaction in old age" Paper presented to the International Congress of Gerontology, Hamburg, 11th-17th July

Lipman, A. & Longino, C.F. (1981) "Family support
    networks in two life care communities". Paper
    presented to XIIth International Congress of
    Gerontology, Hamburg, July
Lopata, H.Z. (1969) "Loneliness: forms and compon-
    ents". Social Problems. XVII, pp.248-262.
Moustakas, C.E. (1961) Loneliness. Englewood Cliffs,
    New Jersey: Prentice-Hall Inc.
Moustakas, C.E. (1972) Loneliness and Love. Engle-
    wood Cliffs. New Jersey: Prentice-Hall
National Institute for Social Work (1982) The
    Barclay Report. London: Bedford Square Press
Power, B. (1979) Old and Alone in Ireland Dublin:
    St. Vincent de Paul
Rosow, I. (1967) Social Integration of the Aged. New
    York: Free Press.
Seabrook, J. (1973) Loneliness. London: Maurice
    Temple Smith
Shanas, E. et al. (1968) "Loneliness, isolation and
    desolation in old age" in E. Shanas et al, Old
    People in Three Industrial Societies. London
    Routledge & Kegan Paul, pp271-276
Sheldon, J. H. (1948) The Social Medicine of Old
    Age: report of an inquiry in Wolverhampton.
    London: O.U.P.
Sullivan, H.S. (1953) The Interpersonal Theory of
    Psychiatry. New York: W.W. Norton.
Tornstam, L. (1981) "Daily problems in various ages".
    Paper presented to XIIth International Congress
    of Gerontology, Hamburg, 11th-17th July.
Townsend, P. (1965) The Family Life and Old People.
    London: Penguin Books.
Townsend, P. & Turnstall S. (1973) "Sociological
    explanations of the lonely" in P. Townsend, The
    Social Minority, pp. 257-263
Tunstall, J. (1968) Old and Alone. London:
    Routledge and Kegan Paul
Wager, R. (1972) Care of the Elderly. London I.M.T.A
Weiss, R.S. (1973) Loneliness: The Experience of
    Emotional and Social Isolation Boston: M.I.T.
Wenger, G.C. (1979) Report on European Symposium on
    the Elderly and the Care System at Jadwisin,
    Poland, 21st-25th May
Wenger, G.C. (1981) "The elderly in the community:
    family contacts, social integration and commun-
    ity involvement". Working Paper No.18 Social
    Services in Rural Areas Research Project,
    University College of North Wales, Bangor.
Wilkes, R. (1978) "General Philosophy and Attitudes
    to Ageing". Paper delivered at BASW Conference
    on Ageing. Social Work Today 9 (45) 25th July.

Loneliness: A Problem of Measurement

Witzleben, H.D. (1968) "On Loneliness". <u>Psychiatry</u>
     21, pp.31-43

Chapter Ten

THE POTENTIAL FOR LEARNING IN LATER LIFE

Paula Allman

The potential for learning at any age derives from
an individual's thinking or cognitive competence.
Therefore, a discussion of the potential for learning in later life must in the first instance derive
from an examination of what happens to cognitive
abilities as the individual ages. In a recent
British study Huppert reported that:

> In an extensive series of tests of learning,
> reaction time and decision making, an elderly
> group was markedly impaired on almost all tests
> compared with young controls. However, on each
> test a number of old people performed better
> than the average for the young group, and on
> many of the tests the very best scores were
> achieved by elderly subjects, even though the
> young group contained many Cambridge University
> students..... An important feature is that all
> the old people who performed slowly were in
> poor health..... An elderly person in good
> health who remains active may be just as
> efficient as a young person in carrying out
> mental tasks. (1982, p.33)

Though these conclusions may appear to be in striking contrast to the majority of findings on age and
cognitive ability in the British literature, they
confirm what has been reported by some American
studies for the past decade. In this discussion I
shall attempt to describe the salient features over
the last ten years of predominantly American research findings and the background to dramatic
shifts in interpretation. In the course of this
discussion I hope it will become clear why it is
important that Huppert's study has at last provided
data derived from our own cultural context.

The Potential for Learning in Later Life

Prior to 1970, a review of the research on ageing
and cognitive abilities would have revealed that
anyone who lived to retirement age could expect to
experience fairly rapid decline in almost every
cognitive or intellectual ability. This evidence
was the result of several inter-related factors
which served to impede a proper understanding of the
relationship between ageing and cognitive competence.

RESEARCH METHODOLOGY: THE FIRST IMPEDIMENT

The most prominent of these impeding factors is research methodology; though to say this is to disguise the complexity of the problem. Until the end
of the 1960's, the literature on adult cognition was
dominated by studies which employed cross-sectional
research designs. Within a cross-sectional design
the performances on psychological or other measures
of several age cohorts (people born in the same
year) are compared at a single point in time. The
researcher attempts to equate the cohort samples on
the basis of various demographic factors, such as
socio-economic class, sex distribution and past
levels of formal education. Before 1970, it was
assumed that, given the appropriate controls of such
demographic factors, cross-sectional findings could
be interpreted as evidence of the qualitative and
quantitative changes that occur in cognitive abilities as a result of chronological ageing. That is,
they were considered to be valid developmental
studies. To interpret such studies as developmental,
it must be assumed that the average performance of a
current cohort of 70 year olds would have been the
same as that of a current cohort of 20 year olds
when the 70 year olds were 20. This assumption
allows the researcher to attribute any significant
variation between cohort norms to developmental
change. The variations revealed through cross-
sectional comparisons usually favoured the younger
cohorts; therefore, the pattern of cognitive
development over the adult life-span was interpreted
to be one of decline with increasing age.

It was only during the 1970s that researchers began
to point to the many problems inherent in cross-
sectional research methodology. For example, focussing on cohort norms disguised the fact that at
least some individuals in the older cohorts performed as well as the average younger subject and some
performed significantly better. (Huppert's 1982
British evidence is in sharp contrast to most other

British evidence simply because she recognised this problem). Nor did the researcher who reported significant differences between the normative scores of successive cohorts bother to return to the raw data to analyse the real differences between performance scores.

> If one has a large enough sample, practically any difference will be statistically significant.... If at the age of 30 an individual is able to produce 40 different words in a three minute period but at the age of 70 one can produce only 36, it is doubtful whether this decrement is going to make a lot of difference in his life. (Schaie, 1975, p.122)

However the most problematic assumption of all was that cohorts were comparable when care had been taken to control factors such as social class and educational experience. To make this assumption the researcher must ignore the presence of social-historical change and its importance for psychological processes (Riegel, 1970). In retrospect, to assume that the experience of being and having been middle or working class is the same for the 20 and the 70 year old, or that attainment of a given level of education in 1930 represents same experience as the attainment of that level in 1980, seems naive. However, until the last decade most research into the cognitive abilities of adults accepted these assumptions. It is important to understand why such acceptance prevailed.

Before analyzing the reasons why the assumptions underpinning cross-sectional designs were accepted, it is worth noting that even in the 1960's there was an alternative but small body of research literature derived from longitudinal studies. A longitudinal study follows a single cohort over a long period of time in an attempt to focus upon the developmental changes in the measured cognitive abilities of individuals within that cohort as they grow older. Results from such studies (e.g. Owens, 1966) usually show evidence of a progressive growth or at least a maintenance of abilities across the adult years. However, designs in this tradition suffer from two biases which led proponents of cross-sectional research to dismiss the longitudinal evidence. One bias results from the tendency of subjects to become 'test-wise' - that is more adept in taking psychological tests by virtue of the fact that they take the same or similar tests at each

measurement time over a period of years. Research
into longitudinal samples has also revealed a tendency for the initially more able to return for the
repeated measurements while the less able drop out.
Thus the sample at the final point of measurement is
composed of a more able distribution of people than
was the original sample. Nevertheless, longitudinal
studies produced results which were in direct
opposition to those produced by cross-sectional
studies; and they accordingly raised questions which
led to more viable challenges to cross-sectional
findings.

ASSUMPTIONS: THE SECOND IMPEDIMENT

Several inter-related considerations allowed the
acceptance both of the assumptions underpinning
cross-sectional research and of the way in which
certain implications were drawn from the research
results. I shall examine these at two levels, the
societal - assumptions which support a particular
social structure - and the disciplinary - assumptions which stem from the nature of psychology. (It
should be noted that the two interact with one
another).
     At the societal level we assume a negative
stereotype, in that the social construction of ageing is linked to fears of death - the undeniable end
result of ageing - but even more pervasively to a
socio-economic structure which, as presently con-
ceived, assigns those who live long enough to roles
characterised by powerlessness, dependency and the
absence of status and purpose. Psychological
explanations of decline and disengagement as natural
consequences of ageing offer a rationale both for
our social construction of ageing and the reality
which our socio-economic structure imposes on older
people. To create an alternative which allowed the
continuance of purpose, status, independence and
power would exclude youth from their assumed right
of ascendency into a system where roles and status
are largely determined by gainful employment.
Challenges to this allocation of roles and status
would demand a drastic reconstruction of the socio-
economic structure (Lasch, 1978).
     But while assumptions embedded in the fabric
of society often remain unquestioned because they
are not even recognised, assumptions at the level of
the discipline are more accessible to criticism and
change. Traditionally, developmental psychology has
focussed on childhood and adolescence and in so

doing has been closely allied to the study of neuro-
physiological (biological) growth. Biological and
psychological development follow parallel routes
during these early periods of life. Biology is
considered to be the main supportive base of intellectual growth during the period of biological
maturation, because malfunctions within the biological systems could impede cognitive development.
It also happens that subjects are most readily
available to researchers during the compulsory
schooling years. At the other end of the life-span
researchers sought their subjects from other types
of captive groups, such as institutions for elderly
people. Unfortunately, what they gained in terms
of ease of access, they lost in terms of representa-
tiveness: they were studying an atypical sub-
population whose performance should not have been
generalised even by inference. Because most of this
sub-population of older people was characterised by
pathology arising from social, psychological and/or
physical origins, the parallels between biology and
psychology were once again in evidence. In the
absence of research on the intervening adult years,
it was easy to assume that the ascending lines of
youth were joined to the descending lines of old age
by an arch which represented a slow process of
psychological and biological decline during the
adult years.
    The youth-centred orientation of psychologists
was directly linked to the establishment of psychology as a scientific discipline. The growth of
compulsory schooling in the early part of this century gave rise to a demand to diagnose the child's
level of ability so that education could best serve
his or her developmental needs. The sub-discipline
of mental measurement developed in order to establish norms for performance at different ages. To
achieve statistical validity for these norms, psychologists needed the large samples which schools
could provide. The psychologists needed the
schools, and the schools needed the psychologists:
a symbiotic relationship which implied that mainstream psychology was centrally concerned with the
establishment and study of norms.
    The practice of psychology thus led to the
views that intellectual development was dependent on
biological maturation and that its systematic study
involved the establishment of norms. These twin
assumptions underpinned the questions that psychologists asked, the approaches they adopted and the
methods they used. It is, I believe, assumptions

which have done the most to impede our understanding
of cognitive development in relation to age. When
psychologists wanted to establish what the cognitive
abilities of older people were, they understandably
sought a pool of institutionalised elderly: in order
to establish norms, they needed large samples.
They had no reason to suspect that the 'inevitable'
biological decline of age might not have a generalised effect on thinking ability. This process of
transferring the established concepts and practices
of the profession to a new group of subjects did not
even seem problematic, in that the assumptions at
the level of the discipline were reinforced by more
deeply-rooted assumptions at the societal level.
     Here, then, are the reasons - as I see them -
why thinking about age and cognition was as it was
until the 1970's. I shall now consider why we have
been able to reverse our thinking at the level of
the discipline, and in so doing to reject our earlier interpretations of the relationship between
ageing and cognition, even though at a societal
level there still persists a negative stereotype of
ageing.

THE PLASTICITY MODEL: THE FIRST REVOLUTION

The most significant challenge to the earlier cross-
sectional findings has come from the work of K.
Warner Schaie and associates. In the 1960's Schaie
developed several new research designs and began to
employ these to study developmental change in the
intellectual or cognitive abilities of adults
(Schaie, 1976).(1) Schaie's 'sequential designs'
involve a combination of cross-sectional and longitudinal designs. At the initial time of measurement a cross-section of cohorts are measured and the
same procedure is repeated at longitudinal intervals.
At each measurement time subsequent to the first
independent samples from the original cohort populations are also measured. With the appropriate
statistical analyses, this addition to the design
allows the researcher to control for the biasing
effects in the longitudinal data, discussed previously, and also to distinguish between age difference and age change. Age differences are due to
the different social and historical experiences of
successive cohorts. Age differences, therefore,
indicate how the average ability of one cohort will
differ from another's. These differences are not
concomitant with the ageing process. Age change
has to do with intra-individual development, and it

is upon these changes that we must focus when attempting to establish what happens to cognitive ability - and as a consequence, learning aptitude - as people grow older.

The results of Schaie's first sequential study have indicated a very much different trajectory for the course of intellectual development (age change) from that predicted by either cross-sectional or longitudinal research (Schaie and Labouvie-Vief, 1974). Rather than a unidirectional sequence of decline or progress, the emerging pattern appears to be an undulating one, representing what Schaie and associates have referred to as 'plasticity' (Labouvie-Vief, 1977). It is this 'plasticity' model which they use to describe the relationship between chronological ageing and cognitive or intellectual potential.

When looking at age difference, it appears that each successive cohort is becoming more and more able, probably thanks to general improvements in the quantity and quality of intellectual stimulation. This finding, however, is related to the norm for cohorts. Schaie (1975) makes the point in terms directly relevant to the learning potential of older people in such contexts as adult, continuing and higher education.

> While it does not follow that all old people have declined intellectually, some indeed have, but so too have some people at age 30. Our longitudinal studies of individuals show that we have some remarkable individuals who gained in level of performance from age 70 to age 84; others have declined from age 20 to age 30.... It is not unlikely that the maintenance and growth of intelligence of an adult may have much to do with the complexity of his environment. (p.121)

The more recent research thus suggests that we cannot predict whether or not an adult of any age has an aptitude for further learning.(2) Whether a person at the age of 60, 70, 80 or 90 has declined, is still developing or has the potential for further development will depend on the interplay of several factors; and this is also true for a 20, 30, 40 or 50 year old. Age, per se, is not the determining factor in the pattern of cognitive development during adulthood: whether an individual is progressing or regressing at any given age, the pattern can be reversed.

Birren (1963) offered a hypothesis about development that goes a long way towards explaining the plasticity model. Birren was the first to point out that we might be in error in joining the ascending lines of youth to the descending lines of old age by an arch. Neuro-physiology might be the prime supportive base for intellecual/cognitive growth either during youth or during times of acute pathology, but at other times the individual's interaction with the social/historical context might be a better indicator of the pattern of his or her intellectual development. This concept of interaction offers an explanation for the undulating patterns of growth - regression - growth which Schaie and colleagues found (Schaie, Labouvie-Vief and Buech, 1973) because the quality and quantity of such interactions will alter both for individuals and cohorts in part as a function of the nature of a society during different historical periods.

Birren's explanation, which derived from a study of exceptionally healthy older men, also helped to redirect attention from the study of cohort norms onto individuals who were ageing successfully. The psychologist who studies the intellectual potential of older people is no longer interested simply in describing what on average older people can do, but is instead concerned to discover what the potential for cognitive development is at all ages of adulthood. The study of those who are ageing successfully may one day lead to an understanding of how the full development of people can be better facilited, and especially how this development can be maintained during the later years of life.

The plasticity model offers two possible interpretations of why the cognitive performance scores of older people are normally lower than those of younger groups. The first is that older people may use their abilities less frequently, so that intellectual skills decline from disuse; the second that older people have as a result of their particular social-historical context never been denied the chance to acquire certain competencies. So one of the assumptions underpinning the plasticity model is that given the appropriate intervention, a lower than average level of intellectual performance can be either reversed or remediated, depending on whether the lower score derives from disuse or absence of an ability. This proposition is of course directly contrary to the facts of biologically based theories of ageing.

175

Several studies have reported the results of intervention strategies designed to test the assumption
of reversibility. This evidence has added further
credence to the plasticity model. Some studies have
used direct modes of intervention - such as the
modelling of concept formation behaviour (Denny,
1974), training in inductive reasoning strategies
(Labouvie-Vief and Gonda, 1976), and the teaching of
mnemonic strategies (Robertson-Tschabo, et al, 1976)
(3) - to reverse or remediate various types of diagnosed cognitive decline. All of them report significant gains in performance scores for older subjects. Other intervention procedures have been less
directly related to cognitive ability. Physical
fitness training, designed to increase the flow of
oxygen to the brain (De Vries, 1975) and pre-experi-
ment familiarization of the subjects with the researcher and the experimental setting (Eisdorfer,
1975), are two examples of benign interventions
which have produced improvements in performance
scores on psycho-motor and/or cognitive measures.(4)
However, since these experimental studies are (like
cross-sectional designs), conducted at a single
point in time there is no evidence to show whether
a complete reversal to an individual's previous
highest level has been achieved. Even so, the
results cast doubt on maturational theories, since
the latter predict that decline with age is irreversible, and hence preclude any effective remediation
once decline has been diagnosed.

CONTEXTUALISM: THE BEGINNINGS OF A SECOND REVOLUTION

Even these more positive interpretations have been
challenged during the past two years. The challenge
in this case is not directed at the research designs
but at the research instruments and the concepts of
intelligence upon which they are based - and
interestingly, it stems from one of the more prominent of the reformers of the 1970s. With reference
to the claim that discrepancies between older and
younger cohorts are due not to developmental change
but to social-historical differences, Labouvie-Vief
says:

> Still, this second interpretation has not been
> completely satisfactory; it has provided a
> relaxed variant rather than a qualitative
> transformation of models of the first type.
> (Here she is referring to maturational models)
> It has retained an implicit and invidious

assumption - namely, that the standards of
competence used to assess purported deficits
were valid in the first place. (1980, p.6)

Labouvie-Vief claims to have come to this realisation as a result of observing older peoples' reactions to the types of tasks which psychologists like
herself were inflicting on them. In some cases older people wanted to insist that the researcher
should make the tasks more meaningful; in many other
cases they simply refused to do the task. Labouvie-
Vief concludes that these older adults were demonstrating a 'kind of intelligent pragmatism' not
often found amongst college-age and younger subjects.
But we must also ask why Labouvie-Vief and other
researchers suddenly began to listen to and observe
the protestations of their older subjects.

A significant change in psychologists' thinking
has in my view underpinned these newest challenges.
A close study of the 1970's literature on ageing and
cognition suggests that, alongside the development
of the new research methodologies and the contrasting evidence they produced, there was much theoretical speculation about the nature of human development and about the paradigms which informed past
and present research.

Up to the mid-1970's all psychological research
took place within either a mechanistic or an organismic paradigm. Referring to research into memory
and learning, Hultsch(1977) observed that

whether the course of cognitive development
during adulthood is characterised by growth,
stability or decline, and whether such functions are linked to biological or environmental
variables is less a matter of 'fact' than it is
a matter of the metamodel (paradigm) on which
the theories and data are based. (p.367)

Most of the cross-sectional and other non-developmental research studies have been grounded in the
mechanistic paradigm which views man as a machine,
the behaviour of which is determined by either
external or internal (biological) variables. In
research on the relationship between age and cognitive ability which follows this tradition the
natural assumption is that the internal (biological)
variables cause cognitive behaviour.

In contrast, development research, both longitudinal and (to a certain extent) sequential is
grounded in the 'organismic' paradigm which views

man as an active agent in his own development.
Development is itself seen as a cumulative sequence
of definable and increasingly advanced stages of
cognitive organisation: so whenever decline occurs
in this sequence it is in the reverse order of
acquisition. The last stage to be acquired is the
first to be lost. Labouvie-Vief (1980) refers to
this notion as the 'first in-last out' or the 'last
in-first out' concept of development. It is based
on a portrayal of development as:

> ....a cumulative series in which lower level
> responses are retained, and must be retained,
> as higher ones are added....The only patterns
> permitted are further additions or deletions of
> the stages on the top. (p.9)

By the mid 1970's a third paradigm had begun to influence theoretical speculation amongst developmental psychologists. This paradigm, contextualism, is
by no means new (see Pepper, 1942), but its adoption
within psychology is. The central focus of contextualism is the historic event - all experience consists of events which have a quality or meaning when
they are considered as a whole. This quality or
meaning derives from the transactions between people
and their context. Contextualism is similar to
organicism, in that both focus on the total structure of thought rather than on the separate components which form the elements of the mechanistic
paradigm. However the contextualist paradigm denies
the existence of any final stage of development;
change and development are continuous features of
life. On this view, moreover, the sequence of
development is not necessarily cumulative - it may
also involve a reintegrative dissolution of earlier
levels so that more adaptive levels of cognitive
functioning may emerge. What constitutes cognitive
competence during adulthood, and even at different
points of the adult's life, may therefore qualitatively differ from adolescent and earlier adult
forms of competence.
It follows that to apply to adults standards of
measurement derived from concepts of child and
adolescent intelligence is an error inherent not only
in the organismic paradigm, but in all research which
derives from it. The researchers who have used
sequential research designs and proposed the plasticity model, though they have recognised the importance of man's interactions with the social/historical
context, have clung to organismic assumptions about

178

the nature of cognitive development and have in
consequence employed measurement instruments based
on those assumptions. Hence Labouvie-Vief's claim
that they have provided a 'relaxed variant' rather
than a 'qualitative transformation' of the maturational model.
    Contextualism will in my view provide the
framework for the important research into cognition
and ageing in the 1980's. A paradigm shift in this
direction has already begun to have a major effect
on research into memory and learning as well as on
the formulation of new models of adult cognition.

ADULT DEVELOPMENTAL POTENTIAL: A CONTEXTUALIST
PERSPECTIVE

Riegel (1973) has proposed that in addition to
Piaget's final stage of cognitive development -
formal logic - adult thought can develop contradictory or dialectical logic, and that this may be a
prevalent and productive form of thought in adulthood. Whereas formal operations, the final developmental stage in Piagetian theory, entail increasing
abstraction and the final resolutions of problems
through systematic consideration of all possible
alternatives, dialectical operations reunite abstract thought with concrete reality and allow for
the simultaneous consideration of alternative and
often contradictory explanations. Rather than
achieving the resolution of problems, dialectic
operations allow for the discovery of problems and
for a receptivity towards questions which have no
immediate logical outcome.
    No one has yet, to my knowledge, developed an
instrument to measure the extensiveness of dialectical thought. Riegel and others have however
pointed to a variety of indirect forms of evidence
for its existence. For example, the natural
sciences - which can be seen as the products of
competent adult thought structures - have evolved
from positivistic stances grounded in formal logic
to relativistic stances grounded in the logic of
contradiction.

> Natural sciences - not to speak of the behavio-
> ral and social sciences - have been plagued by
> implicit contradictions. Since Huygens it has
> been recognised, for example, than phenomena,
> such as interference and diffraction, are best
> explained by a wave theory of light. However,
> polarization (at least prior to Fresnel) is

best explained by Newton's corpusals or emision
theory. Although attempts to synthesize both
interpretations have succeeded, notably in
Planck's quantum theory, modern natural scien-
tists have to come to accept and live with
coexistent, contradictory theories. Some have
not hesitated to admit that these inconsis-
tencies are basic properties of nature rather
than insufficiencies in the knowledge acquired.
(Reigel, 1973, p.347)

It is perhaps on of the most important discoveries
of modern science (natural, physical and social)
that there is no such thing as a final, definitive
explanation. The phenomena of natural, physical and
social life can be validly explained by alternative
and often mutually contradictory theories.

Another source of substantiating evidence comes
from studies of the developing relationship between
learners and their field of study. Perry (1968)
found that college students progress in the study of
their disciplines from absolutist to relativistic
perspectives. And ultimately, whilst recognising
the relativity of knowledge, they move towards
commitment in terms of one position or another.

A similar analysis has been advanced of moral
development in adulthood. Until recently, it was
commonly held that adults had either not developed
beyond, or had in later years returned to, the
conventional levels of moral reasoning defined by
Kohlberg's (1976) theory of moral development. But
Gilligan and Murphy (1980) have proposed an alternative interpretation of the evidence, related to
contextualism and the model of dialectic operational
thought. They suggest that an apparently conventional response may in actuality be a sophisticated
form of judgement which recognises the interdepend-
ence of individuals with their social/historical
context. That is to say, adults confronted with a
typical Kohlberg-type moral dilemma may avoid giving
a highly principled post-conventional response
simply because to do so would seem naive or ideal-
istic in the light of existing social and legal
constraints. Gilligan and Murphy conclude that an
adult's level of moral reasoning cannot be inferred
solely on the basis of his or her moral judgement of
a dilemma. More elaborate questioning is necessary
in relation to the adult's response than is necessary for children or adolescents, because the underlying reasoning involves a complex intermeshing of
abstract possibilities with concrete reality.

The Potential for Learning in Later Life

Contextualism has also (as noted earlier) begun to
have a considerable impact on research into learning
and memory. Since 1975, a number of studies grounded in the contextualist paradigm (Walsh and Baldwin,
1977; Zelinski, Gilewski, and Thompson, 1979;
Hultsch, 1977 and Labouvie-Vief, 1980) have revealed
that although memory competence undergoes fundamental changes over the life-span, these changes can
be seen as progressively adaptive. Labouvie-Vief's
summary of her own research neatly characterises
these recent findings:

> ....we started pilot research on the processing
> of discourse. Our materials were short stories
> and the age-related differences were striking.
> Younger subjects produced detailed, quite
> faithful summaries of the stories; elderly
> subjects produced highly general summaries....
>
> We have since followed up this finding by
> breaking down text structure into a number of
> hierarchical levels and are finding that older
> adults attend to higher-order propositions,
> younger adults to detail. At the same time, it
> appears that the elderly subjects' attention to
> detail is qualitatively different from that of
> younger subjects. First, they report that they
> are uninterested in detail. Second, this lack
> of attention shows in their performance. When
> we built in foils at the level of detail [say,
> the story mentions a white crane lying on its
> side], detail recall is systematically distorted
> in the direction of real world inferences [many
> elderly may recall a pink crane standing on one
> leg]. (p.21)

Hultsch, (1977) argues that whereas research within
the mechanistic perspective has produced evidence of
a decline in memory with age, and research within
the organismic perspective has produced evidence
that decline can be reversed or remediated, research within a contextualist perspective tends
rather to suggest that memory improves with age.
Hultsch, like Labouvie-Vief, would maintain that
earlier forms of competent memory, such as memory
for detail, may be replaced with more adaptive forms,
such as semantic memory (Jenkins, 1974). These
findings clearly support what Coombs, and Smith (1973)
have called a "first in-first out" or "trade-off"
model of development.

IMPLICATION FOR LEARNING IN LATER LIFE

In light of this recent literature on ageing and cognition, I would like to return to the questions raised at the beginning of this chapter about the potential for learning in later life. As has already been noted, the research during the 1970's which gave rise to the plasticity model suggests that age per se should not be used to predict people's aptitude for learning or their potential for further cognitive development. But this answer in itself gives little guidance on practical provision for, and encouragement of, learning in later years.

It is helpful at this point to refer to the results of studies of twins, in which genetic inheritance can be assumed to be controlled. Such studies indicate that both mental and physical activity - but especially mental activity - contribute to successful ageing, as determined by a variety of psychological measures (Jarvik, 1975). The obvious implication is that educational opportunities should not only be made widely available for older people but that the latter should be actively encouraged to participate.

Even if such encouragement were forthcoming, considerable problems would remain - and especially those deriving from the attitudes of providers and of potential learners.

Thomae's (1970) 'cognitive theory of ageing and personality' hypothesises that the way one perceives a change, such as growing older, affects behaviour more than the objective change itself. As a consequence people may begin acting out 'oldness' when there is no real regression in their level of competence. The social construction of ageing will reinforce these perceptions - so too will any learning experience which gives rise to self-doubt, since it will tend to confirm the prevailing negative stereotype. In this is implicit an even more serious constraint to learning in the later years than those created by the social construction of ageing or the older person's acceptance of this imposed stereotyping. It is, I would maintain, a difficulty which lies at the very heart of adult education.

Educational provision for adults is largely grounded on the assumption that adulthood is a non-developmental period of life. According to mainstream psychology, cognitive development should be complete by the end of adolescence: no allowance is made for the types of qualitative changes in thinking which I have discussed. The assumption of the non-developing adult gives rise to a host of educational practices which may discourage adults from learning at levels of which they may be capable and also from demonstrating their uniquely adult competencies. The predominant pedagogy drives from the notion that learning is most effectively assessed by requiring the learner to recall detailed information. Admittedly, examination markers may also look for other types of cognitive competency, such as high levels of analysis and comprehension, but high marks are unlikely to be awarded in the absence of detailed information.

Our concept of education thus clearly derives from what mature adolescents and very young adults are most competent in doing, and from the ways in which they go about learning. The Belbins (Belbin and Belbin, 1972) drew attention to this in their studies of the retraining of older workers. When firms of good intent tried to attract older workers for retraining without changing their established training methods, they merely created failures and reinforced negative stereotypes. On the other hand, when methods of training were adapted to meet the needs and strengths of older workers, the success rate was impressive in that older workers compared favourably with younger ones.

It would be unfair and oversimplistic to argue that the potential for learning in later life exists and that we should therefore increase provision and encourage participation. If our ultimate aims are to increase the quality of life in the later years and to eradicate our negative social construction of ageing, then we must seek to make learning as visible an avocation of older people as gardening or grand-parenting currently are. This goal will never be realised if education continues to be defined in terms of competencies which are irrelevant to the vast majority of older people.

The perspective on ageing which has emerged from the contextualist paradigm and which has appeared increasingly in the literature during the past two or three years promises to have profound implications. The studies of 1970's may have led to a major reappraisal in our thinking about the older person's potential for learning, but this was only the beginning. The most recent research findings call for a more thorough going intellectual revolution. We must start anew to explore the development of cognitive competence during the adult years, recognising that such competencies will be

constantly changing as a function of socio-histor-
ical change. Labouvie-Vief (1980) has, among others,
identified this as a 'trade-off' view of development...."in order to gain a new integration....
(which is relevant in terms of the current context).
...one must give up an earlier one." (p.11) We must
begin to ask in what ways adolescent competencies
may become dysfunctional in adulthood, and seek to
discover the types of reintegrations which take
place. But perhaps even more importantly, we must
revolutionize our concept of adult education and the
approaches we use in the provision of learning
opportunities for older people. If we can succeed
in creating a new approach based on the concepts of
developmental potential and developing competencies
in adulthood, people of all ages will reap the
benefit.

NOTES

1. Schaie (1965) reported on the designs, but
it was not until the early 1970's that evidence
resulting from their employment was available in
published sources.
2. According to an unpublished Open University
survey the age group with the best pass rate in the
years surveyed was the 61-65 year olds.
3. I have not raised, herein, the theory of
Fluid and Crystallized Intelligence (Horn, 1976)
because it is a type of maturational theory that
predicts decline in fluid abilities with age. The
three studies I have just cited pertain to fluid
measures.
4. Further details of the evidence which
supports the plasticity model are given in Allman
(1981).

REFERENCES

Allman, P. (1981) Adult Development: An Overview of
    Recent Research, No.1 in Allman, P. and Mackie
    K. (eds) Adults: Psychological and Educational
    Perspectives Series, Nottingham University,
    Department of Adult Education.
Belbin, E. and Belbin, R.M. (1972) Problems in Adult
    Retraining, London: Heinemann.
Birren, J.E. (1963) "Psychophysiological Relations",
    in Birren, J.E., Butler, R.N., Greenhouse, S.W.
    Sokoloff, L. and Yarrow, M.R. (eds) Human
    Ageing: A Biological and Behavioural Study.
    Washington DC: US Goverment Printing Office.

Coombs, E.H. and Smith, J.E.K. (1973) "Detection of
    Structure in Attitudes and Development Process-
    es", Psychological Review, 80, pp.337-351.
Denny, N. (1974) "Classification Abilities in the
    Elderly", Journal of Gerontology, vol.29, pp.
    309-314.
De Vries, A.A. (1975) "Physiology of Exercising and
    Ageing", in Woodruff, D.S. and Birren, J.E.
    (eds), Ageing: Scientific Perspectives and
    Social Issues. New York: D. Van Nostrand.
Eisdorfer, C. (1975) "New Dimensions and a Tentative
    Theory", in Lumsden, D.B. and Sherron, R.H.
    (eds) Experimental Studies in Adult Learning
    and Memory. New York: John Wiley.
Gilligan, C. and Murphy, J.M. (1979) "Development
    from Adolescence to Adulthood: The Philosopher
    and the Dilemma of Fact", in Kuhn, D. (ed)
    Intellectual Development Beyond Childhood.
    London: Jossey-Bass.
Horn, J.L. (1976) "Human Abilities: A Review of
    Research and Theory in the Early 1970's",
    Annual Review of Psychology, pp.437-485.
Hultsch, D.F. (1977) "Changing Perspectives on Basic
    Research in Adult Learning and Memory",
    Educational Gerontology, vol.2, pp.367-382
Huppert, F. (1982) "Does Mental Funcion Decline with
    Age ?", Geriatric Medicine, January pp.32-37.
Jarvik, L.F. (1975) "Thoughts on the Psychology of
    Ageing", American Psychologist, vol.30, May,
    pp.576-583.
Jenkins, J.J. (1974) "Remember that Old Theory of
    Memory ? Well Forget it", American Psychologist
    November, pp.785-795.
Kohlberg, L. (1976) "Moral Stages and Moralization:
    The Cognitive Development Approach", in Lickona
    T. (ed), Moral Development and Behaviour. New
    York: Holt, Rinehart and Winston.
Labouvie-Vief, G. (1977) "Adult Cognitive Develop-
    ment: In Search of Alternative Interpretations"
    Merrill-Palmer Quarterly, vol.23, pp.227-263.
Labouvie-Vief, G. (1980) "Adaptive Dimensions of
    Adult Cognition", in Datan, N. and Lohmann, N.
    (eds) Transitions of Ageing. London: Academic
    Press.
Labouvie-Vief, G. and Gouda, J.N. (1976) "Cognitive
    Strategy Training and Intellectual Performance
    in the Elderly", Journal of Gerontology, vol.31
    no.3, pp.327-332.
Lasch, C. (1978) The Culture of Narcissism. New
    York: W.W. Norton, Chapter 9.

Morrison, V. (1982) Older Students in the OU, unpublished Survey Research Department Paper no.219 submitted to Disabled Students Committee January 1982.

Owens, W.A. (1966) "Age and Mental Abilities: A Second Adult Follow-up", Journal of Educational Psychology, vol.57, no.6, pp.311-325.

Pepper, S.C. (1942) World Hypothesis. Berkeley: University of California Press.

Perry, W.I. (1968) Forms of Intellectual and Ethical Development in the College Years. New York: Holt, Rinehart and Winston.

Riegel, K. (1973) "Dialectic Operations: The Final Period of Cognitive Development", Human Development, vol.16, pp.346-370.

Riegel, K. (1979) Foundations of Dialectical Psychology. London: Academic Press.

Robertson-Tschabo, E.A., Hausman, C.P. and Arenberg, D. (1976) "A Classical Mnemonic for Older Learners: A Trip that Works", Educational Gerontology vol.1, pp.

Schaie, K.W. (1965) "A General Model for the Study of Developmental Problems", Psychological Bulletin, vol.64, pp.92-107.

Schaie, K.W. (1975) "Age Changes in Adult Intelligence", in Woodruff, D.S. and Birren, J.E. (eds) Ageing: Scientific Perspectives and Social Issues. New York: D. Van Nostrand, pp.111-127.

Schaie, K.W. (1976) "Quasi-Experimental Research Designs in the Psychology of Ageing", in Birren J.E. and Schaie, K.W. (eds) Handbook on the Psychology of Ageing. New York: Van Nostrand Reinhold.

Schaie, K.W., Labouvie-Vief, G. and Buech, B.U. (1978) "Generational and Cohort-Specific Differences in Adult Cognitive Functioning: A Fourteen Year Study of Independent Samples", Development Psychology, vol.9, no.2 pp.151-166

Schaie, K.W. and Labouvie-Vief, G. (1974) "Generational versus Outogenetic Components of Change in Adult Cognitive Behaviour: A Fourteen Year Cross-Sequential Study", Developmental Psychology, vol.10, no.3, pp.305-320.

Thomae, H. (1970) "Theory of Ageing and Cognitive Theory of Personality", Human Development, 13, pp.1-16.

Walsh, D.A. and Baldwin, M. (1977) "Age Difference in Integrated Semantic Memory", Development Psychology, 13, pp.509-514.

Zelinski, E.H., Gilewski, M.J. and Thompson, L.W.
(1979) "Do Laboratory Tests Relate to Self-
Assessment of Memory Ability in the Young and
the Old ?", in Poon, L.W., Fozard, J.L., Cermak,
L., Arenberg, D. and Thompson, L. (eds),
New Directions in Memory and Ageing. New
Jersey: Laurence Erlbaum.

PART TWO. STUDIES OF CHANGING POLICY AND PRACTICE

INTRODUCTION

The contributions here deal with changes in the
perception of need, at the level of both social
policy and professional practice. Each chapter
refers to elderly people in receipt of services:
residential care, nursing, social work support in
the community. In concentrating on the discrepancy
between subjective experience and professional and
official perspectives they continue the preoccupation of the first part with the status of subjective
experience in our understanding of the ageing
process and definitions of need.

The first four chapters deal with Residential
Care. Thane, Means and Smith, in chapters eleven
and twelve, examine the history of provision for the
elderly infirm in Britain, from the nineteenth
century to the late 1940s. They trace the introduction of financial support for the elderly poor, the
demise of the old public assistance institutions and
their replacement by establishments which though
more humane nevertheless did not match the high
expectations of the planners. In the array of interests the elderly were not directly represented and
so were relegated to a "less worthy" position in the
queue for resources.

The chapter by McCoy on short-term care shows
that policy still fails to keep up with need as
expressed by the client group. Although the definition of need has moved beyond the basic level of a
hundred years ago, the provision of short-term care
(its essential value a "reborn certainty", in McCoy's
phrase) has developed in a policy vacuum. Scrutiny
of the characteristics of recipients reveals the
dominance of organisational needs over those of the
individual in the allocation of short-term care.

Part Two.   Studies of Changing Policy and Practice

The picture of official insensitivity is somewhat
modified by Willcocks and her collaborators in the
following chapter. Consumer research, conducted to
inform policy, suggests that attempts are being made
to bridge the gap between provision and need.
The chapters by McCoy and Willcocks bring the
discussion to a different level - that of the professional engaged in supplying care directly. Both
chapters touch on the difficulties encountered by
residential care staff and others in coming to terms
with changing role definitions. This is a theme
developed further in the remaining chapters.
Middleton (chapter fifteen) and Kohon (chapter
eighteen) like Willcocks, find professional staff
unable to relinquish easily their control over
routines, and engage in more collaborative relationships which take account of the emotional and
social needs of residents. In McCoy's discussion,
professional difficulties take a slightly different
form, involving relationships with other professionals rather than clients. Similar issues arise in
the settings described by Dalley (chapter sixteen)
and Taylor (chapter seventeen). Dalley's work on
the concept of the state nursing home leads to the
inevitable conclusion that if one sets up a system
halfway between a geriatric ward and an old people's
home one will have boundary disputes between doctors,
nurses and social workers. The hospice movement
described by Taylor raises the same issues of
autonomy complicated by the fact that the hospice
movement seeks to pose a challenge to established
forms of care while being increasingly dependent on
the N.H.S. for support.
The discussion of residential care is complex
and deals not only with professional and organisational problems but with the intimate needs of
people in communal settings. Willcocks talks of the
pressures of a life lived in public, particularly
acute for the elderly woman whose chief source of
esteem has been her private, and personal, set of
possessions and relationships.
Middleton,in a similar vein,refers to the
anachronism of the communal lounge, often the show-
piece and fiercely defended by professional staff.
She draws attention to the emotional problems involved in communal living. The potential of
sheltered housing for relieving social isolation is
not often realised. Loneliness is often exacerbated
and friendship formation inhibited by poor building
design and professional insensitivity. Middleton's
interest in loneliness and the dynamics of friend-

ship brings to mind Wenger's theoretical discussion in chapter nine and suggests a vital link between theory and practice.

The importance of friendships and mutual support by people whose life situations are similar is seen in the final chapter, by Kohon, Brewster and Chard. Professional social workers in an experimental group accept, with some difficulty, their non-directive roles and the principle of reciprocity and egalitarianism underlying such roles. The group members - elderly clients - meet as strangers but gradually engage in the activities of friendship: mutual support and commiseration, entertainment, and respect for autonomy. Dependence on the social workers is reduced and the communication skills and resourcefulness of hitherto inadequate people strengthened. In the experiment described here, precept is turned into practice with impressive results. It shares with the other contributors a fundamental concern to bring professional practice into closer alignment with client needs.

Chapter Eleven

THE HISTORY OF PROVISION FOR THE ELDERLY TO 1929

Pat Thane

The purpose of this chapter is to provide a brief
outline, for non-specialists in history, of the main
themes in the treatment of the elderly from the
nineteenth century to the nineteen twenties.
The elderly became a widely recognized and widely discussed 'social problem' for the first time in
the late nineteenth century i.e. from around the
eighteen seventies, not only in Britain but in many
other countries. (1) Why was this so ? Plainly old
people had existed in earlier times and provision
had been made for those in need i.e. those unable to
work for their living and without savings or family
to support them. Since the first Poor Law of 1601
each parish had had a duty to support the 'helpless
aged'. Up to the late nineteenth century and beyond, all of those who could, male and female, worked for as long as they were able at whatever employment they could find. When they were past work
they were cared for by their families where these
existed and could afford support. Family responsibility was institutionalized in the New Poor Law of
1834, which obliged close relatives to care for
their elderly, through the withdrawal of poor
relief.
But the elderly did not always have relatives;
not everyone married, not all who married had children; or children died, or migrated far away. There
had been a high rate of geographical mobility in
Britain long before the 19th century, but its pace
and distance increased with the spread of industri-
alization. The mid-nineteenth century was the peak
of migration mainly of young people to the colonies
and it was mostly the young who left the countryside
for the towns, at a still faster pace with the
decline of British agriculture from the 1870's,
leaving behind ageing rural communities (Thane 1982,

Williams 1970)

Old people who had no family to support them
had to look to charity, either formally though the
philanthropic institutions which grew and flourished
during the 19th century, or through the informal
gifts of friends, neighbours or previous employers
(Thane 1982). The last resort when no charity was
available was poor relief, given in or outside the
workhouse. Support by family or friends was most
difficult when old age was accompanied by infirmity,
at which time the alternatives were the workhouse or
the charitable almshouse. It is striking, however,
how many did remain in the care of their families.
Institutional care was then, as now, exceptional.
Indeed Michael Anderson has demonstrated the surprising uniformity over the past three centuries in the
proportion of the elderly population living in institutions. Families cared for their older members
out of duty, affection, or as Anderson has also
pointed out, because they were useful. Old women,
in particular, could help the family by caring for
young children while their mother worked (Anderson
1971). Hence there were fewer old women than old
men in 19th century workhouses despite the permanent
excess of women in the elderly population (Digby
197**8**, Crowther 1981).

Philanthopic and public institutions were imm-
ensely variable in quality. The makers of the 1834
Poor Law had started out full of good intentions
that the aged, as an obviously 'deserving' group,
not culpable for their poverty, should be 'allowed
their indulgences', in contemporary parlance. In
other words they should enjoy more comfortable workhouse conditions, and outdoor relief which was
better and more easily obtainable. In practice,
resources were not often made available for such
relatively open-handed treatment. Inside the workhouse until the later 19th century the aged were
subject to the same rigorous conditions as the other
types of inmate. When they could, by some means,
survive outside the workhouse, the aged were given
outdoor relief more readily than other groups,
though generally of such meagre amounts that their
survival must have depended upon additional help
from family and friends.

Poor Law conditions, however, varied consider-
ably from district to district, though nowhere could
they be described as generous. A major problem was
that poor law administrators were unable to decide
whether their attitude to the aged should be to care
for them or to punish them and their families for

their feckless failure to provide: whether their
role was one of caring or of punitive incarceration.
This dilemma was never solved before the formal abo-
lition of the Poor Law in 1929. Rather, officials
oscillated between the two roles, further confused
by the lack of any official definition of 'old age'
before the introduction of state old age pensions in
1908. Under Poor Law regulations, punitive, 'deterrent' treatment was to be given to anyone physically fit enough for work, a minimal enough definition
of fitness amid the endemic ill-health of the nineteenth century working class. This raised for
officials the difficult and unanswered question of
whether a fit 65 year old should be treated differently from a fit 35 year old.
      There was some expansion of the opportunities
for self-help in old age from the mid 19th century
with the growth of Friendly Society and Trade Union
pension schemes. But these were normally only
accessible to the better paid, more regularly employed elite of workers and existed mainly for men,
rarely for women (Gilbert 1964, Williams 1970).
      None of this provides the answer to my initial
question: why should old age have come to be more
explicitly defined as a social problem at the end of
the nineteenth century ? It is the more surprising
since at that time social conditions in general were
tending to improve. This should, in theory, have
enabled more old people to be either self-supporting
or supported by their families.
      The answer is not, simply, that the aged were a
higher proportion of the population than before.
There was a very slight increase in the proportion
of people aged over 65 in the population in the last
two decades of the century, but the striking increase in their relative numbers came after the First
World War (Baines 1981, Laslett 1977). The answer
lies in the existence of three related processes in
the last quarter of the century. First, there was
a much more general recognition of the complex
causes of poverty. It was seen not as a single problem caused by idleness or personal irresponsibility,
but as a complex of problems, of which old age was
one. Second, there was the increasing difficulty
experienced by some older workers in remaining in
work for as long as they felt physically able to do
so. One outcome of the increasingly competitive
nature of the international economy from the 1870s
was a growing concern among employers to increase
productivity by maximizing worker efficiency. This
led to attempts to exclude from the workforce less

efficient workers, including the old, and to the
gradual introduction of the notion of 'retirement'
from work at a fixed age, generally about 65, rather
than at the age of physical incapacity. Similar
trends can be seen in other countries at the same
period (Thane 1978, Stearns 1977, 1975, Achenbaum
1978, Quadragno 1982). Thirdly, there was the concentration of old people in certain rural areas as
a result of migration which made them locally a very
visible problem, not least for their demands on the
Poor Law.

This combination of events formed the background to growing pressure from philanthropists,
from the labour movement and from employers, for
state pensions for the active aged (Hay 1977, Thane
1986, Williams 1970). This derived both from the
desire to help those elderly people already unable
to find work and, on the part of some employers, to
ease the path towards a policy of retirement. Some
larger employers began to provide occupational pensions for this reason and also because some of the
newer industries were facing for the first time the
problem of an ageing workforce. Smaller employers
were more likely to prefer state pensions given
their more limited financial and administrative resources. There was parallel pressure for improved
institutional care for the aged, but it was weaker,
the economic imperative being rather less.

Institutional improvements, however, came first
in public - i.e. Poor Law - institutions. This was
an outcome of a wider re-structuring of Poor Law
policy from the early 1870s, designed to make a reality of the 1834 principles by providing punitive
treatment for the 'undeserving' and care suited to
the needs of the 'deserving whose poverty was deemed
not to be due to their own fault' (i.e. the very old,
the very young, the sick and infirm and the lunatic).
Ideally, the latter were to be provided for by
charity: but where, as was often the case, it was
not available, the Poor Law institutions should be
suffiently improved to meet their needs and they
were to be encouraged to seek help therein rather
than, as previously, deterred from applying. In
short, Poor Law institutions were to be improved but
there was to be a strict campaign to cut down outdoor relief. The 'deserving' who could survive outside an institution were to be directed to charitable institutions; the 'undeserving' were to be
given nothing. The vigorous pursuit of this policy
through the 1870s and 1880s caused considerable
hardship, especially to the aged and to women, who

then made up a high proportion of recipients of outdoor relief (Crowther 1981, Thane 1982, 1978c)

However, for those who needed institutional
care, there were discernible improvements especially
in richer urban areas. Separate and better infirmaries, childrens' and old peoples' homes began to be
built: In the case of old peoples' institutions
under the Poor Law, this meant that they were better
in the sense of being smaller, and rather more comfortable and less restrictive, though they were
still exceedingly austere. In the 1890s the central
Poor Law authorities recommended improvements for
all over-65s in workhouses: husbands and wives were
no longer to be separated but permitted to share
rooms. They were not to be made to wear uniforms,
were to be allowed to move fairly freely in and out
of the institution and to receive such small luxur-
ies as additional allowances of tea and tobacco.
Such limited privileges were not implemented in all
workhouses, although they remained official policy.
Again, motives for the policy change were mixed.
Officials were moved not only by humanity but by the
desire to outmanoevre pressure for pensions by
proving that the care provided by the Poor Law rendered them unnecessary (Crowther 1981, Williams
1970).

They failed. State pensions were introduced,
after long discussion, in 1908, though with the ut-
most economy. They were very low - at 5s per week,
below Rowntree's estimate of the minimum income required by an individual for a week. They were paid
only to the very old (to those aged 70 or above)
despite the fact that most of the pressure had been
for pensions at 65. They were means-tested, and
people of previously bad character were excluded.
They were non-contributory, financed directly from
the Exchequer. Half a million of the very old, very
poor and very respectable benefitted (Thane 1978b,
Gilbert 1964). For all its weaknesses, the Old Age
Pensions Act was the first measure of state-financed
income support given to the aged separately from the
stigmatizing Poor Law. It was a real, if limited,
gain. It did not help the elderly who needed institutional care, though it assisted some families to
care for infirm relatives. The numbers of old
people in the workhouses dropped after 1908, but not
dramatically. The pensions may indeed have exacerbated the problem of infirm elderly people living
alone who refused instutional care when they were
long past the need for it, especially in a period
when domiciliary services were non-existent. Such

cases caused recurrent scandal, since legally, no-
one could be forced into an institution (Williams
1970, Anderson 1977).

In the nineteen hundreds there was pressure for
the establishment of publicly funded old age homes
separate from the stigma of the Poor Law, partly to
diminish this problem. For example, the Select
Committee on Cottage Homes of 1903 recommended in
their favour and they were the subject of backbench-
ers' Bills in parliament. But nothing was done.
Again, the economic and political reasons for action
were few (Williams 1970).

Both the active and the infirm aged suffered
during the First World War. Inflation eroded the
value of pensions even when they were grudgingly
doubled - they remained at 10s per week until the
next war. Poor Law institutions were turned over to
military uses, with old people thrown out or transferred to less suitable conditions. The death rate
among the aged rose in the early part of the war;
Some, however, gained from the unprecedented employment opportunities offered by the war period, and
others from wartime increases in the incomes of
their families (Thane 1982, Crowther 1981).

Old people, especially males, returned in significant numbers to the workhouse in the nineteen
twenties, many of them because rising unemployment
made it difficult for them to find work or for their
families to spare the resources to care for them
(Crowther 1981). Some pensioners, however, were
better able to survive at home by the later twenties
because the real value of the pension rose with the
fall in the prices of essential goods. Unemployment
indeed led to increased pressure to remove the over-
65s from the workforce. This time, however, it was
pressure from the labour movement as much as from
employers, and was motivated by the hope of releas-
ing jobs for the younger unemployed. This was
Labour Party policy from the end of the First World
War (Phillipson 1982). It was one of the reasons
why the pensionable age was reduced to 65 in 1925 by
the Conservative government. Another important reason was that it provided an opportunity to shift
state pensions from a non-contributory to a national
insurance basis, which was cheaper for the Exchequer
and had been Conservative policy since 1908. The
Old Age Pensions Act, 1925, did not make retirement
compulsory upon receiving the pension. This practice was not introduced until 1946; before that time,
the low level of the pension made such a move unrealistic. Rather it was hoped that the pension

would enable more elderly people to retire earlier on a voluntary basis (Williams 1970). The trend towards increased specialization of institutional care under the Poor Law continued through the nineteen twenties, though rather slowly since government and local authority resources were concentrated on the overwhelming problem of unemployment. Not surprisingly, improvement was greatest and fastest in local authority areas in the South and Midlands where unemployment was least and where the economy began to expand from the later nineteen twenties. The special needs of the geriatrics who made up a high proportion of the aged in Poor Law institutions were, in any case, little understood. Institutions remained bleak and severely unstimulating by more recent standards.

In 1920 30% of all workhouse inmates were aged over 70 (Crowther 1981). The many poverty surveys of the nineteen twenties showed the aged (together with large families) to be an even higher proportion of the very poor than before 1914. This was partly because they comprised a large part of the population (due as much to the falling birth rate as to increased longevity), and because other causes of severe poverty, in particular casual underemployment, had shrunk, whilst the pension remained at bare subsistence level, lower than unemployment relief or other publicly funded benefits (Thane 1982, Mitchell & Deane 1962).

NOTES

1. For a general survey of the position in Britain and elsewhere see Pat Thane (1982).

REFERENCES

Achenbaum, W.A. (1978) Old Age in the New Land John Hopkins Press.
Anderson, M. Family Structure in 19th Century Lancashire Cambridge University Press.(1971)
Anderson, M. "The Impact on the Family Relationships of the Elderly of Changes since Victorian Times in Government Income Maintenance" in E. Shanas and M. Sussman (eds) Family, Bureaucracy and the Elderly Duke University Press, North Carolina. (1977)
Baines, D. 'The Labour Supply & The Labour Market 1860-1914' in R. Floud & D. McLoskey The Economic History of Britain since 1700 Vol.2 Cambridge University Press. (1981)

Crowther, A. (1981) _The Later Years of the Workhouse 1870-1929_ Batsford, London.

Digby, A. (1978) _Pauper Palaces_ Routledge, London

Gilbert, B.B. (1964) The Evolution of National Insurance Batsford, London.

Hay, R. (1977) 'Employers & Social Policy in Britain the evolution of welfare legislation 1905-1914' _Social History_ January

Heclo, H. (1974) _Modern Social Politics in Britain & Sweden_ Yale University Press

Laslett, P. (1977) _Family Life & Illicit Love in Earlier Generations_ Cambridge University Press.

Mitchell, B.R. and Deane, P. (1962) Abstract of British Historical Statistics Cambridge University Press.

Phillipson, C. (1982) _Capitalism and The Construction of Old Age_ Macmillan, London.

Quadragno, J. (1982) _Ageing in Early Industrial Society_ Accademic Press London & New York.

Stearns, P. (1977) _Old Age in European Society_ Croom Helm, London

Stearns, P. (1975) _Lives of Labour_ Croom Helm, London.

Thane, P. (1978) (a) 'The Muddled History of Retirement at 60 & 65' _New Society_ 3. Aug.

Thane, P. (1978) (b) 'Contributory vs. Non-Contributory Oldage Pensions 1878-1908' in Pat Thane ed. _Origins of British Social Policy_ Croom Helm, London.

Thane, P. (1978) (c) "Women & The Poor Law in Victorian & Edwardian Britain" _History Workshop Journal_ November.

Thane, P. (1982) _Foundations of the Welfare State_ Longmans, London

Williams, P.M. (Thane) (1970) _The Development of Old Age Pensions Policy in the U.K. 1878-1925_ Ph.d. thesis L.S.E.

Chapter Twelve

FROM PUBLIC ASSISTANCE INSTITUTIONS TO 'SUNSHINE HOTELS': CHANGING STATE PERCEPTIONS ABOUT RESIDENTIAL CARE FOR ELDERLY PEOPLE, 1929-48.

Robin Means and Randall Smith

(This material has been published in Ageing and Society, Vol.3 Pt.2 and we are grateful to the Cambridge University Press for allowing us to reprint it).

INTRODUCTION

This chapter is the product of our existing research endeavours on an SSRC funded project entitled Welfare Services and Elderly People, 1939-71. The project began in October 1981 and ended in September 1982. Our intention is to trace the development of all those services that were eventually to be located in social services departments in April 1971. One aspect of this work has been to study the impact of the second world war upon welfare provision for elderly people, and how this in turn influenced the political thinking behind the 1948 National Assistance Act which placed a duty on local authorities to provide "residential accommodation for persons who by reason of age, infirmity or any other circumstances are in need of care and attention which is not otherwise available to them".

Is such research merely an interesting intellectual exercise or does it have relevance to existing policy debates about the correct balance of family, domiciliary and residential care for frail elderly people in our society ? We would argue that it has a contribution to make because of its ability to unmask the changing definitions of the welfare needs of elderly people and how they should relate to the balance of input from the state and the family. Contradictory trends will be seen to have been at work. At one level, there was an emergence of a positive, though possibly unrealistic, view of the potential role of residential care i.e. the 1948 Act appeared to offer the prospect of 'sunshine hotels' in which elderly residents retained their self respect and social rights through paying out a proportion of their pension for their board. At another level, however, arguments among politicians and civil servants during the drafting of the bill indicated that welfare services for elderly people were to be treated in a less financially positive way than similar services for children 'at risk'.

PUBLIC ASSISTANCE INSTITUTIONS AND THE 1929 LOCAL GOVERNMENT ACT

According to Engels, the 1834 Poor Law Amendment Act was "the most open declaration of war of the bourgeoisie upon the proletariat" (Engels, 1969:308) with its policy of only offering relief to the able bodied in the workhouse. More recent social historians have stressed the boredom rather than the brutality of workhouse life together with the extent of local variation in practice (Crowther 1981, Digby 1978). However, such research has also emphasised how elderly people often had little alternative but to live in the general workhouse. The fit elderly were treated in the same way as the able bodied, so financial necessity often forced them to enter "the House" during periods of unemployment. Institutional care was also seen as necessary for the destitute elderly who were very frail and sick: the 1832 Commission had spoken of the need for separate institutions where "the old can enjoy their indulgencies" (1) but for a variety of reasons few of these were built.(2) Large infirmary hospitals for the acute sick were established but these rarely offered medical services for the chronic sick. Various government reports in the period 1890 - 1910 (3) spoke of the need for cottage homes and small residential units for the frail elderly but only a minority of local boards of guardians chose to make such provision.

The first quarter of the twentieth century did see major reforms that affected elderly people, especially in the field of pension legislation (Phillipson, undated). However, elderly inmates of poor law institutions were disqualified from receiving a pension unless they were admitted specifically for medical treatment. It was not until the 1929 Local Government Act that major organisational change occurred in the poor law system itself. This act provided that the powers, duties and assets of the 625 Poor Law Unions should be transferred to the county and county boroughs, each of which would be required to form a public assistance committee. The workhouse was to become the public assistance institution. But as Gilbert has pointed out:

From Public Assistance Institutions to 'Sunshine
Hotels'

> In effect the measure transferred the adminis-
> tration of the Poor Law to the major authori-
> ties but left any reform of the Poor Law,
> beyond certain useful but minor administrative
> changes, such as county-wide supervision of
> institutions, to the initiative of the local
> authority itself. Poor Law relief remained
> Poor Law relief and pauperism remained pauper-
> ism except for a few small modifications.
> (Gilbert 1970:229)

Indeed, the law governing the granting of relief was
merely consolidated into the 1930 Poor Law Act,
Section 14 of which re-stated Elizabethan principles
of family responsibility, namely:

> It should be the duty of the father, grand-
> father, mother, grandmother, husband or child,
> of a poor, old, blind, lame or impotent person,
> or other poor person, not able to work, if
> possessed of sufficient means, to relieve and
> maintain that person.

The principle of family responsibility was still to
be upheld and destitute groups, whether elderly
people or not, could only be offered relief after a
test of their means; sons and daughters still had to
make a financial contribution to the upkeep of any
old person received into institutional care.
     Our own arguments about the impact of the 1929
Act upon institutional provision for elderly people
must be tentative because our main research period
does not begin until 1939. Arguably, however, there
is little evidence of reforming zeal from either
central or local government. Some local authorities
built separate units for elderly people, especially
in the period just before the second world war.
Such reforms appear to have been discussed at some
length during the 1937 Public Assistance Conference.
Birmingham, for example, had opened three such units,
in which elderly people were carefully selected for
entry. One home was reserved for "women of the more
gentler type" (4) while another was for men of "the
merit class" (5). However, such reforms seem to
have affected only a relatively small number of
authorities.
     Some pressure for a change in the internal run-
ning of the large public assistance institutions did
exist. Olive Matthews, who was later to be very
active in the Old People's Welfare Committee, called
for a general attempt "to bring more colour" into

the lives of old people in institutions "through contact with visitors from the outside world, by providing occupations as well as entertainments, and by introducing more variety into their food, clothing and surroundings. (6)

In Housing the Infirm, she made detailed suggestions about how the routine of public assistance institutions should be changed along these lines. Some liberalisation may well have occurred in many institutions, although this remains to be confirmed by future research.

One of Matthews' proposals was that pocket money should be paid to elderly inmates, on the grounds that:

> Pocket money gives an added spice to life. It is one thing to be given weekly rations of sweets or tobacco - it is quite another thing to be able to choose and buy for yourself. Many of us remember the pleasure of receiving a small weekly sum when we were children.... It is very much the same for old people in Institutions. (p.13)

A considerable campaign built up around this issue that included M.P.'s, trades councils and some individual local authorities placing pressure upon the Ministry of Health for a change in the regulations. (7) The 1938 Poor Law Amendment Act enabled local authorities to pay up to 2 shillings pocket money per elderly person per week from their rates although the Association of Municipal Corporations opposed the Act, (8) on the grounds that it would be prefer able to withdraw the pension disqualification for those in public assistance institutions (i.e. the AMC did not wish to finance the scheme from the rates). The 1938 Act gave local authorities a permissive power rather than a statutory duty and as late as 1944 Samson (1944) felt able to claim that many local authorities were not using these powers.

So far we have suggested that the period 1929-39 saw some improvements in the treatment of elderly people in public assistance institutions but that these were often marginal. However, one result of the 1929 Local Government Act may well have worsened the position of many elderly people in poor law care. Councils were authorised but not required under the 1929 Act to transfer poor law infirmaries from public assistance committees to public health committees. The object of the innovation was to enable the standard of the work carried out in these hospitals

From Public Assistance Institutions to 'Sunshine Hotels'

to be improved and brought up to that in the best of the voluntary hospitals. Amulree claimed that such progress was soon attained, but only at the cost of their further reluctance to offer treatment for the chronic sick. The end result was that "the Relieving Officers had not the power to order the admission of such a patient into a Public Health hospital, and so the statutory right of admission of the destitute, which was one of the most valuable features of the Poor Law, began to be lost"(Amulree, 1951:12). The result of such policies was almost certainly a shortage of beds for the chronic sick elderly. The remaining poor law infirmaries tended to concentrate upon them as a group but lacked sufficient beds and skilled medical personnel to cope with the overall demand. One solution to this problem was to force the chronic sick to live in public assistance institutions. McEwan and Laverty (1949) provide an excellent description of how this system worked in Bradford in the period just before the establishment of the National Health Service:

> In the Public Assistance Hospitals (The Park and Thornton view)....patients are discharged or returned from the chronic sick wards to the ambulant or "house" section....In the Park, where the chronic sick wards were overcrowded, the most fit (but often frail) patients had to be sent to the ambulant wards to make room for admissions to the hospital section. There was, in consequence, a proportion of sick or disabled people in the ambulant section, where they had to remain, often confined to bed, there being no room for them in the hospital.
> (page 7)

McEwan and Laverty were quite clear that this pressure on beds for elderly patients had been increased by the redesignation of several municipal hospitals in Bradford after 1929. As they explain, "many of the new and aspiring municipal hospitals got rid of their undesirable chronic sick...., sending them to Public Assistance Institutions to upgrade their own medical services", (page 8)

To summarise this first section, it would seem fair to suggest that the residential care of frail elderly people prior to 1939 had severe limitations. The growth of pension legislation had eased the situation of some elderly people outside the institution: the bulk of elderly people remained in the community with or without such financial help. For

a minority of those in residential care, smaller
units were available although access was usually
restricted to candidate considered to be socially
above the average. There was confusion about the
boundaries between sickness and frailty. Above all,
as Roberts pointed out, most elderly inmates continued to sleep "in large dormitories, sat on hard
chairs, looked out on cabbage patches diversified by
concrete, were separate according to sex and, except
on one day a week, could not pass the gates without
permission" (Roberts 1970:26)

The Impact of the Second World War upon Residential Care for Elderly People

The 1931 census indicated that England and Wales had
a population of 39,952,000 and that 7.4% of these or
2,962,000 were over 65 years of age (Marsh 1965)
Only a small proportion of the 65+ group would have
lived in public assistance institutions. Poor
Relief Annual Returns indicate that 59,600 persons
sixty-five and over were receiving institutional
relief in England and Wales on 1st January 1939
(Williams 1981). We will now show how the Second
World War undermined the position of those already
in institutional care, increased the need of many
elderly people for support from the State, and led
to a reformulation of attitudes amongst officials
towards residential provision for elderly people.

Titmuss (1976) provides a detailed account of
the planning for the Emergency Medical Service
before the outbreak of the Second World War. This
was dominated by a fear of the huge casualties that
could be expected from air attack. Estimates of
civilian casualties proved far greater than the
actual figures. A target of 300,000 beds for an
Emergency Medical Service was agreed upon by the
Ministry of Health and this required the discharge
of 100,000 patients from existing hospitals on the
outbreak of war. When war was declared these
instructions were rigorously carried out, and
140,000 patients were discharged from hospitals in
just two days. The age composition of the patients
is not known but many of them may well have been
the elderly chronic sick.

From this point on, many beds in public and
voluntary hospitals were reserved for civilian war
casualties and the civilian sick were denied access
to them. This created enormous pressures in the
first twelve months of the war, especially in
London, but the situation became much worse once
bombing raids began during the autumn of 1940.

From Public Assistance Institutions to 'Sunshine Hotels'

As Titmuss explained:

> The problem of the aged and chronic sick had
> been serious enough in peacetime; in war it
> threatened to become unmanageable. Thousands
> who had formerly been nursed at home were
> clamouring for admission to hospitals when
> families were split up, when homes were damaged
> or destroyed, and when the nightly trek to the
> shelters became a part of normal life for
> Londoners. Yet everything, except humanitarian
> considerations - which often take second place
> in war - spoke against these poorest and most
> helpless members of the community. Because
> they occupied beds for indefinite periods it
> was wasteful to admit them to specially
> equipped and staffed emergency scheme beds.
> To nurse them was not only uninteresting but
> often unpleasant; the work soon dampened the
> enthusiasm of newly enrolled V.A.D.s who had
> expected to nurse soldiers and not incontinent
> and senile old people. It was moreover argued
> in the jargon of the day that the emergency
> hospital service must give priority to 'poten-
> tial effectives'.

One method of coping with this situation was for the
chronic sick patient to be transferred from a hospital bed to a public assistance institution; this
led to a loss of pension rights.

As already indicated, the bombing raids of
autumn 1940 greatly worsened the situation. These
raids brought numerous stories of hardship among
chronic sick and elderly people, especially those
with nowhere to go but public air raid shelters.
The Lancet indicated how:

> The shelter became a dormitory instead of a
> temporary refuge. To the most popular, people
> came from long distances, bringing their bed-
> ding, and friends found places for old people,
> the bedridden and infirm while the queues
> waited outside. Gross overcrowding has result-
> ed, and the lack of sanitation and sanitary
> supervision, of heating and ventilation,
> coupled with lack of sleep, nervous strain and
> improvised meals, has brought the danger of
> typhoid and dysentery, and, more menacing
> still, respiratory diseases. (9)

From Public Assistance Institutions to 'Sunshine Hotels'

A committee under Lord Horder was set up to investigate conditions and recommended after only four days that certain groups such as "the aged, the infirm and the bedridden" should be evacuated because their inclusion in shelters added to the difficulty of supervision, increased the risk of health and lowered morale, while they were perceived as "a serious encumbrance in the presence of an incident". (10)
    Four thousand old and infirm people were transferred from London to emergency hospital beds in country areas in the next 2½ months. However, the scheme was not a success. Many elderly people objected to being moved out of London. Others were not in need of hospital care. The overall size of the problem was too great for the Emergency Medical Service to cope with. The scheme was suspended in early December 1940 and never re-opened. Instead, the Ministry of Health attemped to redefine which elderly people it was responsible for. Increasingly, the Evacuation Division of the Ministry argued that it should only take responsibility for those elderly people made homeless by the bombing and not for the infirm elderly in general. As one Principal Assistant Secretary explained to a colleague:

> It is difficult to provide alternative accommodation for old and infirm people for the major reason that the government are bound to come to the conclusion that this group cannot be included as priority cases under the Evacuation Scheme....I think we must start by seeing what can be done for the homeless people who are our own responsibility. (11)

Instead, elderly people were to be encouraged to make private evacuation arrangements and billeting allowances were made available to the households where they stayed. (12) However, this was a more feasible option for reasonably fit elderly people than for the more infirm and chronic sick. The latter had little alternative but to struggle on in their existing communitites or to seek admittance to a hospital (if a bed could be found) or a public assistance institution. It now has to be asked how the latter were influenced by these renewed pressures from potential inmates, several of whom, Titmuss suggests came from a more middle class background than had normally been the case in the past.
    Two examples of the changing climate of opinion about public assistance institutions will be given before we go on to consider one of the main

From Public Assistance Institutions to 'Sunshine Hotels'

influences upon this change, namely evacuation hostels. Our first example comes from April 1944 when the Women's Institute complained to the Ministry of Health about a Northamptonshire Public Assistance Institution whose inmates were not allowed to wear their own clothing. The Chief General Inspector issued the following instructions to his regional inspectorate:

> As a result of enquiries it appears that there may in some areas be an impression that the use by the inmates of their own clothing while in an institution is contrary to Article 29(3) of the Public Assistance Order, 1930. That paragraph, however, requires only that such clothing as is 'taken from an inmate shall...be labelled and deposited in a suitable place for restoration to the inmate on discharge'. It does not require clothing to be taken from an inmate, and the Minister's view is that whenever this is practicable an inmate should be allowed to retain his own clothing if he so desires, and it is suitable. (13)

By the time of this internal memorandum, the whole issue of future residential provision was being considered by the Chief General Inspector through his role as adviser to the survey committee on the problems of ageing and the care of old people. The survey committee, set up in 1943, was financed by the Nuffield Foundation under the chairmanship of B. Seebohm Rowntree, and from the beginning the Ministry of Health agreed to offer full co-operation to its deliberations. This survey committee provides our second example of the changing climate of opinion towards Public Assistance Institutions. The publication of Old People: Report of a Survey Committee on the Problems of Ageing and the Care of Old People (14) took place in January 1947. The report notes that the survey was set up because of "cases of aged persons dying in circumstances of great squalor and loneliness because local authorities, although asked, have been unable to fulfil their legal obligations to receive them into an Institution". (page 63) One section of the survey report looked at residential care for elderly people and pointed out that many public Assistance Institutions were built in the early, decades of the nineteenth century, and were structurally inadequate.

From Public Assistance Institutions to 'Sunshine Hotels'

> Day-rooms in such Institutions are usually
> large and cheerless with wooden windsor arm-
> chairs placed around the walls. Floors are
> mainly bare boards, with brick floors in lava-
> tories, bathrooms, kitchens and corridors.
> In large urban areas such Institutions may
> accommodate as many as 1,500 residents of
> various types, including more than a thousand
> aged persons. (page 64)

This part of the report received considerable press
coverage.(15) An editorial in The Times on 15th
January 1947 spoke of the 'Claim of the Aged'. The
Daily Herald ran a feature on 'Old People Exploited
in Homes', The Daily Express referred to 'Scandal of
Old Folks' Homes' and The Daily Mail claimed 'Old
Folks Live in Shadows'.
     All this represented a significant shift from
the view recorded in our earlier Titmuss quotation,
about the need to give preference to 'potential
effectives' before elderly people. The change of
emphasis seems to have taken place at the level of
newspaper debate, ministerial utterances and day to
day practice: the reasons for it are complex and we
are still in the process of trying to unravel them.
We shall attempt to look at the development of one
aspect of residential care during this period,
namely evacuation hostels. These reflected the
changing attitudes of the war period towards elderly
people, and were also an important influence upon
planning for the abandonment of public assistance
institutions. The Nuffield Survey claimed that "all
normal old people who are no longer able to live an
independent life should be accommodated in small
homes rather than in large institutions", (16)
suggesting that these should cater for between 30
and 35 residents. This belief in the economic
viability of small residential units had been greatly forwarded by the experience of the evacuation
hostels during the war.
     One problem with evacuation hostels is that it
is difficult to provide a neat definition of them.
They were run by both government and voluntary
organisations: some provided help for evacuees, some
for the homeless, some for the frail and some for
the completely bedridden. A hostel meant different
things to different organisations and part of the
debate between the public and voluntary sector, as
already suggested, concerned whether the frail and
bedridden could expect any special treatment during
war-time. However, the crucial feature of all such

From Public Assistance Institutions to 'Sunshine Hotels'

hostels was that people were seen as residents not inmates; they were not covered by any of the poor law legislation and they did not have to give up their pensions.

The first hostels were set up by local governments, especially in London, as a response to the crisis created by the first bombing raids. Many elderly people made homeless by the raids were too fit to be admitted to a hospital bed under the Emergency Medical Service but too frail to be placed in a normal billet. Unless alternative accommodation could be found, they would 'block up' the Rest Centres designed to look after people during the immediate disruption caused by an air attack. At first provision was very scattered, but by July 1942 the provision of local authority places had expanded to 1855 beds in London and 4,945 beds (17) in the rest of England and Wales. Nearly all these places were reserved for elderly people made homeless or evacuated as a direct result of the war, rather than for the infirm elderly in general. A similar emphasis upon the war homeless and evacuated could be found in the work of the first voluntary organisation to enter this field. By July 1942 the Friends War Victim Relief Committee had 27 hostels for the aged, with 305 places.

A November 1941 pamphlet on the London County Council homes made it clear that Evacuation Hostels were only for war victims and that the regime of such homes was to be very different from the average public assistance institution. This pamphlet laid down the following conditions for admission:

1. Candidates must have been rendered homeless by enemy action.
2. They must be without friends or relatives able to provide them with permanent accommodation.
3. They must be unsuitable by reason of old age or infirmity for normal billeting.
4. If infirm they must not be suffering from any specific illness necessitating their confinement wholly or in large part to bed or calling for continuous treatment from a doctor.
5. They must contribute to their maintenance if able to do so. The full cost was given as 30s per week. (18)

Once admitted, residents were to enjoy far more freedom than that available to most inmates of public assistance institutions. They could be "visited by their friends at all reasonable times"; they could also go out whenever they wished, and could take up to 14 days' leave without being considered to have left the home.

As has already been indicated, voluntary organisations were encouraged by the Ministry of Health to establish hostels for elderly people made homeless by the bombing. Indeed, a special committee on the Aged and Infirm was set up by the Ministry of Health to improve liaison between the voluntary and public sectors over hostel provision and voluntary billeting. However, the N.C.S.S. representative on the committee consistently argued that there was a need for general hostel provision for the elderly infirm. Such proposals were, we have noted earlier, opposed by the Ministry of Health representatives: one Assistant Secretary argued that "we have not available the resources that would enable us to undertake to provide for the aged infirm as a class". (19) However, this theme was not dropped by the NCSS or by its offshoot, the Old People's Welfare Committee (OPWC). OPWC had been set up in October 1940, with considerable support from the Assistance Board, after a conference called by the NCSS on the Welfare of the Aged. (20) The OPWC was able to persuade the Assistance Board of the general need for an expansion of hostel provision by voluntary organisations because of the general need of the infirm elderly. It was also argued this could only be achieved if each resident could be guaranteed a supplementary pension of 30/-. The Board proved willing to defend the new policy against the criticisms of the Ministry of Health that it was wrong to encourage the indiscriminate growth of such hostels, especially since many would be in areas in danger from future bombing raids. (21) In December 1941, the Chairman of the Assistance Board announced to an NCSS conference that:

> The Board have had under consideration the
> position of pensioners who are not in need of
> continuous medical or nursing services but are
> nevertheless so shaky that it would clearly be
> in their interests that they should have
> special care and attention which may not be
> available in their homes. We have, therefore,
> arranged to facilitate the setting up of
> hostels for old people who cannot otherwise
> secure the attention which they need. We have
> agreed to increase the supplementary pension

normally given to a sum which should be sufficient to provide the person with an income of
30/- a week. (22)

This was very different from the fate of the inmate
of the public assistance institution, who lost his
pension rights and the freedom to make decisions
about a whole range of everyday issues such as
clothing and visits. The residents of hostels were
no longer to be restricted to people made homeless
by the war: they could now come from the group who
would normally enter a public assistance institution. Hostel residents would not only keep their
pensions but would have the supplementary element
increased. The one thread that seemed to link the
two types of provision was the attitude to relatives:
the 30/- hostel places were only to be available to
those "who, on account of infirmity or extreme old
age, require special care and attention to an extent
which, having regard to all the circumstances it is
not reasonable to expect should be provided by their
relatives". (23)
    Both the Ministry of Health and the local
authority associations were at first hostile to the
30 shilling hostels. In April 1942 representatives
from the public assistance departments of the London
County Council, Surrey, Kent and Middlesex told
Ministry of Health officials that:

1. Public Assistance Authorities in the Home
   Counties can, even in existing circumstances, provide for all old people requiring hostel treatment.
2. Local authority homes are superior to anything that a voluntary agency would provide.
3. The poor law stigma is over-emphasised.
   (24)

It is doubtful if Ministry of Health officials were
completely convinced by such arguments. The
Evacuation Division saw their task as dealing with
the homeless, and so claimed that the new hostels
were nothing to do with them. The Poor Law Division
of the Ministry of Health had a more ambivalent
attitude. At one level, there was a feeling that
"the provision of homes for the aged is properly a
function of local authorities to be undertaken as a
charge on the rates". (25) There was also a feeling
that the OPWC might be setting up a separate system
of residential care for "a privileged class of
necessitous aged persons", (26) The working class

were going to public assistance institutions and the middle class to voluntary hostels. At the same time, these hostels may well have been seen as good for civilian morale as well as a safety valve. They offered an alternative to long-established institutions which the inspectorate must have known were out of keeping with the brave new world of Beveridge. (27) Evidence we will present later indicates that some officials in the Poor Law Division really did see the PAI's as a landmine that could explode in their faces with newspaper scandal headlines.

By late 1943 and early 1944, complaints were beginning to pile up at the Ministry of Health about conditions in PAI's. Articles were being written which contrasted the large "workhouse" with the small voluntary hostel for 20 or 30 people. Rackstraw - in Social Work (London) - for example, painted a picture of a hostel in Hampstead where "crotchetiness and cantankerousness seem to dissolve in this calm" (Rackstraw 1944) She concluded that "if all the Poor Law Institutions could be turned into factories and these small hostels or Homes peppered all over England, Scotland and Wales, what a much happier country it would be, not only for the old people themselves, but for their relatives and friends, and also for those not yet old who begin to look forward to the future with apprehension and dread".

The relation between this type of article, individual and pressure group complaints about PAI's, and the setting up of the Nuffield Survey is difficult to unravel. Certainly, the hostels provided a yardstick against which to compare the PAI's to their detriment, not only because residents did not lose their pension rights but also because such hostels showed the feasibility of units much smaller than most PAI's. It is significant that, fifteen months before the publication of the Nuffield Survey, the Chief General Inspector not only stressed the need for change to his inspectorate but also stressed the key role that the voluntary sector might be able to play in this process. His memorandum stressed that "voluntary agencies can help local authorities substantially by trying out various forms of institutional assistance for the 'new poor'". (28) It goes on to consider the welfare of the aged, in which "the most prevalent disease is boredom" for those in PAI's, and argues that their burden can best be lightened by keeping them active and interested through good diets, plenty of books, and suitable games. It also notes that "the term 'resident' in place of 'inmate' has advantages". Such elderly residents "would probably be best housed in small Homes and the experience of wartime emergency services and experiments such as Mrs Hill's (29) voluntary hostels in Middlesex and East Ham Homes for bombed-out people suggest that small Homes can be not only more satisfactory to the residents but at least as economical in cost if a suitable unit is chosen". The memorandum does however identify two major obstacles to the development of hostels along these lines, namely lack of staff and lack of premises.

Over the next fifteen months, before the publication of the Nuffield Report, the Ministry of Health received a growing pile of complaints from pressure groups, local authority associations and professional associations about the inadequate hospital and residential provision for elderly people. The National Association of Administrators of Local Government Establishments, for example, stated they were seriously concerned at the prospect of uncoordinated policy over hostels for elderly people. (30) In April 1946, the Association of Municipal Corporations informed the Ministry of Health of the following resolution passed by the Social Welfare Committee:

> That when the forthcoming legislation relating to the amendment of the poor law is under consideration provision should be made to enable local authorities to provide hostel or similar accommodation for aged persons who may not be capable of being entirely on their own, insofar as such accommodation and any domestic assistance that must form part of the provision cannot at present be provided under the Housing Acts. (31)

In July 1946 the National Old People's Welfare Committee (formerly OPWC) informed the Ministry of a resolution "that old people requiring nursing care are often unable to gain admittance to hospital". (32) In October 1946 the National Association of Local Government Social Welfare Officers attacked "the present deplorable conditions whereby the aged and chronic sick are deprived of the necessary care and attention to alleviate their pain and discomfort". (33) The publication of the Nuffield Survey followed in January 1947 and encouraged an even greater volume of complaints from M.P.s, individuals and organisations. (34) The response of the Ministry of Health to such criticism was Circular 49/47 on the Care of the Aged in Public Assistance Homes and Institutions. (35) The circular drew the attention of local authorities to the Nuffield Survey and mentioned forthcoming legislation (i.e. the 1948 National Assistance Act), but stated that in the meantime public assistance should consider what action could be taken immediately to improve arrangements for existing elderly residents. The circular called for the resumption of the building of small homes and made it clear that the minister would be prepared to consider schemes for the acquisition and adaptation of suitable premises for this purpose. The daily routine of the larger homes should also be improved to provide more freedom, especially in the following areas: a) Visiting hours every day of the week. b) Residents to be allowed to wear their own clothes c) Each resident to have his or her own wardrobe, chest of drawers or locker d) Clocking in and out regulations under Article 70 of the 1930 Public Assistance Order to be ignored. The circular also called for a general smartening up of the inside and outside of all P.A.I.'s through better chairs, pictures, handrails etc.

The issuing of the circular does not appear greatly to have reduced the concern of ministry officials at the workings of many of the larger P.A.I.'s, which could be open to scandal. On 9th October 1947, senior officers from the Poor Law Division met under the chairmanship of the Assistant Secretary who explained that:

> ....the purpose of the meeting was to consider methods of securing a more effective 'follow up' to the reports made by the Inspectorate of their visits to Homes and Institutions for old people. The care of the aged was arousing considerable public attention, and the Department must not lay itself open to charges of inactivity such as were implied in the Curtis Report (36) in regard to the supervision of Children's Homes. (37)

The officers agreed on the need for a careful filing of complaints from inspectors about homes, and for a follow-up system to make sure that the response of the local authority was known. The meeting ended with the compilation of "a list of authorities considered likely to require stimulus, in order that the relevant administrative files might receive special and early attention".

THE 1948 NATIONAL ASSISTANCE ACT

The new legislation mentioned in Circular 49/47 was the 1948 National Assistance Act, Section 21 of which placed on local authorities the duty to provide accommodation to all who needed care and attention, regardless of their financial circumstances. The central message of Nye Bevan (Minister of Health) when introducing the Bill to Parliament was that "the workhouse is to go" and to be replaced for the elderly by "special homes", to be run by "welfare authorities", for up to 30 residents the "type of old people unable to do the housework, the laundry, cook meals and things of that sort". (38) The whole tone of debate in both Houses reflected pleasure at the ending of the poor law.

Brown (1972) argues that this created a situation in which "they welcomed the new...welfare departments whichwere to replace it in a markedly uncritical way". (page 17). At first glance this does not appear to be a justified comment , especially in so far as the issue of payment for accommodation is concerned. The Beveridge Report had spoken of the need to abolish the poor law code but had not spelled out the implications of this in terms of local authority residential provision. In March 1946 the Social Services Committee of the Labour Cabinet set up an interdepartmental committee on "The Break Up of the Poor Law" under the chairmanship of Sir Arthur Rucker (Deputy Secretary, Ministry of Health). (39) The committee produced its report in July 1946. (40) Paragraphs 51-74 dealt with maintenance in institutions and argued that "as a further step towards breaking away from the old association of parish relief and in particular the conception of an institution for 'destitute persons', we think that a resident in a local authority's Home should keep charge of whatever income or other resources he may have and pay the authority for his accommodation and maintenance". This "conception of a 'hotel' relationship" would require most pensioners to pay to the local authority 21/- a week from their 26/- pension and to keep 5/- for pocket money". The Rucker Report suggested that this reform should be combined with a sweeping away of previous rules about family liability towards those in institutional care. The Report asserted "that the present extensive liabilities under the Poor Law should be brought to an end, and that for the purposes of assistance under the Bill....there should be a simple liability of spouses in respect of each other".

The 1948 National Assistance Bill followed these proposals, and so contained substantive reforms for elderly people in residential care. At the same time, media and parliamentary debate about the new 'hotel' relationship was highly unrealistic in relation to the resources the state was willing to spend on new residential building. The newspaper reaction (41) on the publication of the National Assistance Bill on October 31st was one of enthusiasm, and the theme of 'hotels for the old folks' was almost universally taken up. The Daily Mirror story read "State to build hostels for the old folk" while The Star referred to "hot and cold rooms for 21 shillings". Bevan claimed in the Bill's second reading that "the whole idea is that welfare authorities should provide them and charge an economic rent for them, so that any old people who wish to go may go there in exactly the same way as many well-to-do people have been accustomed to go into residential hotels". (42) Bevan went on to express his uncertainty about what to call the new institution. Speakers in the House of Commons had suggested "Eventide Homes" or "Churchill Homes". The Daily Mail spoke of "Wanted - Name for Old Folks Hotels" and went on to suggest "sunshine hotels" while the Daily Graphic said "Homes for Aged to be named like small Hotels". (43)

A feature of hotels, of course, is that they conform to a market model in which costomers are free to choose their own hotel, and that the main criterion of eligibility is the ability to pay for the tariff. People are admitted on a first come, first served basis and one's stay at a hotel can be booked in advance. One is certainly not denied entry because one has a daughter living in the same town. If there is a shortage of hotel beds in a particular area and 'no vacancy' signs become a common feature, new hotels are likely to be built by private firms to serve the unmet need. The experience of elderly people in residential care since 1948 has in the event been vastly different. Could the likelihood of this have been predicted from the material we have looked at for the period 1946-48 ?

It is possible to argue that welfare services for elderly people were seen as a low priority compared to services under the 1948 Children's Act or Part III of the 1946 National Service Act. Local

From Public Assistance Institutions to 'Sunshine
Hotels'

authorities received an exchequer subsidy for
developments in both these groups of services. However, from 1944-46 Ministry of Health officials had
consistently opposed any system of exchequer grant
for new residential buildings on the grounds that
local authorities were not being asked to establish
new services (44) and the Rucker Report argued that
"our proposal under which such an old person will be
put into a position to contribute 21/- to the cost
of his maintenance is therefore in this respect more
favourable to local authorities than anything they
have been given reason to expect". This advice was
reflected in the National Assistance Bill despite
protests from the local authority associations (45)
However, by that time, it was known that the Children's Bill intended to offer a 50% subsidy from the
Exchequer on approved expenditure incurred by local
authorities on those aspects of child care which
were not already the subject of specific Exchequer
grants. Ministry of Health officials accordingly
decided to abandon their opposition to some form of
central government support for new residential
buildings. The treasury officials were not however
willing to share this changed perspective (46) and
so the issue was 'sent up' to Ministerial level for
resolution. The Chancellor of the Exchequer
(Dalton) was at first not very responsive to the
Minister of Health (Bevan). The former attacked the
demands of the local authority associations "which
sometimes became quite shameless" and spoke of the
need "to protect the sorely tried taxpayer". (47)
Eventually in October 1947 a subsidy system along
the lines used for new council housing was agreed
(48) by Cripps who had replaced Dalton as Chancellor.
However, this was only to meet about one third of
building costs, as against fifty per cent of running
costs for children's services.
     This subsidy system was not only less generous
than that available for service developments for
other client groups: the subsidy was in fact only of
value if a major building or adaptation programme
was allowed by central government. From the beginning, serious criticisms of the policy were voiced.
On the publication of the National Assistance Bill,
the Glasgow Herald warned that:

     .....the proposals in the Bill will remain no
     more than proposals until the present period of
     financial stringency is past. The new services
     and new buildings which will replace the old
     Poor Law system and institutions will make

> heavy demands on finance, building construction, and manpower, all of which are not only subject to restrictions but are needed for projects of more immediate importance. (49)

Such views were not completely rejected by Bevan despite the generally optimistic tone of his speech during the second reading. He did warn that "the extent to which we can establish these new hotels for the old people will depend upon the development of our building programme". (50) Several Conservative M.P.'s echoed this point - Richard Law, for example, stated that "this is a very good Bill" but that "its results will depend, above all, upon the degree of economic recovery of this country for which we can hope". (51)

The economic recovery proved slow to occur. The capital building programme, including new residential homes for elderly people, was severely restricted. Despite attempts to adapt older buildings into small residential units, the new welfare departments remained heavily dependent upon poor law staff and poor law buildings, a situation that was to be so ruthlessly exposed in 1962 by Peter Townsend in The Last Refuge. With regard to former public assistance institutions, he found that:

> After 1948 they were going to be abolished. Yet in 1960 they were still the mainstay of local authority residential services for the handicapped and aged. They accounted for just over half the accommodation used by county and county borough councils, for just under half the residents and for probably over three-fifths of the old people actually admitted in the course of a year (Townsend 1962:21).

The 29,600 elderly people in such institutions largely depended on staff who had given a life-time's service under the old Poor Law as well as the new administration; Townsend claimed "it would be idle to pretend that many of them were imbued with the more progressive standards of personal care", and added that "a few among them were unsuitable, by any standards, for the tasks they performed, men or women with authoritarian attitudes inherited from Poor Law days who provoked resentment and even terror among infirm people". (page 39)

From Public Assistance Institutions to 'Sunshine Hotels'

CONCLUSION

The title of this chapter refers to "state perceptions about residential care". This wording is a
reflection of the authors' belief that Britain is a
capitalist society, in which there is an inherent
conflict between capital and labour and in which the
state tends to function in the interests of the
former rather than the latter. However, as Denise
Riley has noted in relation to her research on wartime nurseries, " 'the state' fragments into internal government politics, dissensions between
Ministries of Health, Education and Labour, reaction
to pressure from industrialists, splits between
central and local government authorities" (Riley
1979, 1981). The same situation can be observed in
relation to the development of residential services
for elderly people. The concept of the Unified
State does little justice to the complex reality of
how policies evolve and become modified over time.
The '30 shilling' Evacuation Hostels provide a useful illustration. The Assistance Board was willing
to introduce this reform. The Evacuation Division
of the Ministry of Health expressed opposition but
claimed it was for a group (the elderly infirm) outside their province. The Poor Law Division of the
Ministry of Health was ambivalent but was under
pressure from the local authorities to express open
opposition. There was the further distincion to be
made between establishing a policy and getting it
carried out. By 1945, the Assistance Board was
paying the extra allowance to residents in only 26
such hostels. (52)
      However, to say that there is no unified state
is not the same as to claim that all policy options
are open or that British society is an essentially
pluralist one in which the strongest pressure group
wins the most resources. Frail elderly people do
not have a direct productive role and they are not
involved in the reproduction of the next labour
force. This is reflected in general ideological
assumptions about the position of frail elderly
people in society. Such assumptions are not static
- they respond to changing economic and social pressures as the work of Phillipson and Myles (1981)
among others have shown. However, a key aspect of
these assumptions during the period 1929-48 - as
several examples in this chapter have shown - was
that frail elderly people should be a low priority
for resources compared to the working population and
children: they were not 'potential effectives' and

so could not expect much help. Even the OPWC reflected these assumptions with the following press announcement:

> It may be said - and rightly - that the claims of the children must come first and that the aged are the least valuable lives. But the presence of the aged in bombed areas is both an embarassment to the Civil Defence Services and a cause of anxiety by day and added danger at night to their younger relatives engaged in national service. Their removal to less dangerous neighbourhoods before next winter is an urgent need. (53)

Our comments on the 1948 National Assistance Act also stressed the extent to which frail elderly people were seen as less worthy of resources than children.

At the same time, there is a danger in so stressing the 'low priority' aspect that one reverts to a monolithic view of the 'correct' role of the state in the care of elderly people. Attitudes to this question clearly did change in the period 1929-48. The poor law system was swept away. Pension rights were granted to those in residential care. How can this be explained ? Clearly such changes were deeply embedded in the much broader re-structuring of social services that was occurring at the time in the fields of insurance, health care and education. To draw out all the relevant relationships would be an enormously complex task. However, it is appropriate to stress the importance to state officials of civilian morale during wartime. The OPWC press announcement quoted above implied a need to do something about elderly people because they could undermine the morale of younger relatives. The evacuation scheme introduced after the bombing raids of 1940 reflected a desire to improve in the air raid shelters. This concern with morale seemed to open the scope for change, especially once the initial danger from the German bombing had receded. It is interesting in this connection that elderly people were treated more generously in the later flying bomb attacks (54) when Britain was seen to be winning the war. It might indeed be suggested that sensitivity to the morale of the frail elderly increased when middle class elderly people became more likely to need state residential care. Not only was their family support disrupted by the war but labour shortages in the middle forties meant that it was difficult for them to obtain domestic servants to do the cooking, cleaning etc. (55) Many of them could afford to buy a place in a private home, but places here were also restricted. The OPWC casework service (56) reflected a massive demand from people trying to avoid P.A.I.'s. The perceived deleterious impact of this upon civilian morale was the major reason behind the extension of the home help scheme to include frail and sick elderly people in December 1944. (57)

Finally, we would argue that official concern with civilian morale provided an important lever for certain voluntary organisations to develop experiments in both residential care (e.g. the evacuation hostels) and domiciliary care (e.g. home help service, meals on wheels etc). In relation to residential care, perhaps the most important point to make about the evacuation hostels is that, despite their modest numbers, they developed a positive view of residential care. State officials may have believed that P.A.I.'s were the right place for frail elderly people but we know of no evidence that this view was shared by elderly people themselves. The evacuation hostels, however, offered a very different image of residential care, as pictured through such articles as the one by Rackstraw (1944). They were small, homelike and represented no loss of liberty. This positive image of residential care was also presented by Bevan in the second reading of the 1948 National Assistance Bill: he combined this with a view that places should be available on demand. There was no suggestion that access to such homes should be restricted to the very frail who lacked family support. The voluntary organisations after the war went further, to advocate as a key virtue of small residential homes that they reduced the burden on the younger generation. For example, in December 1945 the WVS announced the building of a series of residential clubs, because of the housing shortage, with the claim that "provision of homes of this kind will also give many young people a chance to start or resume their married lives, interrupted by the war, without the additional pressure of elderly relatives". (58) The Last Refuge (Townsend 1962) stressed the extent to which this positive image was not turned into a concrete reality. Residential care too often remained a form of provision for the frail isolated elderly in large buildings that were years out of date or miles from the rest of the community. The question one must ask. is whether unsatisfactory provision was inevitable and whether

From Public Assistance Institutions to 'Sunshine Hotels'

it will always be so.

NOTES

The material referred to in this paper has been collected largely from the department files of the Ministry of Health. There are two main sources. The main body of the pre 1952 material is located in the Public Records Office. It will be referred to in the notes as PRO files and the PRO index number will follow. However, much of the relevant material is still located at the Department of Health and Social Security, whose files are presently being processed prior to handover to the PRO. These files will be referred to in the notes as DHSS files and their original departmental index number will follow: they will be given a new number on transfer to the PRO.

1. Quoted in Royal Commission on the Poor Laws, The Majority Report, H.M.S.O., London, 1908, p.214.
2. For a general discussion of the lack of provision for the chronic sick in this period see Abel-Smith, B. The Hospitals, 1800-1948, Heinemann, London. 1964.
3. These reports are reviewed in MacIntyre, S. Old Age as a Social Problem, pp. 44-67 from Health Care and Health Knowledge edit. by R. Dingwall et.al Croom Helm, London, 1977.
4. Birmingham Post, June 27th, 1940.
5. City of Birmingham, Public Assistance Committee: Handbook and Diary, 1940, p.15.
6. Matthews, O, Housing the Infirm, published by the author and originally distributed through W.H. Smith and Son, undated.
7. DHSS files, 94003/2A. Public Assistance Institution. Reception and Welfare
8. DHSS files, 94003/7/5. Poor Law Amendment Act 1938: Representations by Associations of Local Authorities.
9. The Lancet, Infection in the Shelter, October 12th, 1940, p.455.
10. Quoted in Titmuss (op.cit), p.450. For an account of shelter conditions and how this led to setting up of the committee see Lord Horder, The Modern Troglodyte, The Lancet, April 19th, 1941, pp.499-502.
11. PRO files, HLG 7/395, Care of the Homeless: Accommodation of Aged and Infirm, memorandum from Wrigley to Lindsay, dated 12th April, 1941.

From Public Assistance Institutions to 'Sunshine Hotels'

12. Ministry of Health (1940), Circular 2060, Evacuation of Civil Population - Special Scheme. A copy of circular and other relevant information is in DHSS files, 94003/1/47, Public Assistance Institutions - General.
13. DHSS file 94003/5/4C, Inmates: Clothing: Memor C.G.183.
14. Nuffield Foundation. Old People, Report of a Survey Committee on the Problem of Ageing and the Care of Old People under the chairmanship of B. Seebohm Rowntree, Arno Press, New York, 1980 edition
15. These clippings are collected in DHSS files 99063/3/2, Social Welfare: Aged and Infirm: General Correspondence.
16. Nuffield Foundation (op.cit.), p.75.
17. PRO files, NLG 7/322, Evacuation of Aged and Infirm. Memorandum from Howell James (Chief General Inspector, Min. of Health) to Ure (Assistance Board), dated 23rd January 1941. These figures are contained in Memorandum R.O.A.737 entitled Hostels for Old People, dated 21st July 1942.
18. Age Concern Archives. Box One, Historical and Early Activities. Pamphlet on L.C.C. Rest Homes dated November 1941.
19. PRO files, HLG 7/395 (op.cit.), Minutes of Committee on the Aged and Infirm, dated 12th March 1941. Memorandum from P. Barter to Sir Arthur Rucker, dated 5th May 1941.
20. For a description of the setting up of the OPWC see Roberts, N. (op.cit.), pp.30-40.
21. PRO files, AST.7/557, Welfare: Homes and Hostels. See correspondence between P. Barter (Ministry of Health) and Stuart King (Assistance Board) between August and October 1941.
22. Ibid, for copy of speech of Lord Soulbury (Chairman, Assistance Board) to NCSS conference on "The Welfare of the Aged", dated 31st December 1941.
23. Age Concern Archives. Box Two, Historical and Early Activities. Letter from Stuart King (Assistance Board) to Secretary, NCSS dated 22nd September 1941.
24. DHSS files, 99063/11/1A, Social Welfare: National Council of Social Service: General Correspondence and Executive Committee 1940-1946. Minutes of meeting between Ministry of Health officials and representatives of Public Assistance Departments from the London Region, dated 24th April 1942.
25. Ibid, memorandum from Turner, dated 28th January 1943.
26. Ibid, memorandum from Lindsay, dated 23rd

From Public Assistance Institutions to 'Sunshine Hotels'

September 1942.
27. Beveridge Report. Social Insurance and Allied Services, Cmd 6404, H.M.S.O., London, 1942
28. DHSS files, 99063/3/5, Accommodation For and Care of the Aged. Contains copy of C.G.1. 115, dated 4th September 1945.
29. Margaret Hill was a member of the OPWC. She describes her wartime experiences of running hostels in Hill, M. An Approach to Old Age, Oliver and Boyd, Edinburgh, 1961, pp.23-39.
30. DHSS files, 99063/3/9. Hostels for the Aged: Correspondence with the National Association of Administrators of Local Government Establishments
31. DHSS files 99063/3/2. Social Welfare: Aged and Infirm: General Correspndence. Memorandum from Association of Municipal Corporations dated 12th April 1946.
32. Ibid. Memorandum from Miss Ramsey (Secretary, NOPWC) dated 23rd July 1946.
33. Ibid. Memorandum from National Association of Local Government Social Welfare Officers, dated 7th October 1946.
34. DHSS files 99063/3/17. Social Welfare: Aged and Infirm: Aged Policy During Interim Period.
35. Ministry of Health (1947), Circular 49/47, Care of the Aged in Public Assistance Homes and Institutions. A copy of this circular and further background material can be found in DHSS files 99063/3/17. (op.cit.).
36. Curtis Report. Report of the Care of Children Committee, Cmd 6922, H.M.S.O., London, 1946. This had been very critical of the treatment of children in care by public assistance institutions and other types of state institutional provision.
37. DHSS files 99063/3/17 (op.cit.), Minutes of meeting dated 9th October 1947.
38. Hansard, Parliamentary Debates, House of Commons, Vol.444, 24th November 1947, Columns 1603-1718.
39. PRO files, MH 80/47. Reference to the setting up of the Rucker Committee is given in "National Assistance Bill: Memorandum of the Minister of Health and the Minister of National Insurance", dated March 1946.
40. PRO files CAB 134/698. A copy of the Rucker Report is attached to the Minutes of the Seventh Meeting of the Social-Services Committee, dated 12th July 1946.
41. These press comments are collected in DHSS files, 94018/1/23 on Break Up of the Poor Law: Press Comments.

From Public Assistance Institutions to 'Sunshine Hotels'

42.   Hansard: Parliamentary Debates, House of Commons, Vol.444, 24th November 1947, Column 1609.
43.   These press comments are also found in DHSS files, 9408/1/23 (op.cit.).
44.   See PRO files MH 80/47, especially paper by S.F. Wilkinson (Assistant Secretary, Ministry of Health) on "The Break Up of the Poor Law and the Care of Children and Old People", dated February 1944.
45.   PRO files CAB 134/698, Minutes of the Tenth Meeting of the Social Services Committee, dated 25th September 1946.
46.   DHSS files, 94018/1/3. Break Up of the Poor Law: National Assistance Bill: The Grant-Aiding of Local Authority Services Under the Bill.
47.   Ibid. Letters from Dalton, dated 8th and 17th October, 1947.
48.   Ibid. Letter from Dalton to Bevan, dated 21st October 1947. PRO files CAB 80/49 is also a useful source of information about the grant aiding arguments.
49.   A copy of this press report can be found in DHSS files, 94018/1/23 (op.cit.).
50.   Hansard: Parliamentary Debates, House of Commons, Vol.444, 24th November 1947, Column 1611.
51.   Hansard: Parliamentary Debates, House of Commons, Vol. 5th March 1948, Column 752.
52.   Assistance Board. Report of the Assistance Board for the Year Ended 31st December 1945, Cmd, H.M.S.O., London 1945.
53.   Age Concern Archives Box One - Historical and Early Activities. Undated Press Release signed by E. Rathbone.
54.   PRO files, HLG 7/333, Evacuation (1944): Aged and Infirm Persons Policy.
55.   Concern about lack of domestic servants was so great that a committee was set up to look at post war prospects, see Ministry of Labour and National Service. Report on Post-War Organisation of Private Domestic Employment, Cmd 6650, H.M.S.O., 1948. London.
56.   Age Concern Archives. Various material in Boxes 1 - 4, Historical and Early Activities.
57.   DHSS files, 99063/8/1A. Social Welfare: Domestic Help to Householders: Discussions with the Ministry of Labour and National Service.
58.   DHSS files, 99073/1/4. Homes for the Aged: W.V.S. Residential Clubs for Elderly People.

From Public Assistance Institutions to 'Sunshine Hotels'

REFERENCES

Lord Amulree (1951) <u>Adding Life to Years</u>, N.C.S.S., London.

Brown, M. (1972) <u>The Development of Local Authority Services from 1948-1965 under Part III of the National Assistance Act</u>, unpublished Ph.D thesis, University of Manchester.

Crowther, M. (1981) <u>The Workhouse System 1834-1929</u>, Batsford, London.

Digby, A. (1978) <u>Pauper Palaces</u>, Routledge and Kegan Paul, London.

Engels, F. (1969) <u>The Conditions of the Working Class in England</u>, Panther, London 1969 edition.

Gilbert, B. (1970) <u>British Social Policy 1919-39</u>, Batsford, London.

Marsh, D. (1965) <u>The Changing Social Structure of England and Wales, 1871-1961</u>, Routledge and Kegan Paul, London.

McEwan P. and Laverty, S. (1949) <u>The Chronic Sick and Elderly in Hospitals</u>, Bradford (B) Hospital Management Committee.

Myles, J. (1981) <u>The Aged and the Welfare State: An Essay in Political Demography</u>. Paper prepared for the Research Committee on Ageing, International Sociological Association, July 8th-9th 1981.

Phillipson, C. <u>The Emergence of Retirement</u> Working Papers in Sociology (No.14), University of Durham, undated.

Rackstraw, M. (1944) An Old People's Hostel, originally published in January by <u>Social Work (London)</u> Reprinted by OPWC.

Riley, D. (1979) War in the Nursery, <u>Feminist Review No.2.</u>

Riley, D. (1981) 'The Free Mothers': Prenatalism and Working Women in Industry at the end of the last war in Britain, <u>History Workshop Journal</u> No.11.

Roberts, N. (1970) <u>Our Future Selves</u>, Allen and Unwin, London.

Samson, E. (1944) <u>Old Age in the New World</u>, Pilot Press, London.

Titmuss, R. <u>Problems of Social Policy</u>, History of the Second World War, H.M.S.O., London 1976 edition.

Townsend, P. (1962) <u>The Last Refuge</u>, Routledge and Kegan Paul, London.

Williams, K. (1981) <u>From Pauperism to Poverty</u>, Routledge and Kegan Paul, London.

Chapter Thirteen

SHORT TERM RESIDENTIAL CARE FOR ELDERLY PEOPLE: AN
ANSWER TO GROWING OLDER

Peter McCoy

An interesting feature of contemporary social policy
is the phenomenon of "reborn certainties". The prevalence of (and subsequent un-researched demise of)
fashions in the provision of care is disturbing. A
buzz phrase is coined - generic social work, intensive home help scheme, intake, care for the carers.
Suddenly everyone must do it and later, but equally
suddenly, no one is doing it any more. Short term
care is a good example of this process. The first
reference available to short term care is in a
Circular (Ministry of Health 1957) dated 7th October
1957, which comments on a Survey of Services available to the Chronic Sick and Elderly in 1954-55,
noting:

> "the survey brought out the great value, for
> chronically ill or infirm old people, of a
> short stay in hospital or Part III accommoda-
> tion as appropriate, as a means of giving the
> relatives with whom they normally reside a rest
> or holiday break and the old people themselves
> a change of environment and routine. The
> Minister hopes that both hospital authorities
> and local authorities will extend their
> arrangement in this direction as freely as
> their commitments allow. Experience in areas
> in which they have been tried shows they are
> greatly appreciated and that they may prevent
> a complete breakdown of the arrangements for
> looking after the old people at home, which
> would result in their needing long term care".
> (para 11, p.4)

Short term care continued to be mentioned occasionally in favourable contexts. For example, A Happier
Old Age, (D.H.S.S., 1978)

227

"Although residential homes are at present
used primarily for long term care, many feel
that, where possible, they should be used to
help enable an old person to return to a more
independent life in the community. This requires prior planning, and the availability of
adequate medical and rehabilitation provision,
also regular reviews of progress towards re-
settlement. It has been suggested that social
workers who arrange admission to residential
homes should maintain regular contact with
residents and play an active part in plans for
their return to their own homes, the homes of
relatives or sheltered accommodation. Comments
would be welcome on ways in which the emphasis
on rehabilitation can be strengthened and on
the roles of social workers and others in this
process."

(para. 5.11 pp.3a)

However, by the time <u>Growing Older</u> (D.H.S.S., 1981)
appears, short stay provision is elevated to the
status of one of the five sub-headings in the three
pages on Social Services, on a par with "care in
residential homes" and "quality of life". It has
reached this elevated position, as far as I can see,
merely by growing in size. Even the final proviso -
that further research is being commissioned - must
be treated with some caution, given the reception by
D.H.S.S. Ministers of research work like the Black
Report, (Black, 1981) and the dissolution of the
Personal Social Services Council, which had a significant research role to play.

This national emphasis is often repeated at the
local authority level. For example my own Authority
had no policy on short term care during the late
1970s, while the number of such placements increased
by 350%. Then in 1981 it decided on a policy of
using 25% of the beds for short term care. It is
perhaps worth remarking that the level of services
in Suffolk is not high, the level of residential
beds per 1000 population aged 75 or over being lower
now than in 1970. Since the number of residential
places is a very simplistic measure, it can also be
pointed out that Suffolk's Social Services Budget is
22% less than the Personal Social Services Component
of Suffolk's Grant Related Expenditure assessment.

Both the national and local level data thus
lead to the suggestion that the organisation's
economic needs over-ride the clients' needs,

especially where fashionable policy seems to reflect the reborn certainty of the appropriateness
of short term care. I would argue that soundly
based research using national and local data and presented in an objective way to decision makers, is an
important means of helping to make old age in a
changing society a dignified and rewarding stage in
the life cycle, rather than the long dark tunnel at
the end of the light which many find it today.

BACKGROUND AND METHODOLOGY

The project from which this analysis is derived
arose out of a strategic review of services for
elderly people in Suffolk (McCoy 1980), in the process of which the growth of short term care placements in the Authority's Part III Homes was noted.
(See Table 1) Over the period in question the
Department had no declared policy on short term care,
so the growth was a "grass roots" one. However, the
overall growth masked different rates and phases of
growth within the six geographical divisions of
Suffolk, and at the time of the strategic review,
different managers held contrasting views about the
objectives, efficiency and desirability of the
practice. Short term care therefore seemed a suitable topic for a research project.
    At this stage contact was made with Isobel
Allen of the Policy Studies Institute, London and
 Duncan Boldy and Diana Kuh of the Institute of
Biometry, University of Exeter. It was agreed that
"short term residential care" was a catch phrase,
embracing a wide range of people entering care for
a wide range of reasons, and that it could be seen,
probably differently, from a variety of different
positions - that of management, of heads of homes,
of placing social workers, of residents and of the
elderly person's primary carer - that person who did
most for her or him when the resident was not in
short term care.
    My position as a member of a Social Service
Department gave me two advantages. Firstly, access
to data was comparatively easy to arrange; secondly,
as the Department had funded a research post, as
against a particular project, it was possible, subject to the decision of the management team, to
carry out this enquiry over a long period, thus
turning it into a longitudinal study. Short term
residential care was defined in relationship to anyone going into a local authority Part III home and
coming out again alive (other than going on to

Table 1. Short Stay and Long Stay Admissions 1972 – 1980 Suffolk and England
Expressed as an Index (1972 = 100)

		1972	1973	1974	1975	1976	1977	1978	1979	1980	1981	1982
SUFFOLK	SHORT STAY	100	116	137	167	193	286	397	446	519	664	706
	LONG STAY	100	115	99	112	107	106	82	93	86	77	109*
ENGLAND	SHORT STAY	100	112	122	130	144	148	179	184	210		
	LONG STAY	100	106	104	102	106	99	99	94	98		

Source: D.H.S.S. Returns   * Figures distorted by opening of a new home.

hospital). However, since a prime interest of the
study was the connection between long term and short
term care, any admissions to a Part III home were
used as the basic unit of data, and these were subsequently sub-divided into different categories.
The project was piloted in one division, starting on
1st April 1980 and was extended to cover a further
4 out of the remaining 5 divisions, for a year, from
1st October 1981. The findings presented in the
following paper relate to the first eighteen months
of the project, in one division.

FINDINGS

In the period in question (1st April, 1980 - 30th
September, 1981) there were 625 admissions of 362
people to residential care in local authority Part
III Homes. It is possible to sub-divide them into
four categories as follows:- Short Stay - those
people who had one or more stays and at the end of
the study were still "in the community"; Immediate
Long Stay - those people who were admitted either
for up to three months' assessment or for immediate
long term care, without prior short term care;
Eventual Long Stay - those people who were admitted
for one or more periods of short term care, at any
time in the past, and were subsequently admitted for
up to three months or for immediate long term care;
Others - those people who had moved out of Suffolk,
died during an up to three months assessment period
or left a home during such a period.

The first important set of findings demonstrates the basic similarity of people in all three
main categories on dependency factors. There were
no significant differences between people in the
three major categories for age, mobility or self
care ability. The average ages on (last) admission
for all categories was 82, a finding consistant with
those of other studies (Allen 1982, Kuh and Boldy,
1981). Furthermore, no differences were found in
mobility scores, based on an assessment of the residents' ability to walk, nor on self care scores,
based on the scale developed for the Chronically
Sick and Disabled Persons surveys (Harris, Cox &
Smith, 1971). The only individual factor that did
distinguish between the short term and the two long
term categories was mental state: a higher proportion of short term care residents were rated "alert"
whereas a higher proportion of residents in both
long term categories were rated "confused" and "very

Table 2. Factors Distinguishing Short Stay From Long Stay Placements.

	Short Stay	Immediate Long Stay	Eventual Long Stay
Scored 6 or more on self care scale	47%	52%	44%
Has mobility problems	50%	61%	52%
Confused or very Confused	5%	19%	17%
Admitted from Hospital	5%	53%	25%
Lives Alone	38%	59%	67%
Lives with Sibling	9%	22%	13%
Lives with Spouse	38%	7%	9%
Lives with Sons or Daughters	50%	20%	32%
Sons or Daughters Distant	10%	22%	15%
In Privately Owned Property	43%	31%	27%
In Sheltered Housing	11%	20%	16%

confused".

Where the categories showed significant differences was in structural rather than personal characteristics. The process of admission was clearly important. Those residents who were admitted from hospital were more likely to receive long term care than people admitted from their normal residence. It is worth noting that residents admitted from hospital were slightly (but not significantly) younger on average, were no less mobile, and no more dependent than residents admitted from their own home. Again the only significant difference was in mental state.

A further differentiating factor was the household composition of the resident's normal home. Those who lived alone were more likely to receive long term care, whereas those who lived with other adults only were more likely to receive short term care. Those who were living with their spouse, or with a son or daughter were more likely to receive short term care; those who lived with a sibling, or whose sons or daughters lived away from that part of Suffolk (Western Division) were more likely to receive long term care.

Another relevant variable was the type of housing occupied by the resident. Those living in privately owned property were more likely to receive short term care, and this was true even if they were not the owner. A higher proportion of residents from Sheltered Housing went into long term care than went into short term care but this was only significant at the 90% level. There was however no difference in dependency, mobility or mental state between those persons from sheltered housing and those from other forms of accommodation, though they were slightly (but not significantly) older.

Table 2. lists these factors

DISCUSSION

These findings, which may cause some surprise in Social Services Department and D.H.S.S., are not unexpected when viewed from a sociological standpoint. According to a study conducted in 1963, the chances of institutionalisation could be plotted on a familial situation gradient (Townsend and Wedderburn, 1965). Nearly twenty years on, precisely the same factors are at work, producing what Townsend (1981) calls the structured dependency of old age. The project reported here stresses that the key role is played not by physical incapacity but by structural factors, particularly by hospital placement but also to a lesser degree by placement in Sheltered Housing, a form of accommodation which featured significantly in Townsend's earlier survey of residential institutions and homes for the aged (Townsend, 1964). Where forms of residential facilities for elderly people are controlled by three separate authorities - health, social services and housing - as part of wider responsibilities, it would be surprising if the needs of the organisations were not sometimes at variance with the needs of the individuals. These data show clearly that organisational rather than individual differences continue strongly to influence placement. Despite the clear evidence over the years, this is ignored in most policy statements on care of the elderly, such as Growing Older (D.H.S.S. 1981), which concentrate on marginal activities - a few hours' more home help or volunteer visiting, a fortnight's short term care - in the hope that they will have a significant impact on processes that have been inexorably developing over eighty to ninety years.

Although that is the major point of this analysis, there are several others worth mentioning briefly. First, are we taking services from established clients in order to bestow them on new clients with demanding relatives ? The view has been expressed that the use of scarce resources (beds in local Authority Homes) for short term care would be better used to benefit people who need long term care. The project so far clearly demonstrates that a significant proportion of the short term care residents are different from those who enter permanently: but it also demonstrates that these different short term care residents have nearly all been receiving some form of domiciliary or day care services from Health or Social Services or Voluntary Organisations. Only 6% received no other service, and half of them were living with their next of kin. Over 50% received home help, for example, and there are no significant differences in this respect between the short stay or either category of long stay residents. Thus the development of short stay residential placement must be seen as an extension of the service labelled domiciliary or day care into the residential establishment, a development also found in day care itself. However, a bed allocated to short term residents cannot also be allocated to a long term resident, and Table 1 shows for Suffolk that, as the number of short term admissions rose, the number of long term admissions fell. It is

worth noting that the crucial element in planning
services is how many vacancies occur, not how many
places there are.

Given that this policy developed in a central
policy vacuum, it is perhaps worth looking briefly
at the views of the people involved at various
levels.

Managers

From the interviews with those involved in managing
the process of short term placements it seems fair
if somewhat critical to say they all felt it to be
a good thing but were not really sure why. A variety of positive reasons were given for the policy.
It was said to be preventive, to liven up the home,
and to foster links with the community: all reasons
which, it could be argued, other services (for
instance, day care) could meet without the loss of
long term beds.

Furthermore, very few managers had a systematic
data base (a point again emphasised at the national
level, where Isobel Allen found little detail available on the financial effects): yet there was no
shortage of strong opinions. Paradoxically, as the
Suffolk data shows, if there is one thing Local
Authorities do rigorously it is to assess, charge,
record and cumulate charges and cost data. The data
I collected shows that short term care raises unit
costs, lowers income and lowers occupancy, but has
little impact on the relatively fixed costs of an
establishment.

Heads of Homes

Interviews with Heads of Homes revealed strong
support for short term care, as part of a package of
services where the Home and the elderly in the
community come in contact before a long term admission is made. It is relevant that Suffolk is a
dispersed County, with decentralised powers, a low
level of day care but a fair number of beds in each
Division, thus allowing flexibility. The heads saw
short term care as part of a domiciliary package,
and considered this aspect of service delivery by a
local Home - particularly where local Social Workers
tended to specialise - to be very important. In
their view, the biggest drawback was that the staffing structure of the Homes involved only three
managerial posts, thus making it harder for them to
develop the wide role in the community that they
felt to be necessary. Heads of Homes particularly
welcomed the flow of information that the expanded

admission forms had generated, but often critised the assessment of physical capabilities as misleading.

Social Workers

For a category of workers whose role as gatekeepers is crucial to the functioning of a short term care policy, Social Workers had a more ambivalent view, not sharing wholeheartedly the "preventive" belief of managers, nor the "resource centre" views that some Heads of Homes entertained for their establishments. A number had strongly negative views of Homes, or of a Home, However, they were aware that short term beds were more easily available than many other facilities, and some considered them better than nothing to bridge the gaps in normal care patterns. Social Workers countered the criticisms of Heads of Homes about physical assessment by saying that the assessment was for a different purpose. The Head of Home needed to know what additional demands, if any, a particular admission would make on staff. The Social Worker needed to assess whether or not the services available were sufficient to maintain elderly people in the community: it did not matter whether they could really climb the stairs, or were as continent and alert as their carers said they were, as long as their carers could and would continue to cope with the situation.

These considerations suggest that there are organisational and career development aspects to the emergence of short term care. Nevertheless, it must also be pointed out that over a third of all short term care residents had had three or more such stays, and that the Social Worker concerned saw their future as one of continuing short term care placements rather than of long term care. The only point of total agreement between these categories of worker was that short term care was of significant benefit to the primary carers of the old people admitted, if not to the residents themselves.

Residents and their Relatives

A small sample of residents and primary carers were interviewed, by a C.Q.S.W. student on final placement, in the two largest Divisions involved in the study. Most comments by residents were favourable, though not unreservedly so. Those who lived alone particularly commented on the food, several of those who lived with carers stressed the value of a break for them, and nearly all made some favourable comments about the care staff.

Such comments have to be set against the general
fairly low level of expectations of residents. One
lady, totally blind, went in for a week's short stay
when her home help went on holiday. To start with
she stoutly maintained that it had been a wonderful
holiday: it later transpired, however, that all had
not been too well, that she had felt too embarrassed
to ask staff to show her to the toilet, and that few
people had talked to her. Even so her closing comments to the interviewer were "Tell the Council I've
said good things about it please".

The interviews with a small sample of primary
carers suggested that by no means all of them saw
short term care as the unqualified benefit that
Growing Older (D.H.S.S., 1981) proclaimed, or that
the professionals believed it to be. Some regarded
it as little more than a rationing process. The
example which follows illustrates that there are
families for whom short term care is not the answer
to growing older:

> The primary carers of Mr Y. (aged 70) are Mr B.
> his son (39) and Mrs B. (36). They have two
> small children (8 and 10) and live approximate-
> ly 30 minutes walk from Mr Y's small flat.
> According to his son, the old gentleman has
> never been an easy person to get along with: he
> was a bossy and unappreciative man demanding to
> be waited on hand and foot. Shortly after his
> wife's death, on his 70th birthday, Mr Y.
> decided to remain in bed until he too died. He
> refused food and drink and only got up to go to
> the toilet. His son visited him daily, before
> and after work, while his wife kept the flat
> clean, shopped, cooked and generally kept
> house. With two small children and a part-time
> job it was a difficult task. She began to
> resent the fact that her husband's younger
> sister did little to help, and neither did the
> other two brothers. Mr Y. was finally admitted
> to the psychiatric hospital. Three months
> later he was discharged (after a case confer-
> ence attended by his son) and declared fit to
> live by himself. It soon became evident,
> however, that this was not the case. He refus-
> ed a home help and meals on wheels and the
> earlier routine of helping him daily began
> again. This time his son was not prepared to
> risk his marriage and family life: "My father
> had his life. We never got on and I don't see
> why I should sacrifice my marriage, deprive my

young children of my time and ruin my health for him now. I do care about him and want him to be happy. He wants to go in to long term care as soon as possible, which would help everyone. Short term care is alright for some but not us. What happens when he returns ? He had only been back a day or two when he went back to his old ways, refusing food etc. If only people could see the strain he puts us under. Please ask in your report for the whole family to be assessed before putting old people on a waiting list for a permanent place. We look alright on paper. Dad is physically fit and we are young. But that's not all that matters, is it ?"

It would seem, then, that beneath the blandness of the statistical data there are people with a real need for help, calling for the sensitive development of a range of activities rather than for a single administratively convenient solution to all problems.

NOTES

1. House of Commons. Minutes of evidence taken before the Social Services Committee, 31st March, 1982, p.64.

REFERENCES

Allen, Isobel (1982) Short-stay Residential Care for the Elderly Policy Studies Institute, London.
Black, Sir Douglas (1981) Inequalities in Health D.H.S.S.
D.H.S.S. (1978) A Happier Old Age H.M.S.O.
D.H.S.S. (1981) Growing Older H.M.S.O.
Harris, A.J., Cox, E. and Smith, R.W. (1971) Handicapped and Impaired in Great Britain H.M.S.O.
Kuh, Diana and Boldy, Duncan, (1981) The Evaluation of Short Term Care for the Elderly in Resident- ial Homes Institute of Biometry and Community Medicine, Exeter
McCoy, Peter (1980) Towards a Strategy for Services to the Elderly in Suffolk Suffolk County Council.
Ministry of Health (1957) Local Authority Services for the Chronically Sick and Infirm Circular 14/57 H.M.S.O.

Townsend, P. (1964) <u>The Last Refuge</u> Routledge and
    Kegan Paul, London
Townsend, P. and Wedderburn, D. (1965) <u>The Aged in
    the Welfare State</u> Bell, London
Townsend, P. (1981) "The Structured Dependency of the
    Elderly: a creation of social policy in the
    Twentieth Century" <u>Ageing and Society</u> Vol. 1
    No.1 p5-28.

Chapter Fourteen

A PROFILE OF RESIDENTIAL LIFE: A DISCUSSION OF KEY
ISSUES ARISING OUT OF CONSUMER RESEARCH IN ONE
HUNDRED OLD-AGE HOMES

Dianne Willcocks, Sheila Peace and Leonie Kellaher

BACKGROUND

The research on which this chapter is based was originally requested by the Department of Health and
Social Security in order to provide data for a re-
vision of the Local Authority Building Note concerning the design of old people's homes (DHSS, 1973).
Interest in the accommodation and environmental
requirements of the residential elderly has been
prompted by a growing body of evidence concerning
the effect of physical environment on the quality of
life of those who live in old people's homes
(Lawton, 1970; Lawton, 1980; Lipman, 1968). A study
was therefore commissioned to provide a systematic
investigation of the relationship between design and
location factors; the social atmosphere of homes;
and demographic characteristics of the residential
mix in a sample of one hundred Local Authority
homes (Willcocks et al, 1982).
    The aim of the sponsors was to encourage Local
Authority architects to design residential homes
which provide a harmonious living environment for
the elderly, and the research requirement was to
obtain reliable information on which to base professional policy and practice. The Survey Research
Unit at the Polytechnic of North London, in conjunction with NOP Market Research Ltd., were commissioned to undertake the project. It involved interviewing at 100 old people's homes in an attempt to
identify the environment and accommodation requirements from the perspective of the elderly residents.
    Over the years researchers have identified a
wide range of needs within the residential world
(see, for example Townsend 1962; Meacher 1972),
thereby contributing to the formulation of policies
which offer a response to these needs. Yet there

remains disturbing evidence of the limited effectiveness of the residential service in contributing
to the life satisfaction of elderly people (Peace et
al, 1979; Hughes et al, 1980). It appears that
there is a policy gap, a mismatch between the intentions of those who formulate policy and the day-to-
day experience of the residential consumer, even
though the recent White Paper on the elderly (DHSS
1981) includes an explicit reference to the potential contribution of imaginative design to the well-
being of residential clients.

RESEARCH DESIGN

The research strategy stemmed from a concern to explore the key determinants of the residential process: characteristics of physical environment;
characteristics of institutional environment; and
the mix of old people within each home. But in addition it set out to address the central problems of
first measuring the attitudes of residents towards
the homes in which they presently live and, second,
identifying their environmental preferences in an
'ideal world' situation.
    We began by adopting a multi-stage sampling
procedure to secure a representative sample of
homes. Outline data was collected on one thousand
homes in twenty-nine Local Authorities from the
following sources: DHSS RA2 returns; postal questionnaires to Social Services departments; postal
questionnaires to individual homes. We thus ensured
adequate representation, in terms of: a rural-urban
spectrum; by region; by size of home; by style of
construction; by level of expenditure within the
Local Authority; and by the nature of the 'regime'
within the home. We then selected a sample of one
hundred homes for further study.
    Interviews were carried out with a represent-
ative sample of ten residents in each home. Dependency was assessed using the Crichton Royal Behavioural Rating Scale (Wilkin & Jolley 1979). Fieldwork
was split into two time periods: 50 homes were studied in June 1980 and a further 50 in November 1980.
In addition to the residents, four hundred staff
were interviewed: half were care staff and half
supervisory staff. Also an appraisal of physical
design and level of amenity in each home was undertaken by a social researcher and an interviewer
checklist was used to elicit the reactions of a
"surrogate visitor" to each home. Finally, in a

sub-sample of homes observation and location studies were conducted to look at social interaction patterns and the daily routine and to explore the relationship between the residential home and the local environs.

An innovative extension of the resident interview was the playing of what we termed the 'ideal-home' Visual Game (Willcocks, 1981). This was a card game devised to stimulate the critical faculties of our often frail and confused elderly respondents and enable them to adopt the role of 'environmental decision-maker'. The aim was to generate a list of environmental features representing consumer preferences for inclusion in the revised Building Note.

This combination of investigative tools and research techniques enabled us to create a multi-dimensional profile of residential homes together with profiles of the people who live and work in them.

RESEARCH FINDINGS

In order to elucidate the processes at work within old-age institutions we begin by examining these profiles of residential life. We then proceed to describe social interactions and activities in and around the residential setting, and finally we develop evaluations of the environment based on residents' consumer choice and statements of preference. These results are summarised below:

1. We found that a significant factor in the macro-environment of homes is the recent tendency to provide larger and more complex designs. This has increased the likelihood of projecting an "institutional" image which in turn has implications for the way in which the community perceives the residential home. Within the increasingly complex structure of the home there does appear to have been a spatial gain by residents in terms of public sitting space and increased provision of single rooms - but the cost of this is complexity and there may be a loss of comprehensibility of the environment as a whole. Small group living, as a device which attempts to scale down and simplify large and complicated environments, has been introduced as homes have become larger.

2. Much of our data on residents characteristics confirms trends that have been reported elsewhere. We found that three-quarters of residents are women;

that men tend to be younger; and yet that men have spent slightly longer in care. This suggests that the admissions process for men may be qualitatively different from that for women. The evidence shows that for women 'loss of home' may be a more problematic experience than for men insofar as more women were previously living alone or in circumstances where they controlled their domestic world. Men were more likely than women to be living in a shared household or alternative institutional setting where entry into care is perhaps less threatening to self-image and less likely to mean loss of identity (Willcocks, 1982). We found little evidence that homes have been able to introduce positive measures to mitigate the harsher effects of re-location from community to residential home. Only one-third of the residents had made a prior visit to the home before admission and just one in five residents was offered a choice of home.

3.   Health states of residents were investigated by means of self-report and using Crichton Royal. We found that levels of impairment are increasing, as is the use of mobility aids. This has important implications for a whole range of issues from physical design requirements through staffing resources to more complex questions of the changing ethos of residential care.

4.   On staffing, we were able to chart the general ambivalence which surrounds the nature of the caring task and the role of residential social work. There appears to be lack of clarity concerning services required of both care staff and senior staff; and there is further uncertainty about the appropriate training needed to equip staff to fulfill their duties. Differing professional inputs can produce incoherent outcomes; in particular there appears to be a conflict between social work values and a medical model of care. An additional problem is the grading of care staff as manual workers, coupled with an expectation that they should attend to the social needs of their clients: this is liable to produce an untenable level of burden. Reflecting this, staff appear to be less secure in their work-role in homes adapted for small group-living.

5.   Resident interaction with the physical environment is for the most part mediated by staff, as is the execution of the most basic activities of daily living such as eating or bathing. These events tend to occur at organisationally appointed times in a manner that accords more closely with the needs of staff routine than with the wishes of residents.

Perhaps the most important constraint upon residents
is the likelihood of sharing a bedroom, at least in
the early stages of residence. Furthermore, choice
and variability in the use of space differs between
men and women, and in terms of length of residence.
Men are generally more physically active than women
and they are better able to assert "territorial
rights" both within the lounges and in sitting-areas
in hallways.
6. On the issue of resident activity, we found
that the majority of indoor recreational activities
are undertaken communally and are often staff-
initiated. The lack of private space in terms of
availability of single rooms and accessibility
throughout the day militate against the pursuit of
more independent and creative pastimes. Domestic
activities were also subject to constraint: relatively few homes appear to provide the facilities for
anything more than token activities, and where these
are possible their use is often subject to staff
approval.
     Outdoor activities are conspicuous by their
absence. Problems associated with resident frailty
and lack of mobility can present major obstacles.
Use of gardens tends to be limited and few residents
venture forth to enjoy local amenities.
7. An appraisal of the social environment revealed
that organisational arrangements and physical attributes of homes can actively promote or constrain the
development of meaningful inter-personal relationships. Thus, new friendships occur more frequently
in small homes and group homes, and in homes with a
high proportion of single rooms and a close integration between public and private living spaces.
We argue that this permits an element of control
over the nature and frequency of social interaction
which is conducive to new friendship formation.
     Small group living was shown to improve the
social climate of homes and also to make the physical environment more manageable for residents.
Groups can however become isolated one from another
unless an easily accessible communal meeting place
was provided. Level of provision within the small
group homes can be seen to encourage both domestic
and recreational activity amongst residents, although the group design is not a pre-requisite for
this more positive life-style.
     Although many good features emerged within the
small group homes, problems were also experienced.
Both residents and staff were less satisfied with
their living and working environments than other

respondents. For some residents the pressures of
small group living were great and they have preferred the relative anonymity of the larger group.
Staff may be less secure in their role within small
group homes. Many staff are untrained in the complexities of group work and - despite their support
for the system - experience increased strain in
their working life as they attempt to adapt to the
less institutional model. The small group concept
demands a degree of staff-resident interaction that
many are unprepared for and problems arise due to
group dominance, personality clashes, greater participation by relatives and misunderstandings over
expectations.
8.   The attitudes of old people to the residential
environment emerged when they took on the role of
'environmental decision-maker' in our card-game of
environmental attributes. Essentially, consumer
choice reflected a desire for the normal,the
unexceptional and the non-institutional, often
challenging conventional wisdom from professional
designers on such factors as the opening and
shutting doors and windows, and adjusting bedroom
radiators for themselves. They also seek the
relatively non-institutional privacy of a single
room and an ordinary bath. In contrast, aspects of
collective organisation such as shared bedrooms
receive low priority, as do the excessively institutional medibath and low-intensity nightlight.
      On the basis of the findings a series of prac-
tical recommendations has been developed which aims,
by reordering residential provision, to enhance the
quality of life for those living and working in old-
age homes.

RECOMMENDATIONS

In developing ideas for an alternative residential
life-style it is important to recognise that residents' control of the physical environment which
constitutes their home territory - and in many cases
represents the limits of their entire social world -
is virtually non-existent. Thus our prime aim is,
while maintaining necessary levels of physical and
social support, to restore residents' opportunity
to exercise environmental control. We found
residential life to be constructed around an assumption that residents will be prepared to live out
their remaining years in largely public settings in
the home. This accords with organisational impera-
tives and facilitates the efficient undertaking of

staff 'surveillance', a caring duty more confidently undertaken where residents are assembled collectively rather than dispersed. Our recommendations seek to reverse this emphasis, so that the focus of the home switches from public communal space to private personal space: the needs of the individual are given precedence over the needs of the group. We also advocate a positive development of the relationship between the home and the wider community; and the introduction of practical support for a new philosophy in residential living (which would imply organisational changes based on revitalised staff training programmes).

There are a number of ways in which a residential home might be designed to accommodate these various changes. We begin by proposing the establishment of a facility that we have termed the Residential Flatlet. This would provide the focal point of the home for an individual resident. In practice this would constitute a larger, more flexible version of the existing single room. It would differ from sheltered housing in as much as it would remain part of an essentially supportive environment: but it would nevertheless offer unmistakable personal territory, lockable from the inside, within which the resident would be firmly 'in control'. Occupancy of this type of facility would allow entry to residential care to correspond with 'moving house' rather than 'surrendering' to admission.

The residential flatlet would be large enough to accommodate some personal items of furniture - even sizeable items such as beds or sideboards - as well as all those personal possessions which evoke important memories and meanings. Sufficient space should also be allowed for residents to sit in comfort, alone or with visitors; and tea making equipment would be provided, though it is not envisaged that the living unit would contain more elaborate cooking facilities as the main catering would be undertaken centrally. However, there is no reason why a centrally prepared meal might not be eaten in the resident's own flatlet.

If the focus of activity in the home is transferred to the residential flatlet, then it would be necessary to build support services around it. We suggest that sanitary services should either become an integral part of the flatlet or adjacent to it. Within each room there would be minimum provision of a washbasin and vanitory unit but ideally, we would recommend a small connecting room containing a shower-plus-wash basin-plus-WC. Alternatively there could be an arrangement whereby two flatlets shared an intervening unit. Access might be direct or from the corridor but consideration should be given to night-time use of the WC since it is envisaged that the adjacent or integral unit would eliminate the necessity for commodes in residents' rooms.

We suggest that catering facilities - these could be provided at two levels - the one providing a regular central service and the other the flexibility of self-catering. Due to the increasing frailty of many residents it is suggested that central cooking and serving arrangements be retained, at least for two main meals a day. A large single dining-room was popular with residents in the survey and appeared to provide residents with a measure of stimulation and social contact. Such a setting not only provides a place for residents to meet at mealtimes but is also the room most likely to be used for communal activities and social functions.

However, there should also be a degree of flexibility over mealtimes and meal preparation. Whilst the residential flatlet would be supplied with electric sockets so that residents could boil a kettle when they wished, residents and their visitors will need somewhere to make snacks or a light breakfast. To provide for this, a small kitchenette and dining area should be available to serve a number of residential flatlets. Access to this area should not involve long walks nor be obstructed by heavy firedoors. It is recognised that most residents would not be able to undertake complicated food preparation, but provision of a kitchenette allows the resident, perhaps assisted by relatives or staff, the option of foregoing a meal and still having somewhere to prepare a snack.

We also recommend the provision of a large lounge to offer an alternative meeting place to the dining room, possibly incorporating part of the entrance hall. Such an area may have a colour TV set, possibly a bar, and would provide a gathering place, where residents could also receive their visitors. It could be of particular value to the older, more frail resident who seems to be more appreciative of large open spaces where interest can be stimulated. It would help avoid the potential problem of residents becoming isolated within their rooms.

KEY ISSUES IN RESIDENTIAL CARE

If the hub of homelife were to be centred around the individual's residential flatlet this would have major implications not only for the design and management of support services within the home, but also for the residential care service as a whole. A number of specific issues can be identified.

Quality of Life for Residents

The research has indicated that residents aspire towards self-determination in the ordinary activities of daily living: they demand a single room; they want to control their own physical environment; they do not look for increased participation in communal activities. A range of findings suggests that consumer satisfaction is enhanced where personal identity is respected and individual rights and freedoms are asserted. It is argued that within the framework of the residential flatlet this is more likely to be achieved.

Gender Differences in Residential Care

The study has shown that in many ways the residential process may be experienced in different ways by men and by women. Women tend to enter care at a later point in the ageing process and for different reasons from men. Consequently, problems of adjustment may prove more onerous for them. Women are less able to 'control' their daily routine in terms of moving around the building freely and participating in meaningful activities, either of a recreational or a domestic character. The quality of new social relationships developed in the home may not adequately meet their needs for friendship, and the nature of the residential visit may not be conducive to the continuation of intimate relationships with outside friends or family. Living in small groups offers the promise of an alternative life-style imbued with activity and meaning. In practice, however, this promise often fails to materialise, as a result of structural and organisational constraints. One means of compensating for problems resulting from 'loss of home' and the threat to the traditional domestic role and identity of women might be the more individual life-style associated with the residential flatlet.

Staff Job Satisfaction

Under present institutional arrangements a major
part of care staff time is taken up with the performance of physical care tasks and domestic chores;
little time is available to meet the social needs of
residents and indeed, there is much confusion about
the extent to which staff members could or should
allocate time for developing supportive social
relationships with residents.

An explicit requirement of the proposed change
would be a shift in the focus of staff behaviour,
allowing more time to be spent promoting self-care
and less time in block treatment in relation to
dining arrangements, toiletting or bathing. A personal programme should be designed for each resident.
Staff could then choose to specialise in a particular aspect of the total care task or evolve a more
varied and satisfying work pattern based on a range
of tasks. This is not to suggest that the physical
care task and domestic chores will disappear.
Residents would however be encouraged to retain
domestic and self-care skills where this is realistic. The broadening of the concept of care would,
it is suggested, ultimately prove more rewarding to
staff members.

The Unit of Operation

In an attempt to combat institutionalisation the
unit of operation for both residents and staff in
old people's homes has been progressively broken
down. This has led to the move to small group living with the aim of fostering a more domestic homely
environment. Yet the study shows that small group
living has, in the main, been only a partical
solution.

Although physical amenities may be much improved - more residents have single rooms - and the
social environment more liberal than in communal
homes, freedom in terms of choice and independent
living has not been much extended. Residents in
group living homes were just as likely to request
changes in bathing procedures and mealtimes were
often inflexible. The prospect of token liberalism
is ever present, and this situation is further
hindered by the impact of staff shortages and staff
changes which become magnified by the fragmentation
into groups. If the group system is to develop then
the attachment of particular staff to individual
units may be all important.

The small group approach demands a flexibility
and level of interaction that may appeal only to

certain types of resident and staff, and although it
may be an important option in residential care it is
one where the complexities should be fully recognised. What happens now is that even in small group
settings the individual remains secondary and that,
even given greater personal space, self-determination is often obstructed by group demands. Because
of this there is still a need to restore the balance
of residential living with the individual as the
unit of operation. Only then will groupings arise
from choice.

Community Integration

The improvement in institutional atmosphere which
might be achieved through the delineation of territory seems likely to result in a better general
image of the home. This would make visiting a more
meaningful and satisfying experience, whether it be
the maintenance of ties with kinfolk and the continuation of existing friendship patterns or the
development of new relationships between residents
and outside voluntary groups. The home would represent a more attractive and structured environment
for outsiders and the spatial arrangements inside
the home would promote social interaction in a more
meaningful atmosphere, either for individual exchanges or for group activities. Furthermore, it
is likely that the dignity and individuality accruing to residents with their own territory would
make it easier for them to establish new friendships.

A probable corollary of increasing visiting to
the home - bringing outsiders in - would be the
generation of increased interest and opportunity for
residents to venture outside the home for social
visiting.

The Home as a Community Resource

The way in which public and private space becomes
divided in the context of residential flatlets would
ensure that residents' territorial rights are not
violated by other, more temporary participants in
the community.

Day-Attenders Research suggests that the conflicting demands and expectations of residents and day-
attenders can have an effect on social relationships
within the home. Day-attenders may look at the
frailty and apathy of residents and fear for their
own future. At the same time, they may envy the
security and service offered by residential care and

make heavy demands on staff time while they are in
the home. Residents may perceive the day-attenders
as intruders and resent their encroachment on scarce
staffing resources.
 A residential flatlet style of living would
help to change, in a positive direction, the image
of the residents for outsiders coming in. The
provision of personal lockable space would protect
residents' rights. It might then be possible for
residents and day-attenders to forge social reala-
tionships as comparative equals, and for staff time
to be allocated more effectively to the different
requirements of each group.

Short-Stay For elderly people coming into a short-
stay bed, either for assessment purposes or for
'holiday relief', the provision of a residential
flatlet would offer a more flexible and less all-
consuming model of residential care. It would make
adjustment to the strange environment easier, since
the discontinuity between community life-style and
the residential life-style would be reduced; and it
would thus enable the maximum benefit to be derived
from the use of short-stay accommodation where it is
combined with long-stay care. It has been shown
(Allen 1982 and McCoy, this volume) that under
current arrangements this combined service can present major problems for staff.

Management of Integrated Dependency Levels
There is a sense in which a system based on residential flatlets might be regarded as a means of protecting the "fit" from the "unfit" and vice-versa,
whilst offering the potential for securing the
interests of both groups individually and reducing
conflict between them. This would provide one
possible framework for acting on recent evidence
(Evans et al, 1981) which advocates a mix of dependency levels.
 Where residential life is experienced predominantly in personal space it would be possible to adapt
rooms to the special needs of clients in a way that
would encourage them to retain whatever skills they
still possessed. In other words, aids and adaptations could be tailor-made and geared to individual
requirements.
 A further advantage of this more individualised
mode of living is that it would enable physical
caring tasks and medical care to be carried out in
privacy. The erosion of dignity associated with
certain treatments or procedures would thus be

reduced.

For mildly confused residents this revised arrangement offers a more focussed structure and the possibility of an increasing identification with social reality in a limited physical space. This can be used to reinforce meaningful aspects of a resident's former life. For those who are more severely disoriented and whose behaviour is potentially 'threatening', either to themselves or to other residents, the residential flatlet would provide a controlled environment in which their needs could be met with sensitivity.

Where staff are able to meet needs specific to the individual rather than adopting a style of care appropriate to some undifferentiated 'mass' of residents, it is suggested that there will be an improvement in morale for both staff and residents in the home.

CONCLUDING REMARKS

This discussion of key issues in the residential service suggests that the Residential Flatlet might offer one practical alternative to existing institutional arrangements, and could help to promote a dignified and less dependent style of living for elderly residents. It would appear to meet many of their physical and social needs; it would also create an environment which is more structured spatially, yet could offer greater potential for flexible use as a community resource, for short-term care and for day attenders. Problems of relocation and discontinuity of daily living patterns would be diminished and the maintenance of existing social and familial relationships could be maintained. Finally it should help to reduce the policy gap: that is the discrepancy between the intentions of those who formulate policies for the elderly and the actual practices of those who deliver the residential services to elderly people in Local Authority homes.

There are two obvious ways of assessing the potential of the Residential Flatlet, namely incorporating the implicit philosophy of the flatlet within an existing home, or by experimentation with a purpose-built innovative design. Perhaps both approaches are necessary if we are to make best use of our existing capital investment in residential homes and also to ensure that future homes provide a physical environment which gives priority to the quality of living for both residents and staff.

A Profile of Residential Life

REFERENCES

Allen, I. (1982) Short-Stay Residential Care for the
    Elderly Policy Studies Institute.
DHSS & Welsh Office (1973) Residential Accommodation
    for Elderly People Local Authority Building
    Note No.2 May 1973 HMSO.
DHSS & Welsh Office (1981) Growing Older HMSO Cmnd.
    8173.
Evans, G., Hughes, B., Wilkin, D. with Jolley, D.
    (1981) The Mangagement of Mental and Physical
    Impairment in Non-Specialist Residential Homes
    for the Elderly Research Report No.4 Psycho-
    geriatric Research Section, University of
    Manchester.
Hughes, B. & Wilkin, D. (1980) Residential Care of
    the Elderly: a review of the literature.
    Research Report No.2 Psycho-Geriatric Research
    Section. University of Mancnester.
Lawton, M.P. (1970) "Assessment Integration and
    Environments for Older People" The Gerontolo-
    gist Spring 1970.
Lawton, M.P. (1980) Environment and Ageing Brooks/
    Cole Publishing Co. Monterey, California.
Lipman, A. (1968) "A socio-Architectural View of
    Life in Three Old Peoples' Homes" Gerontoligica
    Clinica Vol X 1968.
Meacher, M. (1972) Taken for a Ride Longman Group.
Peace, S.M., Hall, J.F., Hamblin, G.R. (1979) The
    Quality of Life of the Elderly in Residential
    Care: A feasible study. Research Report No.1
    Survey Research Unit Polytechnic of N. London.
Townsend, P. (1962) The Last Refuge Routledge and
    Kegan Paul.
Wilkin, D. & Jolley, D. (1979) Behavioural Problems
    Among Old People in Geriatric Wards, Psycho-
    Geriatric Wards & Residential Homes. Research
    Report No.1 Psycho-geriatric Research Section.
    University of Manchester.
Willcocks, D.M. (1981) The 'ideal-home' Visual Game:
    a discussion of methodological innovation
    arising from consumer research with old people
    in residential homes. Paper presented at
    British Society of Gerontology Annual Confer-
    ence, University of Hull, September.
Willcocks, D.M., Peace, S.M., Kellaher, L.A. with
    Ring, S.J. (1982) The Residential Life of Old
    People: a study in 100 Local Authority Homes,
    Volumes I and II Research Reports Nos. 12 & 13,
    Survey Research Unit, Polytechnic of N. London

Willcocks, D.M. (1982) <u>Gender and the Care of Elderly People in Part III Accommodation</u> Paper presented at the British sociological Association Annual Conference at the University of Manchester, April.

Chapter Fifteen

FRIENDSHIP AND ISOLATION: TWO SIDES OF SHELTERED
HOUSING

Laura Middleton

The research which forms the subject of this chapter
was conducted at Liverpool University between 1980-
81. It was funded by Merseyside Improved Housing,
and its aim was to review the operation of their
sheltered housing schemes. This called for extensive interviews with a total of 140 tenants in 4 schemes - A-D Courts - as well as briefer interviews
with wardens and housing assistants and observation
of social events. In C Court, which opened during
the research, tenants were interviewed where possible at home before moving, shortly after arrival
and after six months' residence. The final report
(Middleton, 1981) covered a wide range of topics -
building design, reasons for moving, health, management, the wardens' role - as well as the question of
social contacts, which forms the focus of the present discussion.
      By way of background, something needs to be
said first about the assumptions behind sheltered
housing as a provision for old people. The underlying rationale is that old people have special
needs, over and above those of any person of any age,
for decent housing. Unfortunately there is little
agreement as to what constitutes special need, particularly between professionals and consumers.
      Secondly, it is important to be aware of peopl-
e's reasons for moving to Sheltered housing. As can
be seen from Table 1, they are in general less concerned with communal facilities than with better or
more conveniently located housing. Whether or not
the extras which form part of the package subsequently come to be regarded as an advantage, a disadvantage or an irrelevancy is another issue. It seems
clear, however, that most people's housing requirements could have been met a great deal more simply.
Related to this, tenants were accepting sheltered

housing not as one in a range of options, but - almost without exception - as the only viable means of solving their housing problem. Some had no choice, their old property having been bought by the housing association for renovation, and the sheltered housing being used as the point of decant. In Liverpool, at the moment, much council housing, including some post war blocks, is being demolished, and older occupants moved to sheltered schemes, with little option (other than sitting it out in an unlit, vandalised block until eviction).

Table One: Reasons for moving to sheltered housing.

	% Respondents
Dissatisfaction with housing	34.5
Dissatisfaction with environment	17.4
Medical reasons	10.5
Wish to be nearer family	9.1
Social reasons	6.1
Family problems	5.3
No choice (mostly decants)	14.1
Unclear answers	13.0

Thirdly, in relation to outside contacts with family friends and organisations, those people who were sociable and outgoing tended to be so both within and outside schemes. There were times when choices had to be made between allegiance to schemes and to family. Some tenants retained family contacts rather than trying to form friendships in the schemes. In other cases, to become a participating scheme member involved change in the pattern of family contact. For example, some tenants chose to spend Christmas at the scheme instead of going, as in previous years, to family.

TYPES OF SOCIAL CONTACT WITHIN THE SCHEMES

Several forms of social contact were identified: (a) involving visits to each others' flats; (b) friendships involving mutual expeditions outside the scheme, or to social functions inside; (c) membership of groups; (d) friendships between men and women; and (e) helping relationships.

Friendships involving visiting
In A Court 3 out of 37 respondents said they had visits from other tenants, the reasons being given as "just to sit", "to have a smoke" and "to have a

coffee" respectively. None of these visits were
confirmed by those who were named. Another respondent who said her flat was "never empty" did not
have this confirmed by a single other person. The
only mutually confirmed instance of visiting involved two members of the tenants' committee, the visits
being explained by both as involving tenant committee business rather than social reasons.

Visiting in flats was also rare in B Court.
Eight respondents out of 36 went visiting, 5 to
schemebound tenants. In C Court, out of 45 respondents, mutual visiting was reported by only one pair,
who were related. In addition, a blind tenant was
frequently observed visiting another blind tenant in
her flat, although neither mentioned it when interviewed. When encountered in her friend's flat, the
visiting tenant even apologised for being there, and
remarked that she felt "caught out". No one in D
Court made visits to another flat.

Visiting each others' homes would appear to be
a typically middle class activity, many working
class women taking pride in the fact that they do
not go into other people's houses. (Young and
Willmott, 1957; Townsend 1957; Roberts 1971). This
may account for its low occurrence in the scheme
under study. Another possible reason is the close
proximity of flats, making it more difficult to
operate the normal devices which ease social interaction. It seems faintly ridiculous, for example,
to make prior arrangements to visit someone living
in the same block. An invitation to tea seems less
appropriate when the visitor has not had to travel
to develop a thirst. Again, the existence of the
lounge as a designated meeting place, even though
it is not much used, ma: y militate against the use
of flats for such a purpose.

Friendships Involving Expeditions

The mutual expedition was a common experience of
friendship, whether it involved calling for a neighbour on the way to Bingo, trips to shops, or visits
to clubs or seaside resorts. It is likely that this
type of relationship is more representative of past
lifestyle than home visiting for social reasons.

In A Court several neighbours attend social
functions together, although not necessarily regarding themselves as friends. Fifteen respondents
named a particular friend, 10 of these nominations
being reciprocated. Seven were immediate neighbours;
three lived next door but one. In B Court, expeditions were to shops or, in one case to hospital, and

13 tenants reported such relationships. In C Court such friendships as had been made were between immediate neighbours. In D Court only one friendship was identified, involving sitting together in the lounge, as well as trips out drinking. Some respondents in D Court expressed regret at the deaths of friends since the opening of the scheme, and at the lack of new friendships since.

Membership of Groups

Being a member of a group is at once easier and less rewarding than a close involvement with another individual. The groups that were identified usually centred on one person or a couple.

In A Court two such groups existed. The first, consisting of five members, centred on a woman who was also heavily involved in the Townswomen's Guild. It was showing signs of breaking up, as two of the peripheral members were becoming involved in a partnership which increasingly excluded the rest. This partnership appeared remarkably beneficial to one of them who regarded herself and was regarded by the warden as housebound, but who was involved in several trips out to clubs with her friend, as far away as Blackpool. The leader of this small group used to run a whist drive in her room, which ceased after one member became unable to climb the stairs. Her status as group leader was perhaps confirmed by the fact that the card game was not transferred to a more accessible location.

The other group, a loose arrangement of 10-15 members, clusters round the chairman of the tenants' committee and his wife, who arrange social events in the lounge; it is incidentally made clear that the warden's participation is not welcome. As an aside, the tenants' chairman expressed a strong sense of isolation within the scheme, considering it to be no place for a man, even a married one.

Only one network was identifiable in B Court, of four tenants who shared a landing and went shopping together. Even in this group, however, two members did no speak to each other, having quarrelled some twelve months previously about whether or not to buy the cleaner a Christmas present. In C Court two groups have developed, both surrounding extrovert personalities, of 8 and 6 people respectively. There were no evident groupings in D Court.

Friendships between men and women

Friendships between unattached men and women seem to
give rise to particular difficulties. Several respondents commented on the improper nature of such
relationships, especially if this involved visiting
each others' flats. Even marriage does not necessarily escape censure: a couple in B Court came under
considerable criticism, the man being seen to have
married into the scheme, rather than to have applied
through the proper channels. The marriage is regarded as one of convenience, with the husband merely
occupying the other half of his wife's flat.

In any event, such friendships are rare not
only because of adverse social pressure but because
of a very real shortage of eligible men. A single
man whether unmarried, divorced or widowed, is particularly vulnerable to isolation, because such social life as there is tends to be dominated by, and
geared towards, the majority of female tenants.

Helping relationships

In the light of the general assumption that, within
a given scheme, the fit will help the frail, helping
relationships were rare. Where such a relationship
did exist, it usually involved shopping: assisted by
financial inducement in at least one case in D Court,
where the person concerned preferred to pay someone
else to shop for him than to go shopping himself.

Helping relationships can be difficult if they
are not based on kinship or previous acquaintance.
Although tenants sometimes shopped for sick neighbours, this could give rise to resentment on one or
both sides. Those who seemed over-zealous in their
offers of help, even going to the extent of actively
seeking a recipient, were not always appreciated.
One such person began knocking regularly at the door
of her neighbour, the oldest tenant in the scheme
but by no means the frailest, and in no mood to have
her health checked daily. By the second round of
interviewing, she had diverted her attention to the
wheelchair user living opposite, electing to safe-
guard her interests by vetting visitors - an arrangement which also promised to be shortlived.

In C Court - the new part of the housing scheme - there were instances in which tenants' relatives also helped those in neighbouring flats by
putting up curtain rails, finding meters, coping
with cookers and so on.

THE PROBLEM OF ISOLATION

Although the majority of respondents appeared to have no particular friends, some of them had families or other outside contacts. To them, isolation was not often a problem. Others, however, seemed deficient in all areas of social contact. There were those who were apparently unconcerned by this, but also those by whom isolation was acknowledged as a problem.

Loneliness is not of course peculiar to old age: other vulnerable groups include young mothers, those with physical handicaps - particularly deafness - and those who have lost an established occupational or family role, or who have been bereaved. This fact may be important to bear in mind when solutions to the problem of the isolated elderly are being explored.

The Scale of the Problem

In A Court, 6 out of 37 respondents cited no friends, were named by no one, and had no significant outside contacts. All expressed feelings of isolation. Contributory factors were deafness, ill-health and bereavement. A further 8 respondents expressed a significant degree of loneliness, despite having some contacts. In B Court, leaving aside 3 couples who claimed no significant contacts, 12 out of 36 individuals appeared to lack any social links at all.

In C Court only 10 respondents out of 45 were unable to name friends: this figure had fallen to 8 by the second round of interviews. Isolation seemed a major problem to only three of these, all scheme bound and one with significant hearing loss. Clearly, serious isolation was less of a problem in the new scheme. In D Court, a third of the tenants lacked both family and other outside contacts, but only two expressed problems of isolation. This particular inner city scheme produced more fears about break-ins and the dangerous environment; companionship appeared to be lower in the hierarchy of needs than a concern for the safety of property and persons.

Taken together, these findings indicate a sizeable problem for the individuals concerned, if not so much for the management of the scheme. There seems serious cause for concern here, in that sheltered schemes have facilities designed to ease isolation, and are often recommended by social workers, G.P.s and others to old people as ways of ameliorating their loneliness.

Friendship and Isolation

The Nature of the Problem
Whether the move to sheltered housing will help to
counteract isolation depends on various considerations, of which the most important seem to be the
source of the isolation and the expectation invested
in the move. Two tenants in C Court provide contrasting examples and underline the need to appreciate
the reason for isolation. Both moved in the hope of
making social contacts. One had been isolated physically in her last home, having lived in the single
remaining flat in a derelict block where she was
unable to keep up her earlier connections. The other, who had a succession of disabling illnesses, had
lost friends by her importunate demands for sympathy. As might be predicted, the first has settled
contentedly in C Court, has made many friends and
regards her problem as having been solved; the second, although having more potential sympathisers
than before has failed to make friends and is growing steadily more unhappy as even the most tolerant
of her fellow-tenants begin to avoid her.
There are a number of other issues relevant to
continuing loneliness within the housing scheme.
First, there will always be the occasional individual who seems to thrive on melancholy and isolation
and who, should he or she admit to needing help, may
require skilled and systematic external support.
Even were she trained, a warden would not always be
in a position to help.
Secondly, the type of social contact available
may not be that which is needed. Formal social occasions may do little to offset feelings of friend-
lessness, or to offer new opportunities for intimacy, especially when the number of people involved is
uncomfortably large. Thirdly, since friends are a
reference group with which an individual tends to
identify closely, there is a reluctance to make
friends who seem old or frail, as this would seem to
reinforce one's own identity as an old person (Tamir
1979). Moreover, as a number of respondents pointed
out there may be a reluctance to make close friends,
in the knowledge that bereavement and the pain of
loss - probably experienced already - will be a likely consequence.
Fourthly, friendship outside the family has not
been a significant part of the lives of many respondents - a product both of generation and of class.
Where a lack is felt, it is for one's husband or
family, and so cannot readily be replaced by other
forms of social contact. One respondent in A Court,
although she attends all the communal functions and

is able to get out, still feels isolated because she misses her husband.

COMMUNAL ACTIVITIES

Communal lounges are a noticeable feature of sheltered schemes. However, the activities they provide are not among the primary reasons for moving, and they tend to be regarded with mixed feelings. Many are elaborate showpieces, full of carefully-chosen furniture, but little used on a day to day basis. No other topic, incidentally, seems to give rise to more defensiveness among wardens and housing managers, many of whom would appear to regard a lounge full of tenants as a sign of a successful scheme.

In reality, communal lounges are an anachronism, provided in the past as a compensation for the fact that the individual was given no more private space than a bedsitting room. The intention was to reduce housework to a minimum by having communal areas, to be cared for by a caretaker or warden. Because bedsits and shared facilities proved unpopular, most recently-built schemes provide self contained flats. Lounges nevertheless continue to be provided. Merseyside Improved Housing, for example, suggests that tenants should regard the lounge as "an extension of their own homes...for formal or informal activities or just as a room in which to sit to have a chat together". Wardens are expected to promote communal functions on two evenings a week.

Table 2 suggests that this expectation is realistic, in that casual use is negligible. A variety of reasons can be suggested: (a) Lounges are separate. The lounge does not directly adjoin tenants' flats, and the corridor in between is impersonal space. In one of the four schemes, carpeting and pot plants were banned from corridors, which emphasized the sense of separation. (b) Lounges are shared. It is difficult to regard something as 'an extension of one's own home' when one is sharing it with around 40 other people. (c) Lounges are public. They are furnished by the landlord or, in one scheme, by an outside committee. A number of tenants commented that their lounge was 'too posh'. (d) Lounges are institutional. Their heating and the access to them are beyond the tenants' control, and there are restrictions on use made by the landlord. In the schemes studied this included a ban on commercial activities, a ban on alcohol and a ban on open invitations to outsiders.

Table 2: Respondents Participating in Social Activities

Scheme	Number of Respondents	Casual Users	Regular Events	Total attending events
A	37	0	Music 10-15 Bingo 16-20 Coffee 12-16 Dinner 14	20
B	36	0	Whist Drive 4 Bingo 6-7 Dinner 16	23
C	45	1	Parties/Buffets 39	39
D	22	0	Coffee 11 Bingo 7 Dinner 5-8	11

Perhaps the most significant disincentive for informal use, however, is the implication of loneliness and boredom. The expectation is that these states of mind should be endured privately in one's own flat, rather than paraded in public.

The formal use of lounges is much more extensive than their casual use, perhaps because it is less personally threatening. Organised functions provide a rationale for attendance. Even if one goes for the companionship, it is possible to pretend it is for the coffee or the bingo. Nonetheless it does not suit everyone. Few tenants, after all, have actively chosen to live in a communal setting. More often the communal aspects of sheltered housing are thereby accepted as part of the package deal involved in having to move. The enforced communality was the most frequently cited reason for discontent among the tenants interviewed in the study. Although communal functions are presented as being purely voluntary, the 'normal' expectation in all schemes was that such functions should be attended. The non-attenders were designated as 'unsociable', 'standoffish' or worse: it seemed obligatory to enter into the spirit of things. In keeping with these attitudes, non-participants tended to be apologetic and to offer excuses. Some, in an attempt to ensure acceptability, gave prizes for bingo although they never went. One warden required all tenants to join the social club and to pay the necessary fee whether they wished to attend or not.

A variety of reasons were given for non-participation. Some people did not enjoy large organised events and did not want to meet people in such a setting: they were happier on their own, or with families or long-established friends. Others opted out because of shyness, ill health or deafness. The lounge was often associated with loss of independence because of its resemblance to the lounge in an old peoples' home: a spectre some tenants were actively concerned to avoid. In one scheme tenants reacted against an outside organising committee because it made them feel like objects of charity.

It may be remarked that this pressure to participate, often sanctioned by the wardens, is in direct contrast with the normal patterns of sociability in the community. There, if one wants to join a luncheon club, or play bingo, one can contract in. There is no obligation to justify oneself if one is not interested.

THE PROCESS OF MAKING CONTACTS

Reference might be made at this point to the friendships that have occurred, and what they are based
on. Much of the evidence is drawn from the study of
C Court - the new scheme - where making contacts is
a dynamic process and where people, finding themselves in an altogether novel situation, are not
loath to discuss the processes of getting to know
one another.

The friendships that have emerged have three
main origins. The first is previous acquaintance
not necessarily maintained at the time of the move.
Two respondents in C Court discovered on "viewing
day" that they had been at school together, and re-
sumed a friendship that had lapsed for 60 years.

Proximity is the second major factor which en-
courages friendships to develop. All but two of the
partnerships identified were with tenants opposite
or next door, or in one case, between two people
whose windows face each other. The social dynamics
are obvious: it is clearly easier to meet an immediate neighbour by chance. In the early days at C
Court, much contact was made during the period when
the milk was taken in. Tenants were able to stand
on their own door step, clutching a milk bottle
while engaging in conversation - it seemed entirely
legitimate to stay on one's own territory while
talking to others, and to have some extraneous reason for being there. Potted plants outside flats
serve a similar function. It was surely not mere
coincidence that tenants complaining of isolation in
C Court were those who could not see anyone else's
entrances because of corner locations or fire doors.
Shared characteristics are the third main source of
contact. One friendship in C Court developed between two tenants who, though on the same corridor,
were not immediate neighbours. Both suffered from
near-blindness. Two other partnerships between next
door neighbours were also founded on mutual concerns,
the first pair through dissatisfaction with the
scheme, the second pair through the frustration of
having had to care for a sick child.

This gives us some indication of who are likely
to make friends. The three categories seem significant in A and B Courts also, and the one friendship
in D Court seemed to centre on a common sense of
misery.

At least in the initial stages, some rationale
seems to be needed on which to establish friendship.
This is true not only of the elderly - though many

of the tactics used by working people, or parents, for making friends are not available to them. It is less easy to disguise a desire for friendship and contact as anything else. (The need for disguise is not only a social expectation in a society based on privacy and closed family groups, but also a psychological defence against the possible rejection of friendly overtures, enabling both parties to withdraw without embarrassment). Seen in this context, the formal social gathering is clearly of limited value as a means of making friends: what is most needed is a means of making contact through activities which carry their own social justification.

A laundry room with more than one machine - even if unjustified in terms of economic demand - and with seats, heating and no rota system, would be an ideal focus for informal contact, carrying none of the risk of being seen to parade one's loneliness which is attendant on sitting in the communal lounge.

The provision of as many community roles as possible, whether through membership of permanent or ad hoc committees or through assigned responsibilities such as rent collecting, serving as fire wardens and the like, can also promote contact. A deliberate attempt along these lines to provide legitimate functions in an institution which is otherwise likely to deprive people of them, must obviously require wardens to accept some sharing of their responsibilities.

On a more personal level "helping" can provide a rationale for visiting, even if the help is not particularly effective, and may indeed do little more than to offer such legitimation. As long as the recipient is prepared to collude, a relationship of this kind can offer something to each of the participants. It may even be that the dynamics of such a relationship are easier for some to manage than a friendship based on "liking" or "sharing". This possibility needs to be recognised by wardens, who might otherwise try to intervene on the grounds that the arrangement may be "too much" for the helper, or because someone else might be more efficient.

THE AVOIDANCE OF CLOSE FRIENDSHIPS

Sheltered housing, in providing various means of socialising, may also serve to emphasise the loneliness of those for whom friendship is difficult by making their idiosyncrasies more apparent than they would be in the privacy of a street or block of flats. Those respondents in the study who disliked the social side of communal life felt pressured into participating or inadequate for not joining in. Isolated people were known and talked about. Single men had little chance of developing new friendships - a problem which could only be resolved by a highly improbable increase in the male intake.

A number of explanations might be advanced for the surprisingly low incidence of close friendships. In some cases it might be a matter of deliberate choice, either because family contacts proved sufficient or because the respondent preferred solitude. It might in other cases be because the available constituency is considered inappropriate in terms of age, class or gender. In other cases again, there may be a fear that the pain of loss when a friendship ends will outweigh its benefits while it lasts. Whatever the reason, many tenants seemed more comfortable with a nodding acquaintanceship than with a close involvement. Most schemes seemed to meet this need in one way or another.

The main source of concern would seem to be for those who have a continuous sense of isolation despite the various attempts made to overcome it. Such individuals have less need for an enhanced programme of social events which they feel unable to attend than for individual attention in alleviating their individual problems of deafness, loss of mobility, bereavement, or whatever. Any significant progress in this direction would unfortunately seem to call for a degree of skill, innate or trained, which is not possessed by all wardens.

SOME PRACTICAL IMPLICATIONS

For most of those who apply for sheltered housing, it appears to be the only available solution to their housing problems. The high numbers of disappointed applicants, together with the recognition that the needs of large numbers of sheltered schemes could have been more simply met, suggests an urgent need to build or restore suitable small-scale housing, secure from vandals.

Communal facilities in existing schemes are at best a bonus but at worst an unwelcome burden. Feelings of loneliness tend to be heightened in a communal setting (Rosow, 1968). It would seem sensible to extend the public facilities to people not living on site, so creating more of a community centre than a lounge. Physical separation, together with the appointment of a social secretary other than the scheme warden, would reinforce the distinction: but much could be achieved simply from a general change in attitude.

Finally, there could well be greater emphasis on encouraging informal contact, which is more likely than formal encounters to lead to friendship for those who seek it. Some possible strategies have already been noted - a comfortable laundrette (to which the solitary can go at quiet times and the gregarious at busy ones); the allocation of communal responsibilities to as many tenants as possible; the avoidance, whenever feasible, of rooms whose doors are out of sight of all neighbours. The research findings reported in this chapter clearly suggest that the best course is to enhance opportunities which are already well established and socially legitimated for striking up friendships, rather than to strive to create new and unfamiliar ones.

REFERENCES

Middleton L.   (1981) So Much for So Few: A view of sheltered housing. Institute of Human Ageing, University of Liverpool

Roberts, R. (1971) The Classic Slum. Manchester University Press

Rosow, I. (1968) "Housing and Local Ties of the Aged", in B. Neugarten, ed Middle Age and Ageing. University of Chicago Press

Tamir, L. (1979) Communication and the Ageing Process. Pergamon Press, Oxford

Townsend, P. (1957) The Family Life of Old People Routledge, London

Young, M. and Willmott, P. (1957) Family and Kinship in East London. Routledge, London

Chapter Sixteen

THE NURSING HOME: PROFESSIONAL ATTITUDES TO THE
INTRODUCTION OF NEW FORMS OF CARE PROVISION FOR THE
ELDERLY

Gillian Dalley

INTRODUCTION

The problem of the rapidly increasing numbers of the
very old (75+) is widely recognised throughout all
sectors of the health and social services in Britain. Moves towards the introduction of National
Health Service (NHS) nursing homes can be seen as
one governmental response to this problem. A pilot
programme of three experimental nursing homes for
the elderly was announced by the Secretary of State
for Health and Social Security in February 1982.
They were to be set up in Sheffield, Portsmouth and
Fleetwood and financed jointly by the Health Authorities and the DHSS Special Medical Development
Funds. In Scotland, recommendations for the development of such homes, particularly for the mentally
infirm elderly, had been made since the Millar
Report in 1970. The Scottish division of the Royal
College of Psychiatrists had consistently argued for
their development, and more recently the Timbury
Report (SHHD/SED 1979a) recommended the establishment of what it called continuing care units for the
care of the elderly with mental disability. In
addition, a further official report in 1979 (SHHD/
SED 1979b) recommended that the concept of NHS
provision of such residential care be extended to
the frail elderly as well as to the mentally infirm.
Indeed a continuing care unit for the frail ambulant
elderly was already in operation at one Glasgow
hospital and had been monitored since its opening
(McPherson 1982; McIntosh 1982).

THE NURSING HOME CONCEPT

There seems to have been no unitary development of
the concept of nursing home provision within the
NHS, and consequently conflicting or contradictory
elements within the concept appear in some of the
sources mentioned above. Certain common features
obtain, however: all sources centre on the need for
the nursing home to be a nursing responsibility,
with a nurse in sole charge. There should be no
provision of continuous medical care, and medical
care as and when needed would primarily be the duty
of the visiting general practitioner. The Local
Authority would provide social work support - either
with one social worker being assigned to the home,
or patients receiving social work support from
individually assigned social workers. Finally, the
need is emphasised for a domestic environment to be
established in order that patients feel 'at home'
in what in practice would be their long-term home.
    Differences begin to emerge at this point.
The interpretation of 'a domestic environment' varies between the DHSS outline of proposed pilot
scheme (DHSS 1982) and the more ad hoc arrangements
in the Glasgow setting. This is perhaps due more to
the origins of each scheme than to any difference
in underlying philosophy. The English pilot nursing
homes, if not purpose-built, will be specifically
acquired for that purpose, and will be able to provide a mix of single and double rooms, and activity
areas; personal possessions and own furniture will
be incorporated. The Glasgow unit was set up within
an existing hospital ward, and has had to develop
under those constraints, although emphasis on the
need for privacy, dignity and homeliness is the
same. The Timbury Report mentions and "essentially
domestic atmosphere" for what it calls continuing-
care units, based in purpose-built single-storey
buildings containing a mix of single and 4-bedded
rooms.
    Different sources identify different patient
groups as recipients of nursing home care. The
English pilot scheme will cater for the very frail
elderly (without mental disability) who need continuous nursing care. The Glasgow unit very clearly
caters for the frail elderly who do not need continuous nursing care, but rather, what is called
'continuing care'. The continuing care units envisaged by Timbury, and the Report of the Scottish
Psychiatrists, refer to the elderly with mental

disabilities and talk about Elderly, Mentally Infirm
Homes (EMI Homes). The distinction between different forms of care is crucial, because on that depends the type of staff required for running the
homes. Clearly in a home where continuous nursing
care is provided, the numbers of qualified nurses
required will be high; in a home which provides
'continuing care', unskilled staff, more like care
assistants in Local Authority Old People's Homes,
will suffice, with a back-up of skilled nursing
where required.
    In the case of the Glasgow Unit, all staff are
unqualified and are called care staff in order to
distinguish them from the other unqualified staff in
the hospital - the nursing auxiliaries. They are
responsible to the nurse in charge of the Unit. The
merit of having unqualified care staff to run the
Unit on a day to day basis may be that the aims of
establishing a 'family environment' can be realised.
The care staff are regarded as surrogate family
carers, and as such are not expected to perform any
duties that a family member would not do (i.e. in
terms of skilled nursing). In this sense the Unit,
although based within the hospital and constrained
by the limitations of hospital buildings and equipment, can be seen to approximate more closely to a
'domestic setting' than that of the purpose-built
nursing home, staffed predominantly by nurses.
Moreover, the nursing input in the Glasgow setting
comes predominantly from the District Nursing
Service - on the same home-based principle - in spite of the Unit's location within the hospital and
its close proximity to the hospital nursing service.
    A final difference that can be highlighted is
the expectation in the English scheme that the
Nursing Home will be the permanent and final home of
the patient. There seems to be a greater expectation of movement within the Glasgow Unit - in both
directions. On the one hand it can be seen as part
of the rehabilitation process from geriatric ward
through the Unit back to own-home or Old People's
Home (OPH), and on the other hand it can be part of
a process of delaying a patient's final entry into
a geriatric ward (where continuous nursing care
would be available). The criteria for admission
into the different schemes would clearly be quite
different, and would require different methods of
assessment.
    Nevertheless, the principal common element in
all versions of the nursing home concept is that

provision should be made for the very elderly located at an intermediate stage between own-home or Old
People's Home and the geriatric ward hospital,
offering a domestic, family-oriented environment,
under the management of nurses as opposed to doctors. Clearly, it can be seen as a major extension
of the existing role of the nurse and of nurse responsibility.

Insofar as changes in the work role of one
occupational group are concerned, the introduction
of the nursing home concept will be bound to have
implications for the other occupational groups
traditionally involved in the care of the elderly.
If one group gains in responsibility, others will
lose; if one takes on more duties, others will have
to give up some. It is likely, then, that the
introduction of nursing homes within the NHS will
impinge in a variety of ways on the variety of
professions, occupations and agencies (either directly or indirectly) and that both professional
feelings and territorial boundaries might be affected; if this were to lead to failures in co-operation and understanding then the schemes may not
operate smoothly or successfully.

This chapter provides an opportunity to examine
some health and social work attitudes encountered in
a series of interviews with professionals who,
although not directly involved in the nursing home
issue, were prepared to discuss the concept in a
manner clearly conditioned by their professional
ideologies and operational philosophies. The material used is taken from a series of interviews
conducted with health and social work personnel in
three Scottish regions. Data from the two monitoring reports on the continuing care unit already
established in Glasgow, and mentioned earlier, are
also used.

PROFESSIONAL/OCCUPATIONAL GROUPS INVOLVED

The categories of professions and occupations likely
to be affected by the introduction of NHS nursing
homes are various. For some, it might involve considerable redefinition of roles and aims, for others
it might be slight. Nurses especially would be
affected - both hospital and community nursing
staff. Others would include the consultant geriatrician, and consultant psychiatrist, the GP, hos-
pital- and community-based social work personnel,
OPH staff, and lastly, the unqualified care staff

who would be providing day to day care. Relationships between service agencies (the NHS and the
Local Authority Social Work Department) would also
be involved.

During the course of the study (and not directly concerned with the nursing home issue) it has
become apparent that problems of liaison, co-operation and co-ordination between different groups of
professionals within and across boundaries are seen
as major constraints on the provision of good integrated services for the categories of patients we
have designated as 'dependency groups'. Perceptions
of the problems and of the causes of those problems
centre, in particular, on the different goals and
'ways of going about things' that different professions have. Social work personnel tend to be susp-
icious of health service - especially medical -
hegemony in areas that they feel belong to social
work; they justify their fears over what would
otherwise appear to be straightforward boundary
disputes by pointing out the fundamental differences
in aims, interpretations of causes and methods of
treatment between the two conflicting sides.

Broadly, social work people see themselves as
concerned with looking at the individual in a social
context; social and environmental conditions are as
important contributory factors as the individual's
physical condition. Treatment has to take into
account the social dimension as well as the physiological. They would suggest that they place greater emphasis on non-institutional forms of care and
stress the need for patients or clients to retain
their independence. On the other hand, they would
argue that people trained and working within a
health service setting are dominated by the medical
ethos, emphasising medical solutions to what might
often be social problems and underrating the need
for patients to remain as individuals within their
own social environments. Along with that goes the
view that all health service professions or occupations are ultimately subservient to the medical
profession and that none of them are able to function independently of it. The rationale for that
ultimate control is 'clinical judgement' and
'clinical autonomy'.

In their turn, health service personnel exhibit
a variety of suspicions and doubts about social
work - about social workers claiming to be professionals without a properly developed body of professional knowledge; about social agencies, being

subject to political whim (through the Local Authority system) and therefore being unpredictable and
partial; about the unwillingness of social workers
to be seen simply as welfare assistants, whose role
it is to arrange such things as accommodation, benefits and other services for Health Service patients.
     Thus, in arenas where members of 'both sides'
are expected to work in conjunction with each other
- for example, in a primary care team - problems
over goals and methods are likely to emerge. However, professional boundaries exist even within each
of the two main areas. Conflicts of loyalty and
differences in attitude are seen between hospital
and community-based social workers, between hospital
and community-based nurses and hospital and community-based occupational therapists. The nurse/doctor
relationship, although usually based on an expected
subservience of the nursing hierarchy to medical
dominance, exhibits its own set of tensions - for
example, in the context of the primary care team.

THE INTERVIEW DATA

It seems, then, that when a new concept is introduced which might involve a re-structuring of traditional work roles and responsibilities, these anti-
pathies and suspicions may well come to the fore.
The commonest social work response from the interviews to the idea of the NHS nursing home was that
only homes under social work control could really
work properly, and that NHS homes would be the means
of depriving the social work domain of its clients,
at the same time as providing a worse form of care:

> It's almost a philosophical thing really....
> the hospital regime will always somehow impinge
> on the running of them....people won't get to
> lead independent lives.
> (Social Work Manager)

and again:

> ...It would be a continuation of the geriatric
> unit if nurses were running these homes. The
> majority of nurses coming from hospitals rather
> tend to work on as if they were in a hospital..
> ..one requires to promote much more independen-
> ce with the residents. The average nurse act-
> ually creates dependency, I feel.
> (Old People's Home Manger)

The community nursing view was in some ways similar
- that it was crucially important for the hospital
ethos not to be transferred to the nursing home.
Perhaps because of their community experience, they
were in any case somewhat apart from the typical
hospital-based nursing view:

> I think I have some support (within the health
> service)...in the social work department alth-
> ough they're not supporting me personally
> because I'm a nurse....I think their views are
> more like mine. The majority of people in the
> health service are acute services and we are in
> the minority.
> (Community Nursing Manager)

This made them view the nursing home concept very
positively, especially because of the possibilities
it opened up for rehabilitation. It would be possible:

> ...to get the old people to learn to make their
> own bed...and their own tea...and do their own
> washing. They tried to get them doing what was
> within their abilities and from then they were
> able to get them either home or into an OPH
> once they were rehabilitated. But you see how
> do you rehabilitate somebody in an acute ward.
> It's impossible.
> (Community Nurse)

Some more senior nurse managers viewed the concept
positively for professional reasons. It involved
an expansion of the nurse's role:

> Yes, I think it's an area in which the nurse
> can have full scope of her responsibilities -
> and is able to be partly a nurse and partly an
> administrator.

But this same nurse felt there would only be limited
scope for the development of the nursing home scheme. If a patient needed full-time nursing care,
then it would have to be in an environment staffed
by professional nurses (i.e. a hospital). If 24
hour nursing care was not required then the community nursing service was available to patients in
their own homes. The distinction between continuous
care, and continuous nursing care seems to be a
difficult one to draw and varies between

commentators.
　　A hospital nursing view - unsurprisingly perhaps, given the traditionally subordinate position
of nurses - was that it should not be left entirely
in the charge of nurses:

> It could be done, you know...but I think they
> would need to have somebody overall that they
> could turn to for assistance - medical assis-
> tance and so forth.

Others suggested a return to the old cottage hospital or GP unit principle - forgetting that the
important point about the nursing home concept was
to get away from the hospital ethos and to provide
an environment as much like home as possible.
　　Doctors expressed a variety of views. Some saw
the concept as unproblematic - generally those who
would be unaffected by its introduction. One consultant geriatrician was absolutely against its
introduction; he saw it as an erosion of medical
control. It was necessary to maintain what he called 'the medical grip'. Nurses should not be left to
determine when or if medical expertise should be
called upon; it was entirely a matter for those with
medical skills. This requirement to defer to medical authority was reinforced by a nurse manger who
felt that the nursing home concept could be a useful
addition to geriatric care, but felt there would
have to be thorough consultation with the geriatri-
cians first. Another consultant geriatrician, however, approached the concept not in terms of its
being an erosion of his power, but in terms of its
making an inroad into the social work sphere of
control. As more and more old people were opting
for sheltered housing, the residents of OPHs tended
increasingly to be the frail and confused elderly.
Social Work Departments were not happy with this, he
felt, and would have to rethink the staff/resident
ratios to cope with the psychosocial problems of
communal living of that group. The best solution
would be if:

> ...the residential homes were transferred to
> the health service. It's not a take-over bid,
> I think - it's placing the facility in the
> right arena where people are trained to do that
> sort of job and these people (social workers)
> can go hoofing it around, changing society and
> leading us into the brave new world.

This view was supported by both a nurse manager and
a hospital administrator, who felt that health service control was all-important:

> I think if it finished up being the responsib-
> ility of the health service to look after the
> ill or the unfit - then it could work. Local
> Authorities always bother me, because depending
> on the views of Local Authorities you have a
> varying standard throughout the country.

and:

> I think provided these, if you like, intermed-
> iate homes is what you're really talking about,
> are under the auspices of the health service
> and are staffed by professionals then I don't
> see anything wrong with it.

A District Medical Officer recognised the issue of
'the medical grip', but saw it as a problem which
would be difficult to overcome. He was sceptical
about whether nurses would in the event be allowed
to control the establishments; if they were not able
to, then the nursing home would not be the innovative concept it was claimed to be. Conflicts between different professional interests were damaging:

> I see it happening and I think it can be des-
> tructive, and it has been destructive, there
> is no doubt about that...destructive of the
> whole health service, because it has had an
> effect on its morale - and ill feelings and
> anger between professions.

and later of the nursing home in particular:

> ...There is one big snag in my view, just be-
> fore you start almost...who controls admission
> to these places is crucial to any system you
> want to set up.

If it were doctors who held that power then they
would ultimately be in control.

Such examples, then, show that there are differing views current within a variety of relevant
professions about the feasibility of the nursing
home concept. Many view the idea positively but
others temper their approval with doubts about the
roles and responsibilities of those involved; others

are completely opposed to this increase in health
service control of a category of people they feel
should not be medically defined.

THE GLASGOW EVIDENCE

It is worth looking briefly at some points which
emerge from the two reports already written on the
Frail Ambulant Unit in Glasgow, since this is a rare
example of an NHS unit, approximating the nursing
home concept, actually in existence. Neither report
is concerned especially with documenting attitudes
of professionals towards the unit, but some of the
issues foreseen by respondents in the interviews are
touched on in both reports.

Central to the McIntosh inquiry (McIntosh 1982)
is the emphasis placed on the need to establish
appropriate admission criteria to avoid three problems: first, that of doctors being able to shunt
some of their patients into the unit to release beds
for more acute cases; second, that of patients having to be returned to the hospital ward because they
are too frail; and third, that of making excessive
demands on the unqualified care staff. Mention is
made in the report of some feeling that there was
too much medical input, but that the geriatrician
wished to maintain his current involvement. Here
there are perhaps echoes of the problems voiced by
the DMO quoted earlier concerning the control of
admission and therefore the ultimate control of the
unit. How far would nurses ever, in practice,
manage to establish themselves as being in sole
charge ?

Another problem, highlighting the intermediate
status of the nursing home concept, is the question
of role definition and job title for the staff
providing the day to day care. In the effort to
make the establishment as much unlike a hospital as
possible, it was called a unit and not a ward. Along with that, staff were called care staff rather
than nursing auxiliaries; however, they were employed on Whitley grading at the same level as nursing
auxiliaries and in that sense were fully within the
health service. The Report goes on to say that the
work remit should be expected to approximate that of
care attendants in OPHs, although, it notes, "it can
be defined as having a nursing component in the very
general sense of 'caring' and doing for an individual what he or she cannot do for themselves". The
speculation of the nurse manager quoted earlier

about whether there was much need for this intermediate form of care is relevant here.   There seems to
be a grey area where definitions of care, continuous
care, nursing care and continuous nursing care all
overlap; likewise the appropriate locations in which
this variety of forms of care should take place.
      Both the McPherson and McIntosh reports mention
the difficulty of getting away from the hospital
ethos, especially in the cases of care staff who had
had previous experience within hospitals as nursing
auxiliaries.   Perhaps the fears expressed by social
work personnel have some basis in practice. In addition problems would also arise over the status of
unqualified care staff.   Many people within both the
health service and social work are concerned with
status, professionalism and professionalisation, so
there is a natural tendency to question the idea of
giving unqualified staff greater amounts of responsibility than they would generally be expected to
exercise.   The McPherson Report makes the point that
such difficulties might be avoided as long as there
is only one unit with a small number of staff: but
if the number were to increase over time, there
could well be an 'industrial relations' problem to
sort out, involving the need to create a new category of staff within the wages structure and a
consequent need to define tasks, duties, skills and
comparability.
      Although many of the professionals concerned
appear critical of the nursing home concept, this
does not necessarily mean that the concept itself
is seriously flawed.   There is nonetheless a fundamental problem which has to be faced.   Namely how
to integrate two conflicting principles.   One is the
principle of maintaining the patient in a domestic
environment with surrogate family care being the
main support - the community ethos.   The other is
the principle of professional accountability and the
associated legal liability, in a context in which
care is highly organised and provided by a bureau-
cratic service agency, where the practice is for
roles and duties to be clearly defined, and where
legal liability is strictly delineated
      Some aspects of this basic dilemma could be
observed in the Glasgow Unit.   For example, what was
staff's liability in relation to the issuing of
drugs ?   It was important in maintaining the family
nature of care that care staff be able to hand out
medication, in the same way that a spouse or daughter or son might, following the instructions of the

GP and pharmacist. But the fact remained that care
staff were not family members, and in law this could
create problems. Another problem was in drawing the
line of accountability.   Although in operational
terms nursing intervention came largely from the
district nursing service and medical intervention
came from the GP, the Unit was in fact set up by the
hospital, was physically part of the hospital and
therefore ultimately under hospital control. That
in itself perhaps undermined the validity of the
Unit as a non-institutional form of care; in practical terms, the implications were more serious,
because it could lead to immediate and real difficulties in a time of crisis. The data from the
interviews echo similar worries about role definitions, accountability and the dangers of trespassing
into other people's professional territory.
    Many of these issues may well be avoided in the
DHSS pilot scheme in England. First, the homes will
not be attached to hospitals, and so lines of accountability will not be so ambiguous - as between
community nursing, hospital nursing and medicine
(both hospital and GP). Secondly, problems of
unqualified staff liability will not be problematic
because the homes will be staffed with a mix of
nurses and unqualified staff, and nurses will therefore be on hand to administer drugs and so on. However, this in itself undermines the principle on
which the Glasgow Unit is pre-eminently based - that
of surrogate family care. While the mix of qualified and unqualified staff will solve some of the
problems of liability and accountability, it moves
the nursing home one step further away from the
domestic, family environment which is one of the key
elements in the concept. Ironically, the Glasgow
Unit, for all that it is part of the hospital setting, aims to provide a more homely environment than
that apparently envisaged in the English pilot scheme.

CONCLUSION

The nursing home concept clearly provides the opportunity for an expansion in the traditional role of
the nurse within the NHS. Exactly how that expansion will take place in practice is unclear and will
depend among other things on the policy adopted towards the unqualified/qualified staff ratio, and the
relationship of the nursing home to outside structures. The degree to which the introduction of the

concept will be acceptable to the other professional
and occupational groups likely to be affected also
remains unclear. On the evidence presented here,
unforeseen resistance from a variety of professional
quarters may well emerge.

REFERENCES

DHSS (1982)   Key Factors to be Taken into Account in
     Designing Operational Policies for Experimental
     NHS Nursing Homes for Elderly People
McIntosh, J. (1982) The Frail Ambulant Unit -
     Belvidere. A Report on Resident Dependency and
     Staff Performance, Greater Glasgow Health
     Board
McPherson, I. (1982)   The Frail Ambulant Unit - A
     Labour View, Department of Social and Economic
     Research, University of Glasgow
SHHD/SED (1979a) Sources for the Elderly with Ment-
     al Disabilities in Scotland (Timbury Report)
SHHD/SED (1979b) Changing Patterns of Care: A
     Report on Services for the Elderly in Scotland

Chapter Seventeen

THE HOSPICE CONCEPT AND THE NATIONAL HEALTH SERVICE

Hedley Taylor

In this short chapter I want to raise a number of
issues regarding the role and relevance of the hospice movement. These are: a) The criticism which
hospice principles imply for the present management
of death in ordinary hospitals. b) The role of
hospice care in enabling dying patients to be supported in their own homes. c) The relationship between independent hospices and the NHS. d) The wider
relevance of hospice principles.

During the last ten years, there has been a
very substantial increase in hospice provision for
terminally ill persons in this country. This has
been accompanied by extensive public awareness and
support. Even during a period of economic depression and financial constraint, it has been possible
to raise large sums of money from charitable and
corporate funders and by public appeals in order to
meet the capital costs of hospice units. From only
12 in-patient units in the mid 1960s, there are now
nearly 70, together with over 60 home care services
and 11 symptom control teams based in hospitals.
All this has taken place in a society where death is
supposed to be an unmentionable subject. Clearly,
hospices must be meeting a powerfully felt need.
Also, of course, the hospice movement represents a
fear - that of cancer and death from it. In addition, perhaps it also represents a peculiar kind of
hope - that however unlovely or unsatisfactory are
our present lives, at least the hospice offers the
opportunity of a peaceful and dignified death.

The very success of hospices has begun to raise
problems and produce its own strains. Concern has
been expressed about the indiscriminate prolifera-
tion of independent hospice units - and the implications which this has for future staffing requirements, quality of care, ability to meet revenue

costs, and relations with the NHS.

WHAT IS HOSPICE CARE ?

Hospices, as is now widely known, provide treatment
for patients, primarily cancer sufferers, for whom
the advent of death is diagnosed as being imminent
and therefore the emphasis is no longer on curative
treatment, but rather palliative care. This care
has two main aspects; and the difference between
them is something which I wish to emphasise, as it
is important to my subsequent argument.
    One element is that of pain control techniques
and the accompanying intensive nursing, both of
which are particularly relevant to the situation of
dying persons. The nursing itself consists of fairly standard procedures. The main contribution of
hospices in respect of pain control (and I am here
summarising as a non-expert) has been the success
achieved by the administration of analgesic drugs at
regular intervals before the patients' manifest need
for them arises. This not only avoids unnecessary
pain but - perhaps more important - the anxiety
associated with it. Recent research suggests that
these techniques have been assimilated and are widely practiced in NHS hospitals (Parkes, 1978).
    The other primary element in hospice care is
the emphasis on personal attention to the needs of
the patient and support for the family. The hospice
aims not simply to treat or relieve the physical
symptoms but to create a relaxed, calm environment
in which (to use a now familiar phrase) the physical,
emotional, social, psychological and (where appropriate) the spiritual needs of patients are cared
for and where death can be faced with dignity.
    But this aspect of hospice care, relating to
its holistic and patient-centred approach, is not
claimed even by the supporters of the hospice movement to be distinctive to their own practice.
Rather, they see it as representing a distillation
of the best in general hospital practice - albeit
too infrequently found there. Most doctors and
nurses would protest that they too minister to the
'whole person' - and that the assertion that they
treat the symptoms of disease and ignore the patient is a distortion of reality. The hospice movement, because of its development - largely outside
the NHS - has tended to be viewed in isolation from
other advances in medicine which in recent years
have humanised it. And yet, even granting this the
experience of patients and the weight of systematic

283

observation continue to suggest that something akin to a technocrate 'medical model' does operate, even though its practitioners may not consciously subscribe to it.

If pain relief and personalised medical and nursing attention are the twin pillars of hospice care, the question arises as to how truly the hospice movement is able to live up to its own ideals. From the point of view of the patient and his/her family, the benefits of hospice care may be rather more simple and practical, although no less valued for that. The hospice provides the assurance of a pain-free death in as pleasant and as welcoming an environment as is congruent with medical and nursing requirements, and where the care given combines professional expertise with a degree of personal consideration. A hospice administrator recently described it to me as 'a smaller and homelier version of the general ward - that may not be much, but by comparison it is everything!' During an interview which I had with one distinguished medical director of a hospice (whom I think I caught in a particularly relaxed moment), he reflected wryly on the notion of 'peace and calm':

> 'The institutional routines still have to be carried out; wards have to be cleaned, patients moved around, basic nursing procedures carried out, staff go on and off duty, the television plays on when staff 'switch off', and all around, the occupation of beds is changing'.

It is less the quality of the work which hospices undertake which I have found criticised by fellow professionals - although there have been instances of that - than the rhetoric behind it. But then, few institutions can live up to their own rhetoric, including the National Health Service! It only becomes a problem if those within the institution cannot distinguish the ideals from the reality.

The Institutional Forms of Hospice Care
There are three main organisational forms of hospice provision in this country.

1. In-patient units. These provide residential care, usually short-term, for those requiring it. The aim here is to bring pain and other symptoms under control and to provide intensive nursing care during the final stages of illness.

2. Home care services. These consist of
   specially trained nurses working under the
   supervision of a doctor and supported occasionally by a social worker and other
   para-medicals. These facilities extend
   hospice care and support to patients in
   their own homes. In most cases, the home
   care service acts in a largely advisory
   capacity in relation to the primary care
   team. Together, they have become the front
   line in hospice care and have tended to
   diminish the central importance of the in-
   patient unit. The latter, however, still
   remains as a model of care. It is a key
   symbol in the public mind, and one which is
   particularly useful when it comes to fund-
   raising.
3. Symptom control teams. A small number of
   these have been set up, usually within district hospitals, in order to provide expertise and advice to doctors and nurses, who
   continue to retain actual responsibility
   for the care of dying patients on the ward.
   The team members also liaise with colleagues caring for discharged patients in the
   community.

Home care services and symptom control teams enjoy
a number of advantages. First, they are far cheaper
to set up and run than in-patient units. Second,
their members work alongside NHS colleagues, and
their potential for disseminating knowledge about
hospice principles is correspondingly greater. They
are able to assist larger numbers of patients in the
community and in hospital. Finally, they are in a
position to co-ordinate the care of patients between
hospital, hospice and home.
However, they are heavily dependent for their
effectiveness on the willingness of other professionals to accept the advice and expertise that is
offered, and also on their ability to give patients
the level of medical, nursing and personal care that
is required. For this reason, it is sometimes claimed that they result in a dilution of hospice care
rather than a quantitative increase in it. While
there is widespread support for these services within the hospice movement, there is also concern that
unless they can command the necessary medical expertise and other resources, they may be perceived as
providing an inadequate service, and hence as presenting a poor model of hospice care.

THE MANAGEMENT OF DEATH IN HOSPITAL

At the present time, some 60% of deaths take place in hospital or similar institutions, and the proportion has been steadily increasing over the last 20 years. A number of interrelated demographic, social and medical factors have contributed to this change in the place of death, from home to hospital. The hospice movement, with its emphasis on home care, offers some hope that this process is reversible.

Hospitals are, even at the best of times, alien territory for most patients and their families. Their concentration, moreover, on 'curative' treatment may render them less capable of meeting the needs of dying persons. This is not to say that compassionate and dedicated care is not rendered to terminally ill persons. But it is not easy to find time for the kind of personal attention and psychological support which the situation may demand. The routines and organisation of the general ward are geared primarily to the needs of acute patients; and so are not always compatible with the calmer and more relaxed environment appropriate to those in the process of taking their leave of life.

In recent years, the models of care provided by the hospice movement have begun to influence provision within the NHS through the operation of symptom control teams and continuing care units built within hospital grounds, but mainly through the movement of staff between institutions and the setting up of hospice training programmes.

The hospice movement has also, however, given rise to a spirited defence of the achievements of NHS hospitals in this field and of the suitability of the hospital setting for the care of dying persons, given the appropriate attitudes, training and resources. The provision of specialist institutions for the dying, it is argued, may indeed be counterproductive in the case of some patients. Many doctors and nurses would concede the limitations in the management of death within hospitals, and acknowledge the importance and influence of the hospice movement. But many would also claim that those associated with the movement often fail to accept its limitations, or to recognise the quality of terminal care practice to be found in some NHS hospitals.

DYING AT HOME

Although fewer people are dying at home, the success
of modern pain control methods has led to a shorten-
ing of the period which many dying patients need to
spend in hospital. The majority of patients, instead of taking up expensive in-patient beds during
the last months or weeks of their lives, can be re-
habilitated into their own homes, with a final admission of only a few days. It is perhaps this need
to release hospice beds that has been the main
stimulus to the development of home care services.
This mirrors the development in other areas of health care in the early discharge of patients and the
use of out-patient and primary care services to
maintain them in their own homes. The difference in
the case of the hospice movement, however, is that
it has taken particular care to ensure that the
existing community services are reinforced and that
the necessary specialist support available to patients once they are in their own homes.
        Whether or not a terminally ill person dies at
home or in hospital, the provision of supporting
community care services is vital, since most of the
caring will take place in the home. Given the choice, the majority of people would probably prefer to
die in their own homes, although there is no research evidence on this in the United Kingdom. But even
if this assumption is correct, such choice is unlikely to be based on any serious consideration of the
practicalities involved. We may seek to console
ourselves with visions of a gentle leavetaking,
surrounded by familiar faces and loved possessions.
The reality is likely to be more messy and more
stressful to those we might wish most to protect.
        The ability of relatives to cope with terminal
illness depends on a number of factors: the nature
and intensity of the care required, its duration,
the level of dependency of the patient, and the degree of support available from the medical, nursing
and social services. It is the fear - perhaps justified - that assistance will not be available when
required which constitutes the major deterrent to
relatives providing care in the home. That the hospice movement has grasped this issue and has proce-
eded to establish support services in the home is
one of its major achievements; that one of the few
evaluatory studies undertaken of the home care service suggests that it has limited effectiveness may
be one of its outstanding problems. A current study
may reveal more definitive findings.

RELATIONSHIP BETWEEN VOLUNTARY HOSPICES AND THE NHS

For a number of reasons, voluntary hospices value
their independence outside the NHS. It has given
them the opportunity to develop their own models of
care, and has enabled them to establish standards of
excellence against which other forms of provision
can be measured. In practising outside the stucture
of the NHS they are able to offer a more personal
and flexible service to the patients and their families, and to establish a positive identity in their
local community.
    The dilemma this poses is whether the role of
the hospice movement should be to provide separate
and qualitatively different kinds of services from
those of the NHS hospital, or whether it should
attempt to improve practice with regard to terminal
care inside it. On the one hand, it maybe argued
that the best - if not the only - way to improve
practice within the health services is to establish
the credentials of the hospice movement outside the
existing hospital structure, in that little headway
is likely to be made by attempting to influence the
medical hierarchy from within. Proponents of this
view fear that incorporation within the health
service bureaucracy would stifle the independent and
innovatory spirit of the hospice movement, endanger-
ing not only the welfare of its existing patients
but also its long-term influence.

The weight of opinion within the hospice movement is
not, however, in sympathy with this approach. Although many of the original pioneers felt compelled -
largely because of the hostility to their ideas
within the NHS - to establish their own independent
units, they nevertheless aspired to the general improvement of terminal care facilities and the close-
st possible working relationship with their colleagues the hospital service. This attitude is reinforced by a number of considerations: the views of
sympathetic colleagues within the NHS; a national
policy which emphasises collaboration between the
statutory, voluntary and private sectors; the growing financial dependence of the voluntary hospices
on the District Health Authorities; and the need to
avoid duplication in provision, leading to a lack of
continuity in patient care. Finally, it is the
policy most likely to lead to an overall improvement
in terminal care facilities overall, and so to benefit the majority of patients who require them. The
virtues of this enlightened pragmatism seem

inescapable.

The ad hoc development of hospices has resulted in marked variations in the level of provision across the country. Their growth, moreover, has taken place in the absence of any overall policy for terminal care. Few Regional and District Health Authorities incorporate hospice facilities into their overall planning. This leaves voluntary hospices in an uncertain position regarding both the take-up of beds and funding of them from NHS sources. The difficulty is underlined by financial factors: for example, the annual revenue costs of a small 16-bedded in-patient unit are estimated to be £4,000,000: the budgets of larger units may rise to between £1,000,000 and £1,500,000. The Regional Health Authorities make an allowance for the purchase of specialist facilities outside the Health Service, but funds are not earmarked for special purposes and the Divisional Authorities have responsibility for determining their own priorities. For the foreseeable future, the amount of money available from this source is likely to be very limited. More and more hospices are therefore likely to be in a position of seeking additional funding from other charitable and public sources - all of which have a finite potential.

A number of voluntary hospices are indeed already faced with growing deficits, which they are having to meet by means of public appeals. The fortunate among them may be faced with a serious dilution in the quality of services they can offer, or even with closure. Hospice patients, it must be remembered, are also NHS patients: while the public may be ready to contribute to the capital costs of new facilities, they may be more reluctant to meet the steadily growing revenue costs of services which should in principle be freely available on grounds of need.

Partly in response to this situation, it has become the policy of one of the largest charitable funders in this field, the National Society for Cancer Relief, to provide capital for specialist continuing care homes built within the grounds of NHS hospitals, on the understanding that the District Health Authority will assume full responsibility for the running costs. As a result, about a third of existing hospice in-patient units are now funded in whole or part within the NHS. Other major funders are also beginning to require new projects to seek accommodation with the NHS as a condition of their support, while others again are channelling their funds into the education and training activities of existing hospices. Since there are considerable economies to be gained from providing for the care of patients in large district hospitals, the NHS is likely increasingly to make its own provision for the care of dying patients, rather than to pay others to do so.

While this shift in emphasis may not be to the advantage of some independent hospices, it may bring benefits to that large majority of dying patients who continue to be cared for within the NHS. In their new situation, hospices,if they are effectively to tap NHS support, will need to establish a close working relationship with the District Health Authorities and to offer the complementary specialist services they need. This is clearly the kind of partnership which the Government envisages (2) even though it involves a significant compromise: the hospice movement, in having to work with the existing medical hierarchy, is less easily able at the same time to present a challenge to it. Such a partnership does however have its attractions. Rather than the hospital and the hospice being seen as two separate organisations, one concerned with treatment and the other with care - with the patient's home as yet another significant element in the pattern - one might look forward to an integrated system of terminal care in which hospital, hospice and home may be seen as complementary and closely-articulated ways of meeting the needs of patients as they arise.

THE WIDER RELEVANCE OF THE HOSPICE CONCEPT

Some critics of the present management of death in the general hospital have argued that inadequate terminal care practice reflects a more general failure in the treatment of patients in hospital. The recognition both of the individuality and of the wider needs of patients is relevant to the acute and long-stay wards, as well as to the care of terminally ill persons. It carries particular force in the care of the elderly. There is of course an important distinction between the care regime of hospices and the specialist medical procedures associated with terminal illness. Most doctors and nurses - particularly those working in the field of geriatric medicine - would be opposed to any suggestion that the kind of intensive drug programme administered during the final stages of illness should be prescribed outside a carefully defined terminal condition.

Apart from the anxiety which this might arouse in patients, many hospital staff would reject any move which separated the dying from the mainstream of medical care and created the equivalent of a special death ward in hospital. Gerontologists concerned with health provision for frail elderly people are understandably reluctant to place too much emphasis on the care of the dying. They tend instead to stress the patient's opportunities to retain independence and quality of life, given appropriate support either in his or her own home or, if necessary, in hospital or some other appropriate institution. The danger of this otherwise commendable approach is that it may lead us to playdown the fact that death becomes an increasingly important consideration as we get older. The eventual attainment of a good death is to be valued, as well as the prolongation of a meaningful and active life, and may only be realised if both patients and carers are prepared for it.

The hospice movement, because it has tended to develop in isolation from other advances in medicine, may not have taken adequate account of equally important parallel advances in the field of geriatrics, psychiatry and medical sociology. What all of them have in common is an acceptance by medical and nursing staff of responsibility not merely for the treatment of symptoms of physical and mental illness, but also for the general well-being of the patient. They have together had a major influence on hospital practice: the hospice movement, no less - if perhaps no more - than the others.

NOTES

1. Undertaken by Dr Audrey Ward in the Medical Care Research Unit at the University of Sheffield.
2. Peter Wormold (Under-Secretary, Health Services, Department of Health and Social Security), 'Hospice finance: the position of central government and the National Health Service'. Speech given to the first National Conference on Hospice Finance and Administration. London. April 1981.

REFERENCE

Colin Murray Parkes, (1978) 'Home or hospital ? terminal care as seen by surviving spouses', published in Journal of the Royal College of General Practitioners, Vol.28 Number 186.

Chapter Eighteen

GROUPS OF OLD PEOPLE IN THE COMMUNITY: A PRELIMINARY
REPORT

Jeanette Brewster, Bob Chard and Gregorio Kohon

This chapter describes a project carried out by a
small team on a housing estate with an ageing population. 'The best kept secret in the long history
of social services', read an article in a newspaper
not so long ago, 'is that services are not designed
for people; people have, as best they can, to fit in
with services'. We would agree that there is a need
to do something for the elderly, something different,
and that the way of working in the social services
is lacking something: there is something that we are
not reaching in our relationships with the clients
we aim to help.
     It was this dissatisfaction that brought togeth-
her the workers that form our team. Our experience
with groups, though limited, was enough to convince
us of what could be achieved through group work.
The idea of forming groups in the natural setting of
the community came out of the belief that if one
creates the possibility for people to meet and talk,
they will. Of course, old people might meet and
talk but may not communicate: but this happens a lot
in other places too.
     Two of us, Bob Chard, the social worker of the
team, and Gregorio Kohon, found after a few initial
meetings that we both wanted to work with groups of
old people, but that we did not know how to do so,
or what kind of groups to work with. We also recognised the need for two people to participate at
the same time, and were concerned that those two
should then have the possibility of discussing whatever went on in the group with a third person. At
this point, Jeanette Brewster joined us. She is a
welfare officer, and works - as Bob Chard does - for
the Area 2 team of the Social Services Department of
the London Borough of Camden; they were the two
people who would deal directly with the group.

Gregorio Kohon, a psychoanalyst working for the
Personal Consultation Centre (part of the Camden
Council of Social Service), became the consultant to
the project. Two people in the team was the necessary minimum to preserve emotional safety and to behave thoughtfully in response to both the uncertainty
of how people would react, and the anxiety we predicted and expected from the group and in ourselves
(such as dread of illness, dying and bereavement).
    We started by having weekly meetings that last-
ed between 45 and 60 minutes each. We gave ourselves enough time and space to talk about everything that came to mind connected with the formation
of the group: uncertainties, doubts, insecurities,
conflicts. We decided that our method of work
should be to 'play it by ear', and we adopted this
strategy from the beginning. 'Playing by ear' meant
that the group we wanted to form was not to be a
task-oriented group, there was not to be any defined
activity as such, no formalised discussions, no
planned outings or visits. Although no activities
could be discounted as a possibility, we were not
prepared to decide beforehand what the group should
be or what it should do: the group members would
have enough time to decide amongst themselves what
they wanted. It became clear to all of us, in the
course of our initial discussions, that to set up a
task-oriented group would be a way of not thinking,
a way of trying to resolve certain anxieties that
would eventually come up in any group situation in
which people had to communicate. Our exploration of
this issue was lengthy and demanding, but it clari-
fied what the team wanted: namely, a group whose aim
was to facilitate the communication between the
members, without becoming a therapeutic group. It
was very difficult for the two social workers to get
rid of the ideology of their work - of the feeling
that they should always be doing something, and
therefore that the group they were about to form had
also to be doing something. It took time to accept
that people could just meet and talk, and that one
could stay with the uncertainty of not knowing what
was going to happen, and benefit from it. The purpose of the initial discussions was to help the members of the team with these anxieties.
    Eventually, we were ready to establish the
place, the timetable, and the size of the group we
wanted to form. We wanted a more or less natural
setting in the housing estate where all of our
clients live and, after thinking about different
locations, we agreed on 'the shop'. The shop, as it

is known to everybody in the community, is a small
building in the middle of the housing estate, run by
elderly people, where they can meet, have tea, etc.
- it is a project for which the Area 2 team of workers is responsible. We felt some reluctance in using it as the place for our group meetings, because
we wanted to keep the concerns of our group quite
separate from the activities of the shop. We were
at first tempted to invite some of the people involved in the shop project to join our group, but on
reflection this did not seem necessary: they were
already actively involved, and there were plenty of
other people in the housing estate who could be asked to participate.

Ten people seemed to us the right size for the
group we wanted to form. In discussing the length
of time of the meetings we were confronted with one
specific anxiety in ourselves: the fear of being
'devoured' by loss and death. The need to set strict
time limits did not have much to do with other comm-
itments - as it seemed might be the case at the beginning - but arose mainly from the anxieties that
the work with elderly people provoked in us. We
agreed that the duration of each individual meeting
of the group was to be 1½ hours and that we were
going to keep firmly to that resolve.

As has been noted these decisions, though seem-
ingly simple, were made after intensive work over a
substantial period. It took us twenty-eight weekly
meetings - the equivalent of 3½ days of full-time
work - before we were finally ready to start the
group. But in our experience, however lengthy the
preparatory work, this approach has eventually paid
good dividends.

After we had agreed on place, timespan of meetings and size of the group, we had to decide whom to
invite. The list we drew up was based on clients
known to both social workers, deriving from their
individual case loads. We decided on the following
criteria:

1. That the person should be able to get to
    the shop, with or without help.
2. That the person should not be handicapped
    in his or her ability to participate, i.e.
    deaf, or confused or paranoid.
3. That the person should be retired, and over
    60 years of age.

The most difficult decision in setting up the group
was how to invite people. Since we had not defined

what the group was going to do, this issue stirred
up all the earlier anxieties about what should be
the task of the group, its aims, its purposes. We
had once again to convince ourselves that it was
acceptable to invite people to meet together when we
could not say what the meetings were for. We had to
believe that the invitation alone was of value. In
this connection, the team meetings again played an
important role. Our discussions emphasised the value of learning, and the fact that if the group fell
apart and failed, the effort would still have been
worthwhile, since at least as a team we would learn
what we should not have done. This capacity to be
selfish - in terms of acknowledging our wish to learn and our right to make mistakes - was the most
difficult task that faced us.

After we had compiled the initial list of
clients, we wrote a letter requesting a home visit.
Although we agonized about what to put in the letter, we subsequently concluded that it did not
matter. We said nothing about the purpose of the
visit, and only one client phoned to ask what it was
about. We decided to invite people to join the
group with as brief an introduction as possible. As
we did not know what we were about to do, we were
particularly anxious not to give a distorted picture
to potential members of what they might expect.
In our team meetings we role-played each invitation
beforehand, looking at possible responses.

The work we had done as a team helped the two
social workers to describe the group to the clients.
If pressed to say what the group was going to do, we
fell back on our belief that attendance, on its own,
could be useful and enjoyable. This was our first
experience of working as a team, and it gave us a
useful opportunity to review our interaction and to
recognise the need to support each other, to be in
tune with each other. We took the opportunity to
discuss the results of the home visits in retrospect,
reviewing how useful the role-playing of the interviews had been, and how much our predictions had
been confirmed or had failed us.

We invited 23 people: only one turned us down
immediately, and he was about to be admitted to
hospital and likely to be permanently blind. Before
the first meeting of the group, a further role-play
exercise helped both social workers to get used to
the idea of having to act as hosts.

At the first meeting, 17 people attended. This
was an unexpectedly high rate of response, and made
for an unmanageably large group. It was, we believe,

this consideration which resulted in the immediate
drop-out of 10 participants: the place where we were
meeting was too small to accommodate so many people,
and the limitations of the social workers' time did
not allow the formation of two different groups.

So we eventually had a group of retired people
between the ages of 63 and 83, all of whom were
clients of the local social services team and had
been seeing one or other of our team members with
different complaints at least 5 or 6 times a year,
and sometimes as much as once a month. Four were
women and there were three men. The two social
workers met the group once a week, for one and a
half hours at the shop on Tuesday mornings, and subsequently discussed the meeting with the team's
consultant on Thursdays.

During each meeting, we see a group of older
people who bring not only the worries, fears, problems and frustrations commonly associated with old
age, but also a great capacity for fun and enjoyment. Taken together, these result in a kaleidos-
cope of activity, making it difficult fully to
appreciate what is happening. Leading the group is
difficult and challenging. The present pattern of
the meetings established itself in the early weeks,
with individual members attempting to dominate the
proceedings, cutting across each other in a fight
for time and space and for the attention of the
workers. For the most part, they showed marked unwillingness to listen.

We have gradually found the opportunity to talk
with members about the quality of communication in
the group, and have discovered that the meeting
provides an avenue of expression which they otherwise significantly lack. As one man said 'We all
save up our experiences during the week and this
(the group) provides an opportunity to get everything off our chests'. They do so, however, by seeking refuge in 'safe' topics such as practical and
financial problems, avoiding the uncomfortable necessity of speaking of more personal issues, feelings
and inter-relations within the group.

We have found it difficult to decide how and to
what degree we should impose our own aims of facili-
tating better communication. The rapid tempo of the
meeting often gives rise to a need for order and
control, for which the group members look to the
social workers. Our principal, and perhaps most
exhausting, role has been to represent the group identity and to chair the meetings, ensuring that one
person speaks at one time and to the group as a

whole, and to make room for those less socially able to make their presence heard.

The demand for control has also been associated with the development of the group as a safe place to be. The members seemed to need reassurance that we could handle any issue which might arise. The fear of being called upon to share more personal feelings - or perhaps the fear that they might unexpectedly find themselves doing so - has been a continuing and underlying issue. Ventures by individuals into sensitive areas are consistently met by changes of subject and a flight into safer topics.

This difficulty for members was brought out by one man who, in an initial meeting, reported hearing advice broadcast on the radio by a celebrity who had himself experienced a traumatic loss. The advice was that one should not tell other people one's problems because half of them would not be interested and the other half would gloat over them. The comment was made when the man in question appeared to want to talk about his own problems but did not know how the other members of the group would respond. Would they listen, or would they, like him, be too busy avoiding their own pain ? His intervention gave the workers the opportunity to open up this question.

The individual in question is a valued member of the group, with a lively sense of humour. In one of the earlier sessions, members discussed what needs the meetings could meet. Much was said about what the group might achieve collectively, and a crusading energy emerged around various practical problems. Suddenly, the humourist cut across the conversation with a joke about three men - a Scotsman, an Englishman and an Irishman, who were lost and dying of thirst in the desert. Suddenly before them appeared a Good Fairy and granted each a single wish. The Scotsman thought, and wished to be transported to a distillery in the Glens. With a wave of the wand he disappeared. The Englishman was also granted his wish and found himself luxuriating in a bath of best bitter. Then came the turn of the Irishman. He looked around the desert and thought hard, and finally said to the Fairy,'I really can't think of anything I want, but I feel so lonely I wish those two were back here with me'.

This intervention made it possible for us to introduce the idea of a shared experience of loneliness, as an addition to the list of possible needs to be met by the group.

We started the group in the belief that we were

297

missing something in our relationship with clients.
Our subsequent experience has confirmed this view.
What we have described as a process of flight into
safe practical matters has been a dominant and powerful theme. Its significance was underlined by an
interchange in which a widow complained that she had
no one to fit a new bathroom cabinet for her. After
twenty minutes of animated discussion we realised
that an answer was not wanted. The woman in question successfully made her own arrangements with the
support of other members.

A similar example concerns a member of the
group who had a reputation for being very demanding
of the Social Services Department. She would telephone regularly, requesting help with minor, practical matters which she appeared to regard as major
crises. The consequent home visit by a welfare officer would often take an hour or more and result in
little satisfaction on either side. This same woman
was absent from group meetings for two weeks while
her flat was redecorated. On previous experience,
this would have been presented as a major crisis
with which she could not have coped alone. However,
nothing was heard from her until she returned to the
group. During this time, at least one member had
visited her; others had telephoned with offers of
help, none of which were taken up. When she returned to the group, solicitous enquires were made about
how she managed. She complained at length about the
workmen, the dirt, the inconvenience and the disruption: but it was clear that she had coped because
she had concerned friends behind her. In this, as
in other cases, the group provided what proved in
some ways direct help or the relief of responsibility - namely a supportive reaction which respected
the autonomy of the individual.

Our aim has been to provide a meeting place to
which members can come without necessarily expecting
to receive answers to their problems and where the
group is of greater importance than its individual
constituents. We have been able, we believe, to
provide a therapeutic experience without adopting an
explicitly therapeutic approach. The group has a
committed membership who attend regularly and who
have the opportunity to communicate and to engage
with each other. We often have fun; we sometimes
argue; we sometimes get bored. We have a constant
struggle to understand and help each other, in order
to justify continuing to belong to the group.

The meetings comprise a constant tussle with
opposing forces - a desperate need for others, off

set by a fear of exposure; hopes of finding friends, set against the difficulty of establishing emotional relationships and the risk of losing them once gained; a strong reluctance to accept the reality of lessening abilities, undermined by feelings of powerlessness and redundancy; a reliance on the leaders of the group, combined with disbelief that, as younger people, they could be genuinely interested in or committed to its continuing existence.

We believe that members have fuller lives through their participation in the group, and that they are in consequence better able to live outside it. We have also come to the view that our resulting method of working with old people is more satisfying both for the client and for the worker.

It is for a social worker, especially one concerned with the elderly, to be faced with complaints and problems: his or her client wants a telephone installed, the window-leak repaired, certain bills sorted out; or else the client needs help over which holiday to go on, or how to cope with family conflicts, and so forth. We believe that many of these complaints, however genuine, could often be resolved by the clients themselves: but in practice, the tendency to count on somebody else becomes self-perpetuating and ingrained it would seem that many of those we aim to help turn themselves into helpless people in order to get the kind of attention that would otherwise be denied them. The social workers in their turn find themselves in a situation of helplessness: they have at the back of their mind the suspicion that the leak to be repaired, or the bills that need to be sorted out, are not at the heart of the matter, but have no means of discovering what is.

Our work with the group confirmed our initial expectation that if we had the weekly meetings, then none of the members would need individual sessions with the social worker or the welfare officer to sort out their complaints. Over a full year only one participant had a private meeting with one of the workers - a meeting that was regarded by the other members as an attempt to sabotage the group. Apart from this, all concerns - whatever their nature - were dealt with in the group situation, and were also responded to by the group. If their experience is capable of being generalised, the implications for the Social Services Department promise to be very substantial.

The newspaper article quoted at the beginning (Lemos, 1982) ended with an appeal for new ideas.

And indeed, it is time we changed our way of thinking: it is not new artifacts that we need to provide now for the old people we care for, but new attitudes. We must start to treat them as independent, resourceful people, capable of making decisions, and able to relate to us on an equal basis - however handicapped they are or feel they are. The experience described in this chapter, though limited, is a step on the way towards such a change.

REFERENCE

Lemos, Gerald The Guardian May 26th, 1982.

DETAILS OF CONTRIBUTORS

Paula Allman, School of Education, Nottingham
University.
Martin Blacher, Department of Social Work, Plymouth
Polytechnic.
Kenneth Blakemore, Department of Applied Social
Studies, Coventry (Lanchester) Polytechnic.
Jeanette Brewster and Bob Chard, Camden Social
Services Department.
Gillian Dalley, M.R.C. Medical Sociology Unit,
University of Aberdeen.
Helen Evers, Department of Sociology, University of
Warwick.
Christopher Harris, Department of Sociology and
Social Anthropology, University College, Swansea.
Jennifer Hockey, Department of Anthropology,
University of Durham
Dorothy Jerrome, Centre for Continuing Education,
University of Sussex.
Gregorio Kohon, Personnel Consultation Centre,
Camden Council for Social Services.
R.I. Mawby, Department of Social and Political
Studies, Plymouth Polytechnic.
Peter McCoy, Suffolk Social Services Department.
Robin Means and Randall Smith, School for Advanced
Urban Studies, University of Bristol.
Laura Middleton, Department of Sociology,
University of Liverpool.
Pamela Shakespeare, Centre for Continuing Education,
Open University.
Hedley Taylor, Centre for Policy on Ageing, London.
Pat Thane, Department of Social Science and
Administration, Goldsmiths College, London
Clare Wenger, Department of Social Theory and
Institutions, University College of N. Wales.
Dianne Willcocks, Sheila Peace and Leonie Kellaher,
School of Applied Social Studies, Polytechnic of
North London.

Abel-Smith, B., 222
Abrams, M., 28, 42, 148, 149
  151, 152, 164
Achenbaum, W., 194, 197
AFFOR, 84, 87-91, 93-4, 96,
  98, 102
ageing, study of, 8, 81
  anthropological, 7, 9, 12,
  129-30
  biographical, 7, 13, 161-2
  ethnographic, 28
  longitudinal, 162, 170-1,
  229
  phenomenological, 26, 35
  psychological, 169-84
  scientific, 7, 150, 160-1
ageism, 15, 26, 41
  see also objectification
age relations, 57, 72-3, 97,
  116, 118, 124-5
aggression, 74-5
alcoholics, elderly, 11, 62-5,
  73, 76, 79
alienation, 12, 54, 96, 98,
  147
Allen, I., 229, 231, 235, 238,
  251, 253
Allman, P., 13, 168-87
Amulree, Lord, 203, 226
Anderson, M., 192, 196, 197
Archard, P., 63, 80
Arling, G., 159, 164
autonomy, see independence

Baines, D., 193, 197
Baldwin, M., 181, 186

Balkin, S., 52, 59
Bart, P., 39, 42
Beeson, D., 26, 35, 42
Belbin, E., 183, 184
Belbin, R., 183, 184
Bell, D., 48, 59
Berblinger, K., 146, 147,
  148, 164
bereavement, 40, 260, 267,
  293
  see also loss
Berry, C., 61, 80
Best, T., 9
Beveridge, W., 212, 215,
  224
Birren, J., 174, 184
Black, D., 228, 238
Blakemore, K., 12, 41, 81-
  103
Blatcher, M., 11, 61-80
Blau, Z., 149, 159, 163,
  164
Boldy, D., 229, 231, 238
Bond, M., 30, 31, 42
Bonnerjea, L., 31, 32, 33,
  43
Bottoms, A., 46, 59
Bowlby, J., 148, 164
Bowling, A., 42
Brewster, J., 190, 292-300
Brion, M., 28, 43
Brody, E., 32, 33, 42
Brostoff, P., 58, 59
Brown, G., 146, 148, 162, 164
Brown, M., 215, 216
Buech, B., 175, 186

Index

Burke, T., 61, 80

Cantor, M., 92, 102
Cartwright, A., 29, 42
Challis, D., 151, 159, 164
Chard, B., 190, 292-300
Christie, N., 57, 59
Cibulski, O., 162, 164
class, see social class
Clifford, D., 150, 164
clubs, 11, 14, 18-20, 23-4,
    95, 97, 258, 264
    see also voluntary
    organisations
community care, 9, 25, 30-5,
    41, 234-5, 287
Conklin, J., 52, 59
Cook, D., 52, 58, 59
Cook, F., 52, 58, 59
Cook, T., 63, 80
Coombs, E., 181, 185
Coulter, P., 62, 80
Cox, E., 231, 238
crime, 11, 45-60, 68-9, 83,
    93, 98, 99, 101, 260
Crowther, A., 192, 195, 196,
    197, 198
Crowther, M., 200, 226
Cruickshank, J., 90, 102
Cumming, E., 36, 42

Dalley, G., 189, 269-81
Deane, P., 197, 198
death, 12, 113, 115, 130, 132,
    140, 144, 146, 258, 282-91,
    293, 294
Delphy, C., 29, 42
demography, 22, 27, 30, 32,
    85-6, 98, 286
Denny, 176, 185
Department of Health and
    Social Security, 30, 42
dependency, 8, 27, 34, 35, 37,
    40-1, 106, 109, 120, 121,
    190, 233, 251
    see also independence
De Vries, A., 176, 185
Digby, A., 192, 198, 200, 226
Digby, P., 61, 80
dignity, 78
disengagement, 36, 39

Doerner, W., 57, 59
domiciliary services,
    see community care
Drake, M., 62, 80
dying, see death

Eisdorfer, C., 176, 185
Elder, G., 162, 164
Engels, F., 200, 226
Ennis, P., 48, 59
Equal Opportunities
    Commission, 31, 33, 42
Ermisch, J., 28, 42
ethnicity, 9, 12, 81-103
Evans, G., 251, 253
Evers, H., 11, 25-44, 120,
    123

Fairhurst, E., 25, 27, 42,
    43
family, 16, 22, 27-8, 30-
    33, 35, 37, 71-2, 91, 97,
    106, 158-61, 163, 191-2,
    199-201, 215, 220, 232-
    3, 234, 237-8, 248, 250,
    256, 259, 260, 271, 279-
    80, 287, 299
Finch, J., 31, 43
Foner, N., 95, 96, 102
Fooken, I., 162, 164
Ford, G., 81, 103
friendship, 8, 17, 29, 35,
    49, 69, 70, 95-6, 97,
    112, 133, 153, 158-61,
    163, 189-90, 192, 244,
    248, 250, 255-68, 298,
    299
    see also intimacy,
    network
Fromm-Reichmann, F., 145,
    146, 147, 148, 149, 164
Furstenberg, F., 54, 59

Garofalo, J., 52, 59
Gay, M., 52, 59
gender, 9, 11, 12, 16-23,
    25-6, 30-2, 41, 49, 94-
    7, 99, 156, 192, 242-3,
    248
gerontology, 7, 8, 10, 25-6,
    146, 163, 291

Gilbert, B., 193, 195, 198, 201, 226
Gilewski, M., 181, 187
Gilligan, C., 180, 185
Goffman, E., 109, 123
Goldberg, E., 146, 164
Goldfarb, A., 162, 164
Gonda, J., 176, 185
Grad, J., 147, 165
Grant, G., 146, 165
Grant, M., 148, 165
group work, 9, 292-300
group living, 242, 243, 249-50
Groves, D., 31, 43

Hadley, R., 149, 151, 152, 159, 165
Hall, S., 45, 59
Harel, Z., 162, 165
Harris, A., 231, 238
Harris, C., 11, 12, 14-24
Harris, L., 145, 162, 165
Harrison, R., 41
Havighurst, R., 145, 153, 165
Hay, R., 194, 198
Hazan, H., 135, 144, 146, 147, 165
Heclo, H., 198
Henry, W., 36, 42
Hill, M., 224
Hindelang, M., 48, 50, 59
Hockey, J., 12, 129-44
Home Office, 46, 59
homes, nursing, 269-81
homes, residential, 9, 12, 105-6, 120, 129, 189
    death in, 131-2
    design of, 240-54
    long-term, 77-8
    morale in, 112
    provision of, 195-7, 199-226
    short stay in, 227-39
Horn, J., 184, 185
hospices, 282-91
hospitals, 77, 203-6, 209, 227, 233, 237, 275-6, 279, 290-1
hostels, 64, 67, 77, 208-12, 213, 216, 219
housing, segregated, 55-6
    sheltered, 255-68
Hughes, B., 241, 253

Hultsch, D., 177, 181, 185
Hunt, A., 146, 153, 165
Huppert, F., 168, 169, 185

ill health, 62, 67, 90, 92, 100, 112, 113-4, 136, 140, 146, 153, 264, 293
    chronic, 28, 83, 203, 227
    specific, 107, 209, 221
independence, 10, 19, 40, 77-9, 94, 132, 140, 300
    see also dependency
intellectual capacity, 37, 95, 168-87
intimacy, 152
    see also friendship
Isaacs, B., 147, 165
isolation, 11, 31, 56, 69-72, 82, 91, 96, 102, 120, 159, 221, 244, 247, 255-68

Jacobs, R., 39, 43
Jarvik, L., 182, 185
Jenkins, J., 181, 185
Jerrome, D., 7-10, 27, 29, 43, 159, 165
Jolley, D., 241, 253

Karn, V., 146, 149, 151, 153, 165
Kellaher, L., 240-254
kin, see family
Kohlberg, L., 180, 185
Kohon, G., 189, 190, 292-300
Korzenny, F., 54, 59
Kuh, D., 229, 231, 238

Labouvie-Vief, G., 174-6, 178-9, 181, 184, 185
Lake, T., 146, 149, 165
Lasch, C., 171, 185
Laslett, P., 193, 198
Laverty, S., 203, 226
Lawton, M., 52, 59, 81, 83, 85, 90, 240, 253
Lehr, V., 161, 162, 165
Lemos, G., 300
life cycle, 9, 14, 16, 17,

28, 39, 160, 162
life span, see life cycle
Lightup, R., 27, 43
Lipman, A., 159, 161, 166, 240,
    253
Lippman, W. 108, 123
loneliness, 8, 18, 112, 113-4,
    189, 207, 264
    amelioration of, 102
    experience of, 12, 28-9, 297
    measurement of, 145-67
    stigma of, 23, 266
Longino, C., 161, 166
Lopata, H., 148, 149, 153, 166
loss, 12, 17, 21-3, 94, 102, 113,
    115, 132, 139, 148, 163, 243,
    294, 297
    see also bereavement
Lotz, R., 54, 60
Lowenthal, M., 112, 123

McCoy, P., 188, 189, 227-39,
    251
McEwan, P., 203, 226
McIntosh, J., 269, 278,
    281
MacIntyre, S., 222
McPherson, I., 269, 281
Maguire, M., 52, 60
Marsh, D., 204, 226
Matthews, O., 202, 222
Matthews, S., 28, 43
Mawby, R., 11, 45-60
Meacher, M., 240, 253
Means, R., 188, 199-226
memory, see intellectual capacity
Middleton, L., 189, 255-268
Mitchell, B., 197, 198
models of ageing, 9, 72-3, 132
Moustakas, C., 146, 147, 148,
    149, 166
Murphy, J., 180, 185
Myerhoff, B., 130, 142, 144
Myles, J., 219, 226

National Assistance Act (1948),
    199, 215-8, 220
National Institute for Social
    Work, 160, 166
National Old People's Welfare
    Committee, 213

Nevendorf, K., 54, 59
Newman, O., 55, 60
Nissel, M., 31, 32, 33,
    43
Nuffield Foundation, 41,
    207-8, 212-4, 223

Oakley, A., 28, 43
Obiechina, E., 125, 128
objectification of
    elderly people, 10,
    33, 40, 41
    see also ageism
O'Brien, M., 29, 42
Office of Population
    Censuses and Surveys,
    87, 102
Old People's Welfare
    Committee, 210, 220,
    223
Opit, L., 30, 43
Owens, W., 170, 186

policy, 7-10, 12, 25, 28,
    32, 33, 35, 41, 50,
    55-7, 188, 234, 241
Parkes, C., 283, 291
Peace, S., 240- 54
Pepper, S., 178, 186
Perkins, T., 109, 110,
    123
Perry, W., 180, 186
Phillipson, C., 26, 41,
    43, 196, 198, 200, 219,
    226
Power, B., 149, 151, 153,
    166
practice, 7-10, 25, 31,
    35, 188
Preston, C., 25, 43

Quadragno, J., 194, 198

race, see ethnicity
Rackstraw, M., 212, 221,
    226
Regnier, V., 85, 102
relatives, see family
religion, 12, 94, 100,
    138-9, 143
reminiscence, 142-3

residential care, see homes,
  residential
retirement, 7, 17, 28, 29, 38,
  85, 86, 92, 153-4, 169, 196
Reynolds, P., 48, 60
Riegel, K., 170, 179-80, 186
Riley, D., 219, 226
Roberts, N., 204, 226
Roberts, R., 257, 268
Robertson-Tschabo, E., 176,
  186
Rockwell, R., 162, 164
Rosow, I., 163, 166, 267,
  268
Rosser, C., 14, 24
Rossiter, C., 31, 33, 43
Rowlings, C., 27, 28, 43

Samson, E., 202, 226
Schaie, K., 170, 173-5, 184,
  186
Scott, P., 94, 103
Seabrook, J., 146, 147, 148,
  149, 150, 153, 166
segregated housing, see
  housing
self-image, 54, 121, 243
sex, see gender
sexism, 26, 41
Shakespeare, P., 12, 124-8
Shanas, E., 146, 147, 151,
  153, 154-5, 166
Shapland, J., 58
Sheldon, J., 146, 148, 149,
  151, 156, 166
sheltered housing, see
  housing
Sherman, E., 55, 60
short term care, 227-39, 251
Smith, J., 181, 185
Smith, R., 188, 199-26
Smith, R.W., 231, 238
Smith, S., 83, 103
social class, 9, 11, 15-23,
  29-30, 37, 50, 87-8, 211-
  2, 220, 257
social isolation, see
  isolation
social network, 40, 69, 90-2,
  120, 163, 258
social participation, 17

socialisation, 52, 72-3
socio-economic status,
  see class
Sontag, S., 25, 43
Sparks, R., 46, 48, 50, 52,
  60
Stacey, M., 41
Stearns, P., 194, 198
stereotypes of old age, 25,
  104-23, 145, 171
Sullivan, H., 148, 149, 166

Tamir, L., 261, 268
Taylor, H., 189, 282-91
Taylor, R., 81, 103
Thane, P., 188, 191-8
Thomae, H., 182, 186
Thompson, L., 181, 187
Tinker, A., 28, 43
Titmuss, R., 204, 222, 226
Tornstam, L., 145, 146, 153,
  166
Townsend, P., 19, 24, 28,
  29, 43, 50, 60, 146, 147,
  148, 149, 150, 151, 153,
  166, 218, 221, 233, 234,
  239, 240, 253, 257, 268
training, 57, 122, 130, 245,
  267, 273
Tunstall, J., 147, 148, 149,
  150, 151, 166
Turcinovic, P., 113, 122,
  123
Turner, M., 61, 80
Turnstall, S., 148, 149,
  153, 166

Ungerson, C., 31, 43

voluntary organisations, 9,
  29, 64, 212, 221, 234,
  258
  see also clubs

Wager, R., 147, 166
Walker, A., 28, 41, 44
Walsh, D., 181, 186
Ward, A., 291
Ward, S., 28, 44
Wedderburn, D., 233, 239
Weiss, R., 145, 146, 147,

148, 166
Wenger, C., 12, 145-67, 190
Wicks, M., 31, 33, 43
Wilkes, R., 145, 166
Willcocks, D., 12, 104-23, 189,
    240-54
Williams, K., 204, 226
Williams, P., 192, 193, 194,
    195, 196, 197, 198
Willmott, P., 257, 268
Wilkin, D., 241, 253
Wiseman, J., 63, 80
Witzleben, H., 147-8, 167
Wolfgang, M., 50, 60
workhouse, 191-8, 199-226

Yin, P., 54, 60
Young, J., 104, 109, 121, 123
Young, M., 257, 268

Zelinski, E., 181, 187